Vietnam in My Rearview

Vietnam in My Rearview

*Memoir of a 1st Cavalry
Combat Soldier, 1966–1967*

Dennis D. Blessing, Sr.

McFarland & Company, Inc., Publishers
Jefferson, North Carolina

Library of Congress Cataloguing-in-Publication Data

Names: Blessing, Dennis D., Sr., 1944– author.
Title: Vietnam in my rearview : memoir of a 1st Cavalry
combat soldier, 1966–1967 / Dennis D. Blessing, Sr.
Other titles: Memoir of a 1st Cavalry combat soldier, 1966–1967
Description: Jefferson, North Carolina : McFarland &
Company, Inc., Publishers, 2021. | Includes index.
Identifiers: LCCN 2021021165 |
ISBN 9781476677767 (paperback : acid free paper) ∞
ISBN 9781476642819 (ebook)
Subjects: LCSH: Blessing, Dennis D., Sr., 1944– | Vietnam War,
1961–1975—Personal narratives, American. | United States. Army.
Cavalry, 7th. Battalion, 1st. Company B—Biography. | Vietnam War,
1961–1975—Campaigns—Vietnam—Central Highlands. |
Soldiers—United States—Biography.
Classification: LCC DS559.5 .B54 2021 | DDC 959.704/34092 [B]—dc23
LC record available at https://lccn.loc.gov/2021021165

British Library cataloguing data are available

ISBN (print) 978-1-4766-7776-7
ISBN (ebook) 978-1-4766-4281-9

Front cover: the author sitting on his S-4 Jeep (author's collection)

Printed in the United States of America

*McFarland & Company, Inc., Publishers
Box 611, Jefferson, North Carolina 28640
www.mcfarlandpub.com*

First and foremost, I want to thank my wife of 55 years for having the forethought to save my letters home. Without them this book would not have been possible.

Secondly, I offer my sincerest thanks to everyone I served with in the 7th Cavalry in 1966–1967. I was fortunate to be part of this highly decorated Army unit and am honored to have such fine soldiers as my comrades.

Last, there are no adequate words for me to thank those folks for the service of the loved ones they lost in this savage war. I can only relay a deep sadness that remains within me for the buddies I lost and for every American soldier who made the ultimate sacrifice in the Vietnam War.

Table of Contents

Preface

Somewhere, sometime ... someone, no doubt, will say: "This guy got it all wrong!" Each American soldier's experience in this war was different, whether you were humping through the jungle or one of the multitudes of support forces, each of us has his own story. This terrible war affected every soldier I knew in Vietnam. Some came home with obvious physical injuries and many still suffer with invisible mental trauma. We were all changed in some way; no war leaves its participants unscathed.

After 54 years since my time in Vietnam I may not have everything exactly right, but this is my story as remembered with the help of my 212 letters home. I used my letters as a guideline, helping me remember where I was and what I was doing when each letter was written. I did not include many of my letters because they were mainly personal in nature and only chose letters that had some connection to what was happening to me at any given time.

Because I didn't want to add to my wife's worry, most of my letters just skimmed the surface of what was really happening to me in that terrible war. Writing this book gave me an opportunity to tell the full story of what it was like for me to serve as a combat soldier in an infantry unit in Vietnam.

Putting my experiences on paper has been therapy for me. Each section of the book lays bare my own personal journey and has helped me in some ways to come to terms with a war I often found hard to understand.

1

Fort Gordon, Georgia—
Then Off to War

My journey to the Vietnam War began soon after our son's birth at the Fort Gordon Army Hospital in Georgia in December 1965. Following my basic training at Fort Polk, Louisiana, I was given a temporary duty assignment with the MP Company at Fort Gordon, Georgia. When I graduated from basic training my Military Occupational Specialty (MOS) was infantry and I knew it was only a matter of time before I would get my orders to Vietnam. As anticipated I received my orders for Vietnam when our son was barely a month old.

Early in February 1966 we packed everything we owned into our Chevy II and headed back to California. I did the driving and, other than a four-hour stop in Texas for sleep, we drove straight through to California. It was great to be back in California, but I found the shadow of my upcoming year in Vietnam followed me everywhere; it was hard to truly relax and enjoy my time with my family.

In March 1966 I reported to the Fort of Oakland for deployment to the war. The Fort of Oakland was a dreary, unwelcoming place, where they separated us like cattle and prepared us for our embarkation to Vietnam. The Fort was comprised of gigantic warehouses where huge numbers of soldiers were held in limbo prior to their departure to the war. I don't know how many soldiers these buildings held, but probably 5,000 in each. This was a depressing place; bunks were stacked four-high and letters were hung from the ceiling to help you find your assigned bunk.

Duties such as scrubbing the floors and latrines or KP were assigned to you when you arrived. I was lucky enough to be assigned to a group who assisted new arrivals in the filling out of the necessary paperwork; this mainly consisted of last name, first name, middle initial and U.S. Army serial number.

I was held back a little longer than most of the soldiers departing to Vietnam while the Army did medical checks on me for injuries I sustained during my time as an MP at Fort Gordon.

When my name finally came to the top of the list and I was given my orders to Vietnam, I remember feeling excited and scared at the same time; the unknown is a peculiar thing. These conflicting feelings stayed with me during my entire tour in Vietnam.

Prior to my departure to the war, I vowed to myself to write a letter home each day. When making this decision, I hadn't considered the fact that I was destined to be a combat soldier living and fighting in jungles filled with rain, heat, vicious insects, and many other terrible things not found within the borders of the good old USA. Combat activity and nasty weather often hampered my ability to write letters, but I did write whenever possible.

I boarded a Pan American flight to Vietnam on March 28, 1966, and began my journey to the war. My flight to Vietnam was a strange experience and to this day I cannot remember a name or a face of anyone on the airplane. Everyone was quiet and subdued for most of the flight; this was not what you would expect from a bunch of soldiers who were temporarily out on their own and without any command structure.

Upon landing at Ton Son Nhut Airport in Saigon I knew I was now in a surreal place, one unlike anywhere I had ever been. When the doors opened, I was overcome with the oppressive heat and the terrible smells that engulfed me. When we exited the plane, I can still remember the stewardess chirping, "see you in a year, fellas," as if we were headed off to summer camp for fun and games. Going down the steps

My official Army picture taken at Fort Polk, Louisiana, April 1965.

of the plane I saw a line of soldiers neatly dressed in their fresh khakis preparing to board the plane we were exiting. This plane was their flight home, back into *the world* (what soldiers called anywhere else but Vietnam).

Many of the departing soldiers were carrying war souvenirs and one soldier had a U.S. steel pot with a bullet hole in front. The location of the bullet hole made me wonder how in the heck anyone could have survived a bullet wound to the forehead. I guess this guy must have had a guardian angel, because his forehead didn't show any evidence of an injury.

Seeing those leaving as we were arriving was an eerie feeling; none of them were talking, nor did they look us in the eye. They appeared to me to be lost in their own thoughts, far away from the Vietnam War.

My life up to that point had been somewhat in my control. I remember feeling as though I was now powerless to affect my own destiny during this very long year ahead, and that fact frightened me more than anything else up to this time. I questioned what was in store for me and, at the time, I could not conceivably have known how my year in Vietnam would affect the rest of my life.

While walking across the tarmac towards the buses parked at the edge of the airport, I remember the air felt *thick,* as though we were walking in slow motion. Just before we reached our transport bus, a story I'd heard many times came to mind. It was about a soldier who had just arrived in Vietnam and was killed two minutes later. I'll never know if this story was true, but I admit it made me feel uneasy. I have since discovered that official records show 997 U.S. soldiers were in fact killed on their first day in country.

Upon entering the bus for the ride to the in-processing center, Camp Alpha, one of the soldiers asked the bus driver why there were heavy bars on the windows of the bus. The driver appeared to enjoy answering the question and spoke loud enough for everyone on the bus to hear. "The windows have bars on them to keep the locals from throwing hand grenades into the bus." Wow, what had I gotten myself into? This place was most definitely a different world.

When I arrived at Camp Alpha for in-processing, I held fast to the possibility I might be assigned to the MP Company since I had been an MP at Fort Gordon for several months. But no, the Army needed infantry and I was assigned to the 1st Cavalry Division who were stationed at An Khe in the central highlands of Vietnam. The next evening, I wrote my first letter home.

MARCH 28, 1966. Well I had a lovely trip and as soon as I get a long envelope, I'll send you a map of our route. We went from

Travis A.F.B. to Seattle, WA, and from there to Tokyo, Japan. That is
the long route and what a trip! This place is really something else.
The weather here is hot, and the food is terrible. There's no hot
water (they just got running water a few days ago), plus the water
tastes worse than bad. Other than these minor items, it's nice!
While most of this doesn't concern me too much right now, I hear
things can get worse. Don't worry about me, I am adjusting and
sort of getting used to this place. We're in a compound a little like
the stockade at Fort Gordon, only this one sits right next to the airport, with planes coming and going all hours of the day and night.
Last night I slept out in the open about 25 feet from a helicopter, we
have a landing field here for them and they come and go every five
minutes. I've figured out we are 16 hours ahead of you, right now
it's 6:00 A.M. Sunday morning where you are and 10:00 P.M. Sunday night here. Tell everyone I said Hi and that I'm fine. Be good
and give J.R. a big kiss for me.

Before I left home my wife gave me a new Bulova Caravel wristwatch.
She bought it with three and a half books of Blue-Chip Stamps (these
stamps are now ancient history). I liked being able to keep track of time
and I always knew the date because it had a date display. At first, I enjoyed
the challenge of figuring out what time it was back in California, but this
mental exercise didn't last long because I found myself dwelling on what
my wife might be doing at home and it only made me feel more homesick.

MARCH 28, 1966 (evening). Right now, it's 2:30 in the morning in
California. Tomorrow morning, I move out to the 1st Cav at An Khe.
We leave here at 05:30 hours, man that's early. This afternoon the
helicopters were quiet for about 2 hours and then they began showing up in droves, they must have had a real big air assault. Say, you
wouldn't believe the way the milk tastes here. This morning I went
over to the mess hall for breakfast and was amazed to see quarts of
milk on every table (you know how I like milk). I snagged a quart
from one of the tables, poured a glass full, took a big drink and
gagged. The darn stuff smelled like regurgitated baby's milk. When
I read the label, I discovered this was milk, but it was made from
reconstituted milk products. I think I'll just stick to drinking the terrible tasting water. I better get ready to leave out to An Khe in the
morning.

The morning of March 29, 1966, I caught a flight to An Khe to report
for duty and began my entry into a combat unit. As we were approaching
the base camp of the 1st Cavalry Division (Camp Radcliff), I could see

a huge yellow and black patch painted on side of Hon Cong Mountain. There was no mistaking who was occupying this part of the Vietnam highlands. I was soon to learn that wherever we went, that patch was on display because the Cavalry always wanted everyone to know we were in the area.

First Cavalry Division patch.

I have done some research about the Cavalry Patch and found some interesting facts. The patch was the largest one in the Army when it was designed and approved for use in 1921. The criteria required that it must band men together, be easily recognizable and be a word-picture that would inspire. The patch is shaped like a shield. A stripe is shown ascending from right to left. It represents a scaling ladder for the breaching of castle walls. The horse's head is for the cavalrymen's love for their mount. When the soldier was currently assigned to the 1st Cavalry Division, the patch was worn on the right sleeve. The horse's head was facing forward as if he was charging forward. Once you left the 1st Cav you wore your Cav patch on the left sleeve and faced it backward; this protected the former cavalrymen's rear. The patch itself is affectionately known as the Horse Blanket.

Upon landing at An Khe I reported to Headquarters Group, and then they sent us to endure a boring and unproductive orientation session. Most of the rest of the day was spent in hot tents, filling out paperwork. One of these forms, the next of kin notification, was something I didn't even want to think about.

MARCH 29, 1966. Well here I am, up at An Khe. What a lovely place! I wish I could describe it, but I just can't. Guess we'll be staying the night here and I should find out what unit I'm going to tomorrow. Right now, it's 11:30 at night, March 28 where you are. It seems that everything here comes in cans. We do have soda and beer, but only 7-Up and Flagstaff beer (both warm!). There is no such thing as a Coke. It seems it's going to be a while before I can get a shower, but I managed to get a haircut for about 25 cents.

The next morning, March 30, 1966, I reported to B Company, 7th Cavalry and they then assigned me to the 2nd Platoon, 3rd Squad. My first squad leader was one of the survivors of the battle at LZ X-Ray, in the Ia Drang Valley that occurred in November 1965. My first fire team leader was a sergeant who also survived LZ X-Ray.

On my first day in the 2nd Platoon I was sent to supply and they loaded me up with gear, but didn't issue me a weapon. When I asked our platoon sergeant why I didn't get a weapon, he said there weren't any available. We then were taken out to cut brush inside the barrier line around the 1st Cavalry's base camp at An Khe. This area was known as the Green Line.

Once we were out on the barrier line cutting brush I asked my platoon sergeant what I should do if we were attacked by the enemy since I didn't have a weapon. He wryly replied, "Don't worry. There will be

Front gate at Camp Radcliff—1st Cavalry Division base camp (An Khe, Vietnam), March 1966.

plenty of weapons lying around if that happens. Just pick one up and use it." The remainder of that day we cut brush, not exactly what I envisioned my first day was going to be in the Airmobile Infantry. When I was finally issued a weapon, its origin was unsettling; the armorer told me it had just been turned in because the guy who had it before me had a heart attack. I remember thinking at the time, "I hope this isn't a bad omen."

> MARCH 30, 1966. I don't know what I have gotten myself into. Wow! Well I'm in the 7th Cavalry of the 1st Cavalry Division (it's the Cavalry unit that was at the battle of the Little Big Horn, Wow!) On April 2 we are going out to the Ia Drang Valley and if you read the Cav's recent history, this was a very big battle. Boy I hope Charlie isn't there this time. I wish I could get a picture of this place in your mind. All night long big guns go boom and choppers zoom over-head. It's like it's out of a book or a movie and not real. During the day troopers are fighters & sandbag fillers and at night some are alcoholics. So far it looks like this is the life combat soldiers live. Let me tell you a little about Vietnam, it's got two seasons: hot and dry and hot and wet. That gives you a big choice; and man, when they say hot, they mean just that. I already have sunburned my neck and arms. I would like it if you could send me 4 t-shirts and shorts dyed O.D., I would really be thankful. Also, a few Fizzies other than grape and some stainless-steel blades. Send them by air or they'll never get here. Also, please put airmail stamps on your letters or it takes two months for me to get them.

This letter home brought back the fact that the Army supplied little in way of personal items needed by its guys in the field. Things like fresh underwear were a real treat. Once in the field I discovered we needed to gather our own water from wherever we found it, but any water we got had to have purification tablets added to it for safety. These purification tablets sometimes made it almost undrinkable, so I took a hint from some of my buddies and began having my wife send me Fizzies (flavored sugar tablets that dissolved quickly) and they really helped mask the terrible taste of the water.

When we arrived in Vietnam, we were still wearing our stateside fatigues. They were Army O.D. (olive drab) and clearly not designed to be worn in the jungle. They quickly fell apart once we began humping through the jungle and jumping out of helicopters into rice paddies. Later in the year we were issued jungle fatigues. These were a huge improvement; the material they used dried very quickly and held up well to the jungle environment. We also went into the field with our standard issue army boots (all leather). They were not at all suited for the jungle and the leather rotted right on our feet. Later we were issued jungle boots: made mainly of canvas, they had drain holes to allow the water to drain away from our feet and were much more comfortable.

The 1st Cavalry Division was the vanguard of a totally new concept of warfare identified as Airmobile. The 11th Air Assault tested this new tactical doctrine at Fort Benning, Georgia. This unit was then transformed into the 1st Cavalry Airmobile Division. What this new fighting concept did was to turn the battlefield into a three-dimensional nightmare for the enemy. The Air Cavalry would drop in front of, behind, or even right in the middle of the opposition, stunning and overwhelming the enemy soldiers. This new concept not only was bewildering to the enemy soldiers but also confused their commanders. The North Vietnamese were perplexed by the swiftness of the 1st Cavalry's aerial onslaughts and the very fact that the 1st Cavalry was always on the offensive.

The 1st Cavalry Division was the only division to serve in Vietnam and win a Presidential Unit Citation, this for the operation in the Ia Drang Valley fought by the 1st and 2nd Battalions of the 7th Cavalry in November 1965. During their 82 months of continuous combat operations in Vietnam, there were 25 Medals of Honor, 120 Distinguished Service Crosses, 2,700 Silver stars and far too many Purple Hearts awarded to the 1st Cavalry Division. The Cavalry has a total of 5,410 names engraved on The Wall in Washington, D.C.; each name represents those who gave their all and never came home. It's a sad fact but the 1st Cavalry Division had more soldiers killed in action in the Vietnam War than any other unit serving in it.

Bravo Company of the 1st Battalion 7th Cavalry was a typical infantry company in Vietnam. Although called Airmobile, the 1/7 Cavalry operated much the same as any other infantry unit with one possible exception—we made more air assaults into landing zones than most Army units in Vietnam during the time I was there.

An Army Division like the 1st Cavalry has three brigades; each brigade is comprised of three battalions. A battalion in an infantry division has four companies, always named alpha, bravo, charlie and delta. Each company has four platoons, always named 1st, 2nd, 3rd and 4th. A platoon has four squads: the 1st, 2nd and 3rd squads are rifle units and the 4th is the weapons squad with two M-60 machine guns.

In addition to the three brigades of infantry, the 1st Cavalry also had the 1st of the 9th Cavalry; instead of being called companies or platoons, they were considered a squadron and referred to as 1/9th troops.

The 1/9 Cavalry were the eyes and ears of the entire 1st Cavalry Division and their primary job was reconnaissance. Their job proved to be one of the most important during a war where searching for the enemy was vital.

Somewhere in each battalion and in each company, you would find a Headquarters Group. This important group was comprised of the captain with two RTOs, the XO and his RTOs, a forward observer and his RTO, a chaplain, a clerk, the surgeon and head medic. In addition, the HQ Group had the 1st sergeant, engineers, pathfinders and sometimes miscellaneous reporters and photographers accompanied them in combat situations.

Most of the company operations were sweeps on the ground, beating the bush looking to engage the enemy in combat. I guess you could say we were trolling for the enemy. Whatever you called it, we found ourselves in the 1/7 Cavalry humping through the jungles and rice paddies searching for the enemy and hoping we wouldn't find them. We spent many days without any contact, but occasionally we would come across the enemy. It's the old saying, *hours of boredom, followed by moments of sheer terror*. As any combat soldier will tell you, when you engage the enemy, your only thoughts are, will I survive this and what can I do to protect my buddies.

Early on, all enemy soldiers were called *Charlie*, a nickname derived from the phonetics used on the radio for VC or Victor Charlie (VC also being the abbreviation for Viet Cong). However, we were in fact fighting two different enemies in Vietnam. The NVA (North Vietnamese Army) had soldiers who were seemingly unafraid to die. They were an aggressive, motivated, disciplined, task oriented and well-equipped army. In addition to these hardcore soldiers, we were confronted with the Viet Cong. There was a huge difference between the NVA and the VC. The VC were armed with mismatched weapons and appeared to be poorly trained. They were local villagers and insurgents fighting against their own government of South Vietnam. When the VC engaged us in battle, they were far less dedicated and could disappear in a heartbeat. Most of the time the VC lived in the area where they were fighting and would simply return to their villages and meld in with the locals.

The 1st Cavalry Division had somewhere around 20,000 troops in Vietnam. I am told it took eight or possibly more troops in the rear to keep one combat soldier fighting in the field.

The grunt in any infantry unit becomes the most expendable job in the Army. Once you received your assignment to a squad, you knew you were at the very bottom of the military pecking order. If you were smart, you did your best to listen and learn quickly; the more you knew about your job in combat, the better chance you had of surviving.

The Army used us grunts to overcome the enemy with all available firepower. We used our radio to bring to bear every type of additional resource, such as artillery, ARA, mortars and all sorts of air power. Usually when we were able to overwhelm the advancing enemy forces, they would disengage and retreat into the jungles.

The words *we have contact* crackling over the radio are words no grunt ever wants to hear. This statement seldom meant anything good was going to happen and when you heard it, your mind began to play out the worst possible scenario. Any experienced infantry soldier can tell you that hearing someone had made *contact*, meant your unit would soon be thrown into the fight.

As a *contact* situation developed, more and more troops would be inserted until the Cavalry was able to overwhelm the enemy. Many times, the Cavalry would send in a platoon if they were involved in a hot LZ fire fight (this was the Army term for an LZ receiving small arms fire from an enemy force).

As for armament, most riflemen carried an M-16 rifle, 300 to 400 rounds of 5.56mm ammunition, two fragmentation hand grenades, one smoke grenade, a trip flare or a claymore anti-personnel mine. In addition, we carried personal items, C-rations, and water. Many of us carried extra canteens and I personally made sure I carried an extra two hand grenades (handy weapon that makes a big bang). We had ammo pouches mounted to our pistol belts and they made an excellent place to rest your M-16 in a proper position for firing towards the enemy. Our packs probably weighed around 45 pounds with the added weight of the web gear and whatever personal items we could ferret away.

The morning of March 31, 1966, I departed An Khe, heading towards Plei Me Special Forces Camp. The 2nd Platoon was loaded up on an Army CV-2 Caribou. This plane was developed by the de Havilland Company of Canada as a short field aircraft. This technology was exactly what the Army needed for taking off and landing on very short, dirt runways. The aircraft was a high wing twin-engine and easily recognizable with its high upswept tail. The plane could hold three tons of cargo or 32 troopers. The Cavalry air support for this operation had been the 17th Aviation Company and their Caribous were easy to identify with the large yellow Cav patches on their tails.

Once we loaded up and took off, I had time to observe the others on the plane. Some of the troopers who were still part of the 2nd platoon had been at the big battles in the Ia Drang Valley in November and they clearly did not want a return trip.

Caribou sitting on an airstrip in the Central Highlands—March 31, 1966.

My squad leader was sitting across from me and I could see the apprehension in his eyes. He had been in the 2nd platoon when it was cut off from the rest of the battalion during the battle at LZ X-Ray. During the flight he spoke to no one and no one spoke to him.

Many of those on the plane had been at these battles and had their own terrifying stories to tell. Talking with them was a real learning experience. They were able to bring into focus what being in combat was about. Looking at their faces and seeing their anxiety I knew their return trip to LZ X-Ray was going to be a trying experience for all of us.

My fire team leader had been on the surviving machine gun squad (the other M-60 squad had all been killed); he had been trapped in front of the rest of the platoon and his machine gun squad's covering fire was credited with saving the platoon. I noticed he had a big scar under his eye, and I asked him how he got the scar. He told me he had heaved a white phosphorous grenade and it had hit some branches and bounced back at him. When it exploded the burning phosphorous hit him in the cheek directly under his left eye and temporarily blinded him. He said the other soldiers yelled at him and guided him back inside our lines and the medic used a bayonet to dig out the burning phosphorous from his cheek.

One of the troopers told me a story about thinking he had been wounded, because he could feel something wet running down his leg.

The medic said he was not injured, but his canteen had sustained a mortal injury. Later he heard the spent bullet rattling inside the canteen, giving him a great souvenir and a great story.

> MARCH 31, 1966. Well guess where I am. I'm at Plei Me. I am sure you have probably heard of this place. It's the Special Force's Camp that was hit so badly not too long ago. It looks like we're going to be in the field fighting VC/NVA a long time. I saw my first battle casualty today. I won't describe what I saw because I know how you are about those things. Well, things are lovely here, I'm in a foxhole, my first time since basic training. Wow! What big fun! Well, I'm a battle-hardened vet now, even though I have never fired a shot. I went out on my first patrol. There were only five of us and that's not many. If one of us was hit it would be a mess.

Near Pleiku and the Cambodian border, the enemy was almost always NVA soldiers. They proved themselves to be rough and tough fighters and, in some cases, they were better equipped than we were. Much like us, the NVA were always seeking out the enemy. They were armed with modern equipment and much of their weaponry was equivalent to our own. Luckily for us most of the time they were very poor marksmen. When we engaged them in a fire fight, we often overwhelmed them with our superior fire power. When they were fighting in this area near the Cambodian border, if things got too hot for them, they would simply cut and run back across the border.

To this day I continue to be amazed at the NVA commanders' total lack of concern for the tremendous losses they sustained in this war. They appeared to place no value on human life and just kept sending men to their deaths.

I can remember my first night in Plei Me like it was last week, instead of 54 years ago. This first night was a real eye-opener for me; this was my first time standing guard in a foxhole. I felt the stress of being in a combat unit and the uncertainty of what might happen next kept me on edge. Many times during the night I kept pressure on the trigger of my M-16 and the entire time I thought I was seeing things move out in front of my position. Although I was scared and apprehensive, I was prepared to do my duty and defend myself and my foxhole buddy. During the night my squad leader (who had been at LZ X-Ray) came by to see how I was doing. I told him I was seeing things moving out in front of me. He gave me a tip I would use the entire year I was in Vietnam. He said, "just look to the side at night and things will clear up." I did as he suggested and no question about it, you can see things better.

The 175s, the really big artillery, continued to fire all night long and each time one fired I felt like I was jarred a foot off the ground. Somehow, I had survived my first night in a foxhole without firing a single shot.

When morning came, I looked around at what remained from the battle that had taken place there at the Plei Me Special Forces Camp in November 1965. My foxhole was about 20 feet from the remains of an A-1E Skyraider that had crashed and burned. Nearby I saw the earth had been scarred by a long bulldozer strip. I later learned this was a trench for a mass grave dug to dispose of the hundreds of NVA and VC who had been left rotting after this battle.

That day a trooper in our platoon (a real screw-up) was proudly showing off what looked like a preserved head on a stick; he said it was an NVA soldier. The grotesque head had a long mustache that hung on each side of his mouth, a high forehead and very long gray hair. The Captain came unglued and really chewed out this soldier. When he saw the head, I guess he thought this trooper had cut the head off an NVA soldier's body. The soldier quickly told the Captain he had found the head under a bush.

ARA Huey with 48 rockets on each side, taken at Special Forces Camp at Plei Me.

APRIL 1, 1966. Well, I'm still at Plei Me. I've taken a lot of nice pictures and they should be interesting. Please send me a lot of film because I can't get the good stuff over here. If you haven't sent the other package yet, you don't need to send Fizzies they have them at the PX in base camp. I'm sitting here about 100 yards from Plei Me, you should see all the interesting things lying around here. There are signs of a really big battle. It looks as though we're going to be here for a few days. I guess we're going to be out in the field for at least 30 days which doesn't sound good to me. I think I'm losing weight already, since we're on c-rations now.

Our PX at base camp was in one of those metal shipping containers, nothing like the PX at Fort Gordon. I seldom went to the PX in base camp since they rarely had anything I could carry or use in the field.

The C-rations and I didn't get along too well. Most of them I just couldn't eat, although many times I got hungry enough to try and choke them down. Anyone who has eaten or tried to eat the C-ration version of canned eggs and ham will understand exactly what I mean; just opening the can made you gag. Nothing like the sight and smell of green eggs to whet your appetite. I did like some C-rations, but I pretty much lived on the B-3/B-1 Unit rations. They contained cookies with cocoa and crackers with cheese. Most the guys threw these away and I would go around and collect them.

The accessory pack in the C-rations consisted of sugar, salt, pepper, coffee, cream, two packs of gum, toilet paper, a spoon and a small pack of five cigarettes. Since I didn't smoke, I gave away the cigarettes. In time, I learned which brand each of the soldiers in my squad preferred and looked for their brand whenever I opened my accessory pack. In addition to the accessory pack we were able to select two items from a central sundries box. I tried to take a new pen and writing pad, but each time I was told that my second item had to be a carton of cigarettes. When picking the cigarettes, I was careful not to select a brand that those in my squad liked. I took the required carton of cigarettes and squirreled it away in my pack, knowing someone would really need a smoke when they ran out. I thought of this as a kind of insurance. I figured the guys wouldn't want to lose their cigarette provider.

APRIL 2, 1966. Well, here we are, still dug in around Plei Me. We have moved twice since yesterday. I thought it would be all over by now because we were supposed to go out on a mission this morning, but instead dug in to protect the artillery. Three mortar rounds dropped in about an hour ago. No one was hit (I think). I have learned some new words from the guys, beau coup-dinky dau means *really crazy*, a boom-boom girl means you know what and you can guess what boom-boom means. Number one is the best and Number ten is the worst. We hear a lot of, you are number 10 G.I, Ho! Ho! Yesterday we went to the river to wash and shave, you wouldn't believe how dirty I was, I hadn't had my boots off for three days. No matter how much I washed I couldn't get the red clay stains off my hands, as you can see by the color of this letter. There were a lot of guys going for a swim, but I just cleaned up and left. Later I heard the guys swimming had been fired on by a sniper, luckily no one was injured. My foxhole buddy went down stream and told me there were all kinds of females (in the raw) bathing. Wouldn't you know I'd go to where the snipers were. Tomorrow morning, we go back to the Ia Drang Valley where the big battle took place in November. Don't worry though, this time we're going in with lots of support. Say, if you haven't sent that package yet please put in a couple of pairs of socks and some shoelaces (not leather). Tell everyone I said Hi!

2

My First Air Assault— Back to LZ X-Ray

APRIL 4, 1966. Well we've got an air assault scheduled for today. Charlie hasn't bothered us much yet, but some of the other companies have run into them, Wow! Well it's one hour before we leave for LZ X-Ray. I've got a good job on this one, just secure and hold and tonight we get to guard the mortar platoon. If you were to see me now you wouldn't recognize me. I'm a mess, all covered with dirt from head to toe. In the last five days I've only taken my boots off twice and have never taken off my pants. When we get back to base camp, we will just throw everything away, like socks, underwear, pants and shirts, the whole works can't be worn again. Say, love, mail sure helps out here so if you could please write often!

Later I found out I was wrong about throwing away our clothes; someone was just messing with the FNG (fucking new guy). Shows you though how easy it was for me to believe what other troopers told me. During these early days I was probably the most gullible, but it didn't take long for me to know when someone was messing with me and I soon learned to give as good as I got.

The morning of April 4 we headed out to LZ Albany and loaded up on Hueys for our trip to LZ X-Ray.

By watching and listening to the others from the 2nd platoon who survived this horrendous battle at LZ X-Ray, I learned many survival tips. I believe these discussions with them are part of the reason I made it through my year in Vietnam.

Being an inquisitive person, I asked my squad leader and fire team leader about their experiences at LZ X-Ray. They and others in the 2nd Platoon (now known as the lost platoon), told me stories of this life-changing battle, one in which they all thought they were going to die. By the time I

Hueys at LZ Albany near the Ia Drang Valley on my first mission to the Ia Drang Valley.

got to X-Ray I already knew more than I really wanted to know and the things I had been told by these brave men only amplified my unease about our impending air assault.

As we began descending into X-Ray, I looked at the faces of the survivors and what I observed was not exactly a look of fear, but more one of extreme apprehension.

Suddenly, all hell broke loose. Our 16-ship formation dropped down to tree top level. We could see the flashes of the artillery hitting the LZ and the ARA ships raced pass us, firing their rockets into the LZ and the surrounding tree line. An air assault is a traumatic experience; you seem to go from zero to sixty in a heartbeat. The LZ was now covered with dust and smoke from the ARA ships and artillery fire. The door gunners began firing their M-60 machine guns as our choppers approached the edge of the LZ and with their tracers bouncing everywhere it was hard to know if we were under fire. The skids on our chopper barely touched down and in a matter of seconds the entire rifle company began firing their M-16s (assaulting the tree line). Hot bullet casings were flying around in all directions and we continued to fire until our NCO yelled cease fire and we immediately began heading for the apparent safety of the tree line.

Once everything calmed down and we hadn't contacted the enemy, then there was absolute silence. We knew the quiet wouldn't last long and sure enough the silence was soon broken by our NCO's order to "*saddle up, boys.*"

As we began moving out, I looked around and discovered most of the troopers in our platoon were younger than me. It was clear that although many of them had been trained for combat they just did not seem to understand the true danger of being a grunt in Vietnam and lacked the focus necessary for combat. I realized their youth would probably work against us when we did find the enemy and decided it was time for me to try and take control of my own safety and do everything in my power to assure the safety of those around me. I began relaying some of things the seasoned troopers had passed along to me, and I guess because I seemed to know what I was doing many of the younger soldiers began to listen to me. I discovered later that many of them thought I had been in Vietnam a lot longer than them.

This air assault into the Ia Drang Valley was my first look at what it was like to be an airmobile grunt in Vietnam. The noise and sudden onslaught of chaotic activity gave me a clear picture of what might lie ahead of me. I tried not to dwell on the thoughts of being killed or injured here, but I had already decided that escaping this war in one piece was probably a long shot. Luckily, this time, there were no enemy forces present. When things settled down, my eyes remained glued on the survivors of the battle at LZ X-Ray and I saw nothing but sadness in their eyes. I imagine many of them were experiencing a form of survivor's guilt, remembering those troopers who had been lost there.

APRIL 4, 1966 (evening). Well, so much for my first air assault. No contact. We are dug in deep and we know Charlie is near. I could see some action soon. We test fired our rifles yesterday evening and my foxhole buddy and I each had a 20-round magazine in our M-16, we both emptied our rifles and were able to cut down a good-sized tree. Today when I jumped off the helicopter in the assault, I was carrying a box of ammo and when I hit the ground one grenade I was carrying hit the ammo box and broke the pin off the grenade. I thought for sure I was a dead man, but quickly realized that the pin had to be pulled before it could go off. That little lesson really had me scared. While digging my foxhole today I got sunburned. We're really deep in VC territory so I've got to set up really good tonight. Our PX rations came in today so I'll have plenty of writing paper.

Since my time in Vietnam I have studied the history of the battle at LZ X-Ray and discovered what a truly horrific scene it must have been.

This was the landing zone where the 1st Battalion 7th Cavalry and attached units held out against a numerically far superior enemy force in November 1965. The enemy had only one mission on that day, which was to wipe out an American Army unit. General Giap, the commander of the North Vietnamese Army, told his soldiers to kill everyone upon contact and they tried to do exactly that.

This battle at LZ-X-Ray was the first in Vietnam between a large regular NVA unit and a large U.S. Army unit, the 1/7 Cavalry. The 2nd platoon of B company was cut-off from the rest of the battalion during this first major battle. My current platoon sergeant had saved the platoon by calling in accurate artillery fire. I believe he really should have been awarded the Medal of Honor for his leadership and valiant effort on that day at X-Ray. I have since discovered he eventually was awarded a Distinguished Service Cross. There were many heroes in this battle, but as it turns out only one Medal of Honor was awarded—to Lt. Marm for his action to personally attack a machine gun emplacement hidden behind a giant anthill, where he took out about 18 enemy soldiers.

In studying that battle I believe if the NVA had been able to flank the battalion, which they were trying to do, the whole battalion could have been lost. Had they played their cards right, the NVA had enough manpower to wipe out the entire 7th Cavalry. Luckily poor enemy tactics and leadership proved to be the savior of the 7th. When the 2nd platoon of B company had been cut off from the rest of B company, the accurate artillery shells slashing into the center of the enemy battalion of NVA had kept the NVA from being able to flank the rest of the 1st of the 7th Cavalry and had saved the day. Had the NVA succeeded in wiping out this one cut-off platoon, then swept around to the company's flank, this could have had a much different outcome. This battle came close to becoming another Little Big Horn, only this time in the Ia Drang Valley of Vietnam.

Historians have tried to understand why the NVA were willing to suffer such a hideous loss just to overrun one American unit. After the war, General Giap contended this battle was a learning process for them.

During this first battle for X-Ray against the 1/7 Cavalry the NVA abandoned on the field of battle: 57 AK-47 assault rifles, 54 SKS carbines, 17 Degtyaryov automatic rifles, four Maxim heavy machine guns, five RPG 2 rocket launchers, two 82mm mortar tubes and an enormous amount of ammunition. It is said that the NVA prided themselves in never leaving anything behind, let alone weapons and ammunition. So, this battle in the Ia Drang Valley must have been considered a tremendous loss for them. During the three-week Pleiku campaign, November 1965, the North

Vietnamese were estimated as having 3,516 soldiers killed, 1,178 wounded and 157 soldiers captured. The First Cavalry lost 304 troopers killed and 524 wounded. These would be considered tremendous losses for any army in the world.

The man in charge at X-Ray, Lt. Col. Hal Moore, seems now to have been the right person at the right time during this operation. Colonel Moore had been a West Pointer and he bordered on being the over-zealous type that many grunts didn't like. The problem as I see it between an officer's point of view and that of an average grunt, was the officers were duty-bound to carry out orders with little, if any, blurring of the lines. In Vietnam our officers were ordered to seek out the enemy and kill or capture as many as possible before the enemy disengaged. Grunts themselves took a more pragmatic approach and although we felt it was our job to engage the enemy when necessary, at the same time we tried not to do anything stupid that might result in our being needlessly injured or killed. We did our best to keep one another safe and live to fight another day.

Colonel Moore stated his intent was to accomplish his mission at LZ X-Ray with as few casualties as possible. I believe he was very brave, and his bravery went a long way in earning the respect of the average grunt. He was there to make the tough decisions when the shit hit the fan at a battle which many commanding officers might have found overwhelming. Colonel Moore was smart and understood the finer points of combat better than many of his peers. He proved he was not afraid to take chances if he thought he could overwhelm the enemy. He clearly took a huge chance at LZ X-Ray and his combat skills helped in keeping his battalion from being overrun by the enemy. Had the enemy commanders known they really had the upper hand and that with their sheer numbers they could have circled the battalion, there would have been no troopers left alive to tell the story of LZ X-Ray.

> APRIL 5, 1966. Well, we're still here at the same landing zone and it looks like we'll be here until tomorrow. We went out on patrol this morning and you should see what we found. Old Charlie was really dug in. We found a hole with 26 cases of ammo, 33 mortar rounds, over 4,000 rounds of small arms ammo and 2 cases of machine gun ammo. You've probably already read about it in the newspaper, they like to let the world know when we capture anything from the enemy. Wow! Here I am in the middle of nowhere and I get a letter from you. You can't imagine how much your letters mean to me, especially out here in the jungle. Every time you go to the refrigerator and get an ice cube I want you to think of me, since

I've been here I have only been able to get warm things to drink and out here in the field everything is HOT. You better believe I'll be glad to get back to you and the land of ice water. Better jump off before I throw this borrowed pen away.

The hole we found that I mentioned in this letter was a reinforced bunker full of ammo. The word came down from the chain of command for us to drag the ammo out of the bunker and hike it down the hill to LZ Victor. Then I was told the engineers were going to blow the stuff up in place. I thought how stupid because moving this ammo from the bunker was done in roasting tropical heat. I just didn't understand why we had to hump all the ammo down the hill, just so some of the brass could look it over before it was blown up. Guess the brass felt walking up the hill in that awful heat was too much for them. Blowing the bunker and ammo in place would have killed two birds with one stone, instead of leaving a serviceable bunker behind for the enemy to use against us in the future.

Up to this point I had the naïve view that the Army would never put me in harm's way without a good reason. My view changed drastically over the first couple of months in country. What finally removed my last bit of innocence was learning what it meant to be assigned to a listening post. Basically, a couple of soldiers were assigned to a listening post and ordered to sit outside of the perimeter at night. These soldiers were sacrificed to an attacking enemy force as an early warning for the rest of the unit. Being assigned to a listening post was probably one of the most dangerous of assignments any grunt could have during any war. This tactic is probably still used by U.S. infantry units during combat, even though we now have many electronic warning systems that could and should remove the possibility of needlessly putting our soldiers in harm's way.

When I was first assigned to a foxhole, I learned the other guy in my foxhole had already seen action. I thought this was great news until I spoke with his prior foxhole buddy. He told me that when this guy was under fire, he would just stick up his rifle and shoot without looking while staying down in the foxhole. It might be OK to seek the cover of your foxhole when receiving heavy fire, but you do have to occasionally look out to make sure you're still firing at the enemy. After learning this unsettling bit of information about my foxhole buddy I no longer had much faith in his ability to help me if we came under fire.

Foxholes were two-man positions, meaning each of us had to pull guard half of the night. We settled on an eight-hour watch; he was to stand watch from 2100 hours until 0100 hours and my watch was 0100 hours until 0500 hours (first light). When we were out in contested areas it was mandatory for all of us to participate in stand-to each morning at the very first light. All our gear was to be on, with rifles at the ready and every soldier on full alert and prepared for action. Morning was the most dangerous time because the VC would use the cover of darkness to creep up close to our positions and then attack before or right at daybreak. The first night I went to sleep when first watch began because my foxhole buddy was set to wake me for my watch. I was surprised when he didn't wake me until around 0200 hours. When I asked why he didn't wake me on time at 0100 hours, he just ignored my question. During my watch as it grew lighter that morning, something slowly started to materialize in front of me. I was stunned when what I was seeing came into clear focus—three U.S. tanks sitting about 100 yards away from our foxhole. I can tell you, I am 100 percent certain those tanks had not been there the night before when his watch began at 2100 hours. This discovery of the tanks made me mad as hell; there was no way those tanks could have moved in that close to us without making a good deal of noise. My foxhole buddy clearly must have gone to sleep on his watch. Every soldier had to trust and believe his foxhole buddy would, at the very least, stay awake and vigilant during their assigned watch. Sadly, some troopers I came across during my year in Vietnam just didn't have any sense of duty to their fellow soldiers. The other guy in my foxhole that night fell into that category. I asked my sergeant for a new foxhole buddy and told him what I believed had occurred the previous night. Fortunately, I never had to pair up with this guy again.

APRIL 6, 1966. Well, went out on patrol again this morning and didn't find a thing. We did burn some more huts. We're known as the burners, because every time we go through an area, we burned everything standing. Man, they sure hate to see us coming. I found this paper out on patrol today. It's a message trying to get the Viet Cong to give themselves up, too bad it works on so few. It tells a story of VC looting and killing and tells how he should think of his family. My goodness its cool here today it's only about 100 in the shade. I'm still trying to get over that sunburn I got the other day. This overbearing heat only helps to make things more miserable (if that's possible). I hate to chase Charlie because sometimes we might catch up with them. I would rather wait for them, but that's not the way to win. You only need to read up on Custer and the Battle of the Little Bighorn to know what happened to 7th Cavalry while seeking out their perceived enemy. Their entire unit was wiped out while waiting for re-enforcements who never came. Well, all I can say is I hope history never repeats itself.

We called the lean-to's we found out in the sticks hooches. Any time we found them in a contested area, we burned them. These areas rarely contained civilians anyway and burning them denied the NVA troops use of the little shelter they might provide.

While patrolling many of the contested areas we often encountered the native people called Montagnards, the "mountain people" of Vietnam. They lived very primitive lives, much like our early American Indians. With little or nothing in the way of clothing, many of the men wore loincloths and the women wore little more than a cloth wrapped around at the waist. They were true scavengers and sought out trash heaps for anything they might be able to use. As the war progressed, we often found them wearing our discarded clothing; apparently T-shirts were popular items. Below is a picture of some of the Montagnard rummaging through trash. Most were wearing T-shirts.

The Montagnard people were mostly neutral, but they would and did fight on either side when they thought it was in their best interest. Sometimes we would find them using the NVA hooches as their own, but

Montagnard people in the Central Highlands of Vietnam.

because they were built and used by the NVA we were ordered to burn them all.

> APRIL 7, 1966. Well, we're still in the Ia Drang Valley and it looks like we'll stay until at least tomorrow. When you send your next letter could you put some pre-sweetened Kool Aid (bugs bunny type mostly root beer). Also, once in a while, could you put in a double-sided stainless-steel blade, sometimes we're out in the field for a long time and I run out. I'm sending you a pill and I want you to take one quart of water and drop this pill in it and shake it up, then let it set for 15 minutes. Then taste the water and you'll see what I've got to drink, doesn't it taste good! Now you know why Kool Aid is such a big deal over here. I had a real easy day today, we went out on patrol, then came right back.

The mail, but not packages, we sent home didn't require paid postage. All you needed to do was write *Free* where the stamp usually went. Being a Scotsman at heart, I really couldn't believe how great it was to send my letters home and just write *Free* for the postage.

As stated in my last letter, I sent home a purification tablet for my wife to try. One tablet put into a canteen wasn't too bad, but sometimes we were required to use 3 or 4 tablets and it made the water almost undrinkable. Sometimes I had to force the water down my throat. When we put 4 tablets in the water it could only be used to wash out your mouth, otherwise it would make you gag. I saw grunts gagging and throwing up just trying to drink this heavily treated water. I've got to say, until Vietnam I never really appreciated the fresh/clean water we have at home.

The ability to rely on getting decent water to drink was only one of the many miseries my tour in Vietnam forced me to endure. Vietnam was a land full of creeping, crawling and stinging insects, full of hostility. The flies weren't too bad, but the mosquitos drove me nuts. It often seemed as if the mosquitos were invincible: they followed us everywhere like a kind of insect fog. Then there were the leeches; I hated them most of all. You couldn't feel them attach to you and didn't even know they were sucking your blood. Sometimes, you didn't notice them until they had doubled or tripled in size. I found the best way to get them off quickly was to use good old G.I. mosquito repellant. This was great stuff; it not only repelled mosquitos, but was good for leeches and many other insects. Unfortunately, this golden liquid was extremely hard to get. The troops in the rear got it, but us grunts in the field rarely got any. Eventually I asked my wife to send along some bottles of 6–12 repellent from the camping store. I found the

6–12 worked nearly as well as the G.I. repellent and at least I had something to help keep the critters off me.

> APRIL 10, 1966. Well, just got this writing paper. For some reason it's hard to get, as you may have noticed I haven't written for a few days. I'm up to four air assaults as of yesterday. So far, Charlie has been hiding. We got some sniper fire yesterday, consisting of three shots. We're down by Pleiku and I'm sure you may have heard of it. We're in an area close to Happy Valley. If they say anything in the papers about the 1st of the 7th you should cut it out and keep it. If you can, get two copies and send me one. I went to services on Good Friday and today Easter Sunday. I'm sitting here in my foxhole eating class A chow (that means they hand you a paper plate when you go through the chow line), drinking Falstaff beer (warm of course) and writing this letter. Last Friday, they really had us done in. At 2:30 in the afternoon they decided to walk us back to the main landing zone, 7000 meters away. It was 110 degrees and we had no water. Now on an L.A. street it might not be too bad, but in the jungle it's really bad news. We only stopped three times, so the medevacs could take out the ones who dropped. This lovely Army. Then we went back to Plei Me and fumbled around in the dark trying to find where we were supposed to be (remember no water yet, only now we also had blisters on our feet). We didn't get any water until about 10:30 at night. Tomorrow, there's going to be action, we're taking an air strip right on the border. We stand-to twice each day, once in the morning at 0530 hours and the evening stand-to takes place as the sun goes down at 1930 hours. Stand-to is a necessary pain in the butt, we know it's when Charlie is probably most likely to try and attack. It's evening stand-to right now, but the sarge said I can finish writing in my foxhole. I can barely see. We've got a new saying here, it means the same as *sorry about that*, it's *toy-coy-zip*, you say the toy-coy in a normal tone and the zip in a high pitch. You now can hear toy-coy-zip quite a bit, proves nobody is perfect.

This was the first time since being in Vietnam I let 3 days go by without writing home. I ran out of paper. Our sundries delivery, which included such things as pens and paper, was sporadic and not on any kind of schedule. We often ran out of things we used and sometimes relied upon. Since I found I couldn't count on the Army supplying things I needed, I had my wife supply them for me. My earlier letters were written on paper my wife provided. When I was in the field, I was at the mercy of the Army's questionable delivery schedule and learned to scrounge around to find things

I needed to survive. All of us in the field knew that most everything we might need was readily available to the soldiers working in the rear areas and this fact was a constant irritant to me. Oh well, we learned to make do with what we did receive, and I was lucky enough to have my own personal supply line back at home.

The march back to the main LZ that I talked about infuriated us all. All you could hear from the troopers was *don't do it the right way, do it the Army way.* As usual someone had dropped the ball and didn't even think about the fact that most of us had little or no water.

The 7th Cavalry left LZ Victor at battalion strength and walked 7,000 meters to LZ X-Ray. I was on point for the whole battalion. When we were about halfway to X-Ray, they called a halt to the march. When we started moving again, I happened to look over my shoulder and saw a soldier catching me fast. I could tell this was no ordinary grunt, his clean freshly pressed fatigues and .45 caliber pistol told me he was not coming to the front for combat. Well, it turned out to be the brigade commander, Lt. Colonel Moore. When he caught up with me we talked as we walked along. First, he asked if I was doing all right and if I had any water? I replied I was OK, but I did not have any water. He then asked my opinion about several things; it was nice to know he would take time to talk to me since I was only a private first class. He grumbled a little about the grunts who couldn't take the heat and had to be taken out on his personal chopper. He told me he got off his chopper to make room for the troopers who needed to be evacuated.

I framed a handwritten letter General Moore sent me after the war. The General wrote, "I remember walking point with you in the Ia Drang." I was pleased to hear he remembered our walk in the sun that day in April 1966.

General Moore co-authored a book titled *We Were Soldiers Once ... and Young.* The book describes in detail the battle of LZ-X-Ray that took place in November 1965. This book is considered by some to be the definitive book on infantry tactics during combat in Vietnam. I've read it many times and learned something new each time.

I understand that Lt. Col. Moore started the Mad Minute tactic that later caught on with many combat units while in the field in Vietnam. The Mad Minute tactic required all weapons in the company, with the exception of the machine guns, to open fire at a pre-designated time. This usually took place right before or right at daybreak. This tactic accomplished a couple of things. First, it let us test fire our weapons so we would have confidence they would fire when we really needed them. Second, if the enemy had spent all night crawling up on our position, this barrage of fire made them think they had been detected. Often after the Mad Minute had commenced, they would either fire back or jump up and give their position away. When they jumped up, they became easy targets and were effortlessly dispatched. This tactic saved many army units by taking away some of the enemy's advantage of using the dark of night to sneak up on us. Bottom line, it was a fun thing to do. Just imagine, being able to blast away spraying the brush without the fear of someone putting a new hole in the middle of your forehead.

The position of point man is considered by most grunts to be a dangerous assignment. Many soldiers figured if you were on point, you probably would not survive heavy contact with the enemy. I had a different opinion about walking point, I always wanted to know what was up in front of me and at the time thought I had a better chance of survival if I could hear and see the enemy coming. The one time I never wanted to be on point was when the platoon had to hack through thick brush or the dreaded elephant grass. Slashing through the brush made so much noise that if the enemy were in the area, they could set up a quick ambush. Walking point under these conditions pretty much assured you would be the first to contact the enemy and most likely be badly wounded or killed by their ambush.

The flank position in the platoon was a job I definitely didn't like to do. This assignment required a soldier to either walk on the left or the right flank of the platoon, barely in sight of the patrol. The flank position's job was to upset or spring any ambushes that might be attempted on the sides of the platoon. Walking on the right or the left of the platoon meant you had to make your own trail, since no one was breaking ground through the jungle in front of you. Because you were making far more noise than the rest of the platoon, your safety was in your hands. You had to be super vigilant and make sure you didn't step on anything that could go boom or wander into a punji stake pit.

When we were near Pleiku at camp, we were considered the Palace Guard (which meant we were guarding the highest-ranking officers of the division). This was good duty; in fact, it's probably the best duty any infantry soldier could hope to have. Camp Holloway was named in honor of Chief Warrant Officer Charles E. Holloway. The attack that took place there on February 6, 1965, provoked the U.S. to become more involved in the ground war in Southeast Asia. Our stay at Camp Holloway was short-lived. The Army always had more dangerous things planned for their infantry.

We set out on our next mission, Operation Mosby, on April 11, 1966.

It was a search and destroy sweep of the Cambodian border involving Pleiku and Kon Tum provinces. Operation dates were April 11 through April 17, 1966.

> APRIL 12, 1966. Well, I made my fifth air assault yesterday. This one was something else. Rounds bouncing everywhere. So far, we have gotten three NVA. Just a few minutes ago a lot of gunfire went off and then over the radio the 3rd platoon reported they ambushed one lonely NVA. Can you imagine a whole platoon opening up on one lone sole. He didn't even know what hit him. I might be back at the Golf Course (base camp) by the 15th for my Birthday. I'm counting the hours till I get home. I'm going to want a big tall glass of anything with ice. I don't know where I am right now, but I think we're close to the border. I'm sending home some things they have dropped from airplanes here to try and get them to surrender. Last night a plane went over broadcasting in their language. It was weird, you could hear children crying and women wailing coming from the sky.

Following this last air assault, the 3rd platoon had set off a tremendous ambush at this location in the middle of the night. Some of the soldiers related the following details: during the night a group of NVA came walking down the trail and hit a trip wire and this set off a trip flare, an anti-intrusion device we used that displayed a very bright light. These NVA were carrying flashlights and weren't shy about using them. When they hit the first wire and the flare went off the whole group just squatted down in the middle of the trail and were jabbering back and forth in their singsong sounding language. According to the story tellers it appeared this group of NVA had no idea we were in the area. When the M-60 machine gun squad saw the flare go off they had dug their foxhole in the center of the trail and blocked the NVA's progress. Finally, the Cavalry troopers on the ambush threw out a cluster of hand grenades and opened fire. Then the whole platoon made a hasty retreat to the safety of the company perimeter. Some smart trooper had torn a white t-shirt into strips and then tied them along the faint trail that lead back to the rest of the company. This proved to be a great plan, as the trail itself was almost invisible in the dark. I was positioned next to where the platoon came into the company area, about 100 meters from the ambush site. The next morning, we found some blood trails leading away from the ambush site; no enemy dead or wounded were found in the area. We had sustained no casualties on our side.

Later that same morning a lone NVA soldier came along carrying a rifle by its barrel over his shoulder and a large rucksack on his back. He really didn't stand a chance when about half the platoon opened fire on him.

The NVA soldier's weapon was a carbine, much like our own World War II M-1. Their carbines were made by the Chinese, or at least they had Chinese characters stamped on them. Even the ammo for this rifle looked like the U.S. carbine's ammo. The rifle had ended up with a hole through the barrel that looked as if it was had been drilled by a machine shop. Once again, our M-16 rifle proved to be the superior weapon. We later learned this lone NVA soldier was most likely an officer. This was how the NVA operated, platoon commanders would often be two or three days out in front of their respective platoons. They would then meet at a predetermined location and join up with larger units just prior to their attack. This tactic was used to try and defeat our accurate and devastating air support and artillery, which was known to continuously rain down substantial firepower on the enemy whenever we were in a contested area.

When we were in contested areas like this operation, near the border, we would dig our foxholes as deep as possible. One of our units then would be sent outside the perimeter to set up an ambush. These ambushes would usually be set at a preselected spot, such as a well-used trail or where two trails crossed. Those who set the ambush would then lie in wait for the enemy to come along. On ambush there was no sleeping and you needed to be 100 percent on alert. So, all night long the unit lies in wait without moving or making any noise. If you think that's easy, try it sometime.

If the enemy came along and set off the ambush, every trooper in the ambushing patrol would hit as hard as possible with claymores, grenades and rifle fire. As soon as the firing stopped, the entire patrol would jump up and run like hell towards a predesignated location. Why run? The top reason was you just never knew if you had ambushed two or 99 or 1,000 NVA or VC. If the ambush was unsuccessful the patrol would return to their platoon at daybreak and continue business as usual. Whether your ambush was successful or not, the next day you just trudged on without any sleep.

On April 13, 1966, a U.S. Special Forces soldier advising an ARVN unit was killed along with 14 ARVN soldiers who were with him. They were operating in the Ia Drang Valley very near the Cambodian border not far from the 1/7 Cavalry area of operation.

APRIL 13, 1966. Well we're still at the same spot and they just brought in some more C-rations and that's bad news. I just got two letters from you, each with Fizzies. I love you. Say, these Fizzies are really going to help. The only water we can get comes from the streams; I wouldn't even let Pup drink out of it without a couple of purification tablets in it. These Fizzies really do help this awful water taste a little better. I really think the Army is screwing up! Da Nang is an R&R center (rest and relaxation) which are usually very well secured, but we're right in the middle of Cong land, out by ourselves, near Pleiku right on the Cambodian border and its bad news here. If you find a map go roughly one hundred miles northwest near the border and that's where we are.

The postal system in Vietnam was confusing. At times it worked like clockwork and other times it seemed as though our mail was stuck somewhere out there in limbo. Sometimes we would go a week or so and get nothing, then suddenly we would receive multiple pieces of mail all at once. It always was a surprise to me that the mail seemed to come through to us just when we really needed a boost. The weather would be miserable, the enemy would be near and then out in the middle of nowhere that big orange bag of mail from home would be delivered. Getting mail from home was often the only bright spot in my week.

I mentioned C-rations in my latest letter. Unfortunately, as grunts in the field we knew what a fresh delivery of C-rations meant. More C's equaled more time in the field. No matter what type of C-rations you ate, they were all bland and almost tasteless. I eventually did find a way to improve the taste of the C's. I wrote my wife and had her send over some bottles of A-1 and hot sauces. Over time as my condiment collection grew, I found a clever way to transport them. I safely carried them from place to place in an empty claymore bag (with its long shoulder strap it was easy to carry). Word soon got around and my condiment bag became a big hit with the other guys. Eventually you could find it being passed around the platoon during chow time. Occasionally a guy from one of the other platoons would come looking for me and ask to borrow my condiment bag.

To open our C's the Army supplied us with a P-38, a rather crude tool, but it did the job. You held it between your thumb and forefinger and rocked the little blade back and forth around the edge of the can. A grunt never wanted to lose his P-38 since there was no other way to open your C's. Most of us carried it on our dog tag chain (in fact, to this day I still have mine attached to my dog tags).

To cook the C's the Army supplied something called a heat tab. These were said to work great; they were flameless and caused no smoke. Unfortunately, we never got any of them, but apparently the guys in rear got them first and kept them. As grunts in the field we had to find other ways to heat our C's. Someone discovered that you could use a pinch of C-4 explosive mixed with a little dirt and water to slow its burn and then you could heat water in less than a minute. When C-4 wasn't available, we used the pellets from an artillery shell for fuel. We made our own little stoves to use for heating C's. I made my stove out of an empty 2-inch high C-Rat can. I would turn it upside down and punch holes in the top to allow for ventilation. Taking my time, I used a beer can opener and made some interesting designs on my stoves.

APRIL 14, 1966. Well, here we are outside some Special Forces Camp, I don't know where. They gave us two cans of cold beer and one can of pop tonight. (I traded one can of pop for two more beers … so I'm feeling fine). Tomorrow, we go back to base camp. I don't have any idea where we are right now, just that we are near Pleiku. I hope your package has come when I get back to base camp. Well I'm going to make it back in time for my Birthday after all. I'm hoping I can get into An Khe to get you and Tina something. Looking forward to getting back and taking a shower, I haven't had one for two weeks (aren't you glad you're not near me).

3

Back to Base Camp

APRIL 15, 1966. Well here I am 22 whole years old. Right now, we are back in base camp. No telling where we are going next. That last place we were at was Plei Rang. The wet season is coming up soon, so I guess they're going to try and squeeze in another operation before it hits. They tell me when the Monsoon Season starts, it rains day in and day out. Tell me what you have been doing. You know I hardly remember what California is like. I'm sitting on my cot listening to the recorder. I'm going to try and make a tape for you today.... Well lover, I've got a few things to do, so I better sign off. P.S.—that dot in the picture is a helicopter.

I don't know why, but when I did try to make a tape for my wife, I got halfway through it and didn't know what to say. I know that some of my hesitation was a result of not wanting to explain some of the things I had seen, in order to not cause her further worry. Truth be told, I just didn't want to put her through the same pain I was feeling. You can paint a different picture of what is truly happening to you when you're writing a letter, but it was next to impossible for me to hide my anxiety on a tape recorder.

My next operation took place on the edge of Happy Valley. I was on point and I smelled smoke and immediately raised my hand to stop the forward progress of the platoon. The LT worked his way forward through the heavy brush and came up next to me and asked what the holdup was. In a hushed voice I told him I smelled smoke, which was possibly from a cooking fire. We knew there were no friendly troops in the area we were patrolling. He then asked a couple of the others standing around if they smelled anything and they said they didn't smell anything. Our LT had learned to trust my abilities, so he put two squads online (side by side) and started sweeping forward.

The platoon began to push forward and all at once froze in place. Sure enough, one squad had popped into an opening in the jungle with a couple of hooches. There was food still cooking on the fire and a huge stack of punji stakes piled high on the ground next to the hooches. The whole platoon stood around talking in subdued voices, everyone knew how close the platoon had come to surprising the enemy soldiers who had been there.

One of the guys who always called me Home Boy, because we both were from southern California, had picked up several enemy crossbows and gave me three of them. I strapped all three to my pack, but only one survived humping through the jungle during this mission. I still have the crossbow and a couple arrows. This crossbow is a thing of beauty; it was hand-shaped out of what looks like mahogany and I could see whoever it belonged to must have polished it regularly.

This incident established my ability as point, and I was gradually realizing there were some nice aspects to being assigned permanent point. I discovered the LT had begun to appreciate my value and if I spotted something, he would call me back and not leave me out there as cannon fodder. Another plus to working point—you were first up for any booty we found.

I was fortunate to have perfect vision and because I didn't smoke, my sense of smell was better than many of my comrades. In addition to these necessary abilities, I had been diagnosed as having green deficient color blindness. Although color blindness is normally considered a disability, it proved to be a real advantage for me. The camouflaged enemy bunkers stood out to me and I found them easy to spot.

The biggest danger for a point man is the possibility of being shot by a sniper. In a small ambush, the sniper usually shoots the first person he sees, then runs like hell. On larger ambushes, often the snipers let the point man go by, so they could hit the main body of the enemy forces.

APRIL 17, 1966. I got five letters today, so I guess I've got to write. Guess what, I got your Birthday card today, so here it is just a little late…. We're going back out in the field tomorrow, but it's not bad this time because we are just going to secure the airport. It's not a bad job at all. The LT (our platoon leader) and I went alone to recon the area. I'll act as a guide for our squad to lead the platoon when they get out there. I've got some good action shots, but nothing that you couldn't look at…. You asked about the jungle boots. No, I haven't got any, but I saw plenty down in Saigon on guys with desk jobs. I did get a used pair of what appeared to be mechanics pants, when my stateside fatigue pants finally fell apart. Guess your letter did some good!

I often sent home pictures to my wife and occasionally they were shots of combat activity. When I mentioned the action shots were nothing she couldn't look at, I was simply fulfilling a request she made of me before I left for Vietnam.

My wife's uncle had been in World War II and had sent many pictures of dead bodies home. Her memories of having seen these pictures displaying the carnage of war still bother her. Her uncle came home from the war a haunted man and spent most of his life in and out of Veteran's Hospitals for his mental problems.

I promised my wife I would not send home any pictures of dead or wounded soldiers. Looking back now, I'm glad I didn't send these types of pictures. Many of my memories of combat in Vietnam are hard enough to deal with, without subjecting myself and others to a personal visual record of the terrible things I have imprinted on my mind.

The note about finally getting replacement fatigue pants has an interesting back story. When I wrote my wife about my fatigue pants being ripped and almost falling off me, she wrote a letter to Baxter Ward, a local newscaster in Los Angeles, telling him about my infantry unit having to go without replacement fatigues. Mr. Ward then wrote a letter to the Pentagon. A colonel at the Pentagon responded to my wife directly, telling her he appreciated her making him aware of the supply delays of my unit in Vietnam and that the Army was doing its best to get new clothing supplies out to the infantry divisions in Vietnam. Soon after this letter exchange, miraculously, we received jungle fatigues. As is the Army's way, a huge pile of new and barely used fatigues were dropped off for us to dig through and find our size.

Sadly, no one even mentioned the huge black market that existed in Vietnam. If you had the means and access to Saigon, you could purchase new jungle fatigues and jungle boots; this was long before they were issued to us in the field.

While we were back at base camp, we received a great duty assignment. We were sent just outside the base camp perimeter to guard the An Khe airport. They sent us to guard the mess hall supplies being stored at the airport before they were distributed to base camp.

While guarding these supplies, I witnessed mindless waste. Some of our soldiers were opening #10 size cans of peaches, drinking the juice and throwing the peaches away. It goes without saying this was the last time they allowed us to guard anything that could be opened with a P-38.

Our unit was much better at guarding the artillery supplies. After all, you can't eat ammo. Besides, what possible use could you have for an artillery round?

APRIL 18, 1966. Well, I sent out a package to Tina this morning, so it should be there in a day or two. I made a tape on the recorder, so you should get one soon, so you can hear what I've got to say. You know what would be nice, if when you get the recorder make four or five tapes with tunes on them and send then in a box to me. I sure wish I had some more songs out of those 45's of yours. It's really nice to be able to sit down and hear those songs that we used to listen to together. It makes me forget about this hell hole. Well, the monsoon season is just about upon us.

APRIL 19, 1966. Happy First Anniversary! Well, I got your package this morning and you're a life saver. I needed those shorts and T-shirts. Also, that electric razor is just perfect. It will save some wear and tear on my poor old face....

Shortly after writing this letter we were put on alert. Anytime Headquarters put us on an alert it could be bad news. It usually meant someone, somewhere was in trouble. We were often called upon to help someone else get out of whatever trouble they had gotten themselves into. Luckily for me, though we were often put on alert during my year in Vietnam, none of the alerts we received ever resulted in our being sent out on a rescue mission.

APRIL 22, 1966. Well, looks like I'll be out in the field the 26th. We went out yesterday morning. We came out by truck convoy and I was in the front of the first truck. This morning we moved to about the halfway point. We are guarding bridges which the VC have already blown up. Last night we went out on a squad ambush. That's only nine of us plus the F.O., I'm glad we didn't see Charlie. I can't imagine what would happen if a whole bunch of them came along the trail where we had set an ambush. You wouldn't believe what this U.S. Government is doing here. They have built a little village of about twenty buildings and it's guarded by M.P.'s and only American G.I.s can go in; it's called Sin City. The Army inspects the working girls and lets them work in this village as prostitutes. An Army doctor checks each girl once a week and gives free shots when needed. The U.S. Army owns the whole thing and if your caught going downtown for your boom-booming, the M.P.s will arrest you. Well, such is life in Vietnam. I'm getting along fine right now. We're in a real good spot and we might stay here awhile, even though we're in the field, we're pretty well off.

Sin City. Wow, I just couldn't wrap my mind around the thought that the Army allowed this place to exist and worse yet, that the Army built and ran the place. The central business of Sin City was of course to provide boom-boom girls (prostitutes) for American G.I.s. There was a bar there, but most of the guys spent their money doing you know what.

This place was verboten to me by my own choice. I guess it made sense for the Army to be able to check out the girls, but this just rubbed me the wrong way. The government was now participating in the oldest profession in the world. Well taxpayers, choke that down if you can.

As soon as the 2nd platoon hit base camp, the troops were turned loose and about half of them would head for Sin City. If you wanted to socialize with your buddies, you pretty much had to show up there. I did go a few of times, but decided it wasn't for me. Going there was just too much of a temptation for a young man of 22.

I never told my wife about the last time I visited there; guess she'll know about it now. I was sitting with some of the guys having a beer and every so often, the girls would come around and solicit me, although they all pretty much knew I didn't Boom Boom. Most of the time they just left me alone, not wanting to waste their time. On my final trip to Sin City, there was one girl who kept trying to slide onto my knee and I kept pushing her off. She really persisted and eventually she was sitting on my knee. I knew she was young and I asked her how old she was. She said she was 15. She started whispering in my ear that she wanted to go in the back room with me and Boom Boom. At first, I told her no, then told her I didn't have any money. But this little girl was persistent and told me she loved me and there wasn't going to be a charge. Now these were business ladies, working girls, and they never just gave it away. I must admit I was tempted, but somehow I was able to resist. I retreated out of this bar/whorehouse and made it back to the company area inside base camp and could still be classified as a Vietnam virgin.

A couple of hours after I returned, the first of the platoon members started to straggle back. The first guy coming through the tent flap picked up the first thing he could find and threw it at me. When I asked, "what's the problem?" he replied that my buddies had passed the hat and raised 500 piasters (a little less than five U.S. dollars) to pay that little girl to get me into the back room. When they found out she failed her task to entice me, the boys of course tried to get a refund, but she refused. The guys who chipped in for the girl got involved in a major melee and I guess every one of them got thrown out of Sin City by the Army MPs. Worst of all, they were barred from Sin City for the rest of the day and that made them even angrier. I found out what they had paid that little girl was nearly twice as much as the Boom Boom's fair-traded rate of 300 piasters per round at Sin City.

There was much talk among the troopers about the rampant venereal disease being spread by the Vietnamese hookers, particularly the incurable strains of VD rumored to exist among the girls. It turns out, and I believe, these rumors were planted by commanders to try and slow the guys down. Of course, it was impossible to slow some of them down when it came to Boom Boom. Most of the troopers in Bravo Company savored the favors of the local working girls at one time or another during their year in Vietnam. I must admit I was very tempted a couple of times during the year, but I did good. I know many guys probably think I'm lying, but the truth is the truth, and I never was unfaithful to my wife during my year in Vietnam. Besides, the mere mention of getting VD scared me to death.

Somewhere around this time we were guarding along Highway 19, not far from Pleiku. We had a new sergeant who had just taken over the squad. He slipped up on me while I was standing guard duty during the night and accused me of sleeping while on guard duty, which I denied. He then told me I was lying. I took guard duty very seriously and his accusation really pissed me off. I told him that the next time he slipped up on me and I saw him in front of my position, I would put a half a magazine in him or at least one round right between his eyes. I really had seen him gliding along in the shadows and of course I wouldn't have shot him, but I guess I could have acknowledged his presence as soon as I saw him and avoided the whole argument.

> APRIL 24, 1966. Well, I got a nice letter from you today and it even had perfume on it. It sure smelled good, like a letter should. Just two more days and we're an old married couple. How about that! … We went out on patrol again this morning and guess what happened. I sat down on a burned-out stump and after about 15 minutes I looked down and saw hundreds of ants were trying to run me off. One of those bastards bit me in my left ball, wow did that hurt. Our medic thought it was funny. I didn't tell you, but while we were in the Ia Drang a big red ant took a hunk out of my right ball, guess I have a matched set now.

These red ants in Vietnam were ferocious and they would attack anything. If you held up a lit match to them, they would attack into the flame and die. Brave little suckers, not at all afraid to die, but stupid; maybe they were NVA trained.

> APRIL 25, 1966. Well, this is my last envelope, so I don't know if I'll be able to find one tomorrow or not. One day until our

anniversary. I sure wish we could be together, but we'll just have to have a double celebration next year. I was out this morning guarding a bridge that had been blown up (I can't imagine why). Whoever blew the bridge up knew what they were doing, it looked like a perfect job because there was little left of it. We test fired our weapons this morning and I really made this M-16 talk. I was shooting semi-auto at a can and the can was bouncing in the air, but later I looked the can over, and it didn't have a single hole in it. You should hear this thing on full-automatic, it really throws some ammo. Last word is that we'll be out here till the 29th and then no telling where we're headed…. Wow! they just delivered cold beer, Schlitz "the beer that made Milwaukee famous." My goodness it's cold. Along with cold beer and soda's, we got hot rations, BBQ chicken, peas and mashed potatoes and gravy, man, are we living. Most of the time when we get cold beer in the field (which isn't often), there's no charge for it, but this was one of the few times they charged us for it. It cost me 60 cents just to get in line to buy it and 20 cents per can. Guess they want to make sure we don't get drunk. After all, no commander wants his soldiers drunk while they are in the field. You wouldn't believe how dark my face and the back of my hands are now, they look dirty all the time. This afternoon I was back guarding the blown-up bridge, when a three-wheeled car, like a golf cart stopped by us. There were six girls and one guy on the cart. The guys in camp saw them and started streaming off into the bushes in groups of twos and threes, hum, I wonder what they were doing? How about that, a whorehouse on wheels. Oh well, you know you have a good husband and besides that, I was on guard and couldn't leave my post. This Vietnam is for the birds. It looks like rain, its thundering and lightening all over the place…. You know being with the artillery does have its advantages, like big guns booming all night and keeping you awake. I think I'd like to stay here the rest of my tour, just kidding! Oh well, guess I better sign off before it starts raining.

I know I talk about drinking beer all the time, but the truth is I rarely had more than 2 or 3. Most of the time any beer we did get in the field was warm and it just didn't seem right to drink a warm beer, but it was better than nothing. When we were in base camp, I would let loose a little and occasionally had too much beer. (I never drank hard liquor.) I am certain that keeping my wits about me not only saved me a lot of grief and aggravation, but probably was responsible for keeping me alive during my year in Vietnam.

Our next operation took place near Bong Son within the Binh Dinh

Me guarding a bridge that had been blown up by the VC or NVA.

Province, Operation Bee Bee, conducted between April 26 and April 28, 1966. It was a show of force by the First Cav's third brigade and the 1st of the Ninth.

> APRIL 28, 1966. It looks like we are going to go in tomorrow. I don't know if that is bad or good. Every day we have been walking up this mountain pass. Today I rode all the way up in a truck and all the way back. You know the "Grapevine," well this mountain road is about like that, only with more curves. I'm told that many years before this, the French lost two regiments in this pass to the Viet Minh who were the predecessors of the VC. It's a perfect place for an ambush, but now there's an ARVN Fort at the very top....

This mountain pass I talked about is the Mang Yang Pass on Route 19, between An Khe and Pleiku. One of our platoons in this same area came across a large clearing full of little white crosses. None of the crosses were identified by name and at first, they thought they were the graves of the French soldiers who had been killed there. Upon further observation, it was concluded they must be Viet Minh graves because the clearing was not overgrown and still appeared to be carefully maintained.

Our next operation was Operation Browning, a daylight raid upon enemy forces that took place near the Binh Dinh Province on April 29, 1966, and included the third brigade and the 1st of the Ninth.

My third squad walking on patrol of Highway 19 near Mang Yang Pass.

Nothing really came of this operation. I am told one of the other platoons did encounter a sniper who got off a couple of shots before retreating. The good news is no one was injured.

> APRIL 30, 1966. I got two letters from you yesterday and one today. Wow, I'm in seventh heaven. I sure enjoy getting mail from you. Yes, I did get those pictures of J.R. and he is just beautiful…. Say lover, I'm glad to hear you got a tape recorder. Have you played my tape yet? You haven't said either way. Do I ever love getting your packages. When you send them try to keep them under 5 pounds and you can mail them regular mail because they still go air mail from San Francisco to Vietnam anyway. I would rather receive two or three little packages, than one big one….

> MAY 2, 1966. Well, here we are still sitting outside Pleiku. There's no telling how long we are going to be here, but I'm hoping we go back into base camp soon, I could really use some fresh underwear. The last couple of days I haven't had any mail, guess the Army is messing up again. I'm glad to hear you got to play my tape….

Hygiene in the field in Vietnam was nothing like bivouac in basic training. When duty calls, you grab your toilet paper, your entrenching tool and of course your weapon. When you're finished, you cover every-thing up before you leave.

It was always great to get back to base camp, with its semi-civilized hygiene facilities. There, you could find ammo tubes that were sticking about two feet out of the ground at a 45-degree angle, properly referred to as piss tubes. The showers at the latrines consisted of three or four 50-gallon barrels mounted over a shower stall. Most times the water was ice cold and if you waited until you thought it had heated up a little by the sun, the water was all gone. I really didn't take too many showers there anyway, the stalls were always filthy dirty. When I did take a shower, I pre-ferred to go to a shower point by the river; they were almost nice. Occa-sionally I would just go for a swim in the river to clean up at the swimming area. The latrines at the river were made with cut off barrels that caught the crap. It's unbelievable to me, but disposal of this human waste was a highly sought-after job. Each morning they doused the sludge with diesel fuel and burned it. Troopers who wanted out of the field, often volunteered to burn and stir the sludge while it was burning. The stench was almost unbearable.

Getting clean clothes in the field was a pipedream. We had one set of jungle fatigues and one pair of jungle boots. For obvious reasons, we never washed our fatigues. Most of the time, the only way a soldier in the

SWIMMING AREA

1. No swimming under any conditions if h
2. The "buddy system" will be used by a in the water. Even large groups or pe individual with the groups will have (
3. A line will be used to mark the dou will go beyond this line.
4. There will be no diving except in river bottom is rocky and irregular and outcroppings both above and just belo extremely hazardous in most parts
5. Intoxicating beverages will not be con
6. Lifeguard stations will be equipped blankets, and one vehicle for emergency In addition, bamboo poles and ring i pool for use by anyone assisting a pe
7. Horse-play is prohibited.
8. No glass bottles will be allowed in th
9. u

Me at swimming area at An Khe.

field could get a new or clean set of fatigues was when they brought them out to the field. Their delivery service for the clothes was interesting; they would drop the shirts in one pile and the pants in the other. We would go pick out a shirt and pants that fit and then throw the old used stuff into another pile. We were required to carry extra socks, but I had this thing about taking off my boots for any reason. From time to time I would air my feet out, but I feared if we were attacked and I wasn't wearing my boots and died, well, let's just say that's not how you're supposed to end up in the cavalry. I paid a heavy price for my phobia about removing my boots: when I returned home, my feet were in bad shape and to this day, I still have problems with them.

The razor I mentioned a while back was a gift from my father-in-law. He had been in Normandy during World War II and knew it was something I could really use in the field. The razor was battery powered and came with its own case and mirror. It sure was nice being able to keep my beard down without having to use cold water to shave. I have no memory of what happened to it. I suspect I just gave it away when I left Vietnam.

> MAY 3, 1966. Well, I really overdid it last night, they have a local beer here called Biere Leroux and its powerful stuff, I think it gave me a double hangover. Some idiot fired off his weapon last night, that seems to happen every time we come in from the field, I don't think anyone was hurt. Sometimes I think it's safer in the field fighting Charlie, instead, of some clown accidentally shooting you in base camp. At least Charlie's a bad shot. I got a real surprise yesterday, they told me they finally got an ice machine in base camp. I can't believe it, but for the first time, we had ice in our iced tea at the Mess Hall. The beer was extra cold, and you know me and cold beer. This time when we go to the field, we'll be gone a long time (at least 25 days), so you might drop a pack of Kool Aid in every letter. The water in Bong Son is terrible.

There were two choices of local beers. Both were OK, drinkable anyway. One was the Biere Leroux I talked about in my letter. Since it came in quart bottles it was easy to get carried away and imbibe a bit more than you should. The other local beer, Ba Muoi Ba or "33," came in regular long-neck bottles. The cokes were nothing like you would recognize, though the bottles looked the same. The dark mix of the drink would settle to the bottom, leaving the clear at the top. As part of their service to G.I.s the coke seller would shake it up for you, then knock the cap off with a metal bar as gracefully as a sommelier pulling a cork. The mixed product looked like coke

Me and a young Vietnamese girl who was selling cokes.

but was minus the fizz. The young boys and girls who opened our beers and cokes had a way of striking the caps and knocking them into the air like missiles. Sometimes they even iced them down for us, but this was rare. Most of these boys and girls were 8 or 9 years old and just looking for a way to earn extra money for their families.

4

Bong Son Battle— All Hell Breaks Loose

Our next operation, Davy Crockett, was a search and destroy mission, conducted by the third brigade of the First Cavalry and the First of the Ninth, plus an ARVN Scout Company. It was near Bong Son, within the Binh Dinh Province, and took place from May 4 until May 16, 1966.

We had been guarding Highway 19 between An Khe and Pleiku for a while and were ready for a new mission. We didn't know at the time just how devastating this next mission would be for those of us in the 2nd platoon.

Usually when our battalion would move out for a combat operation, we would be flown there by C-130s, C-7 Caribous, Chinooks or Hueys. This trip, however, we used a different mode of transportation. On May 4 the whole battalion boarded open deuce-and-a-half trucks, and then headed east towards the ocean and Bong Son. The trucks held about 20 or so and were open in the back. We were loaded in with half of us standing and facing outward with our weapons at the ready in case of an ambush. The remainder of the troopers were sitting down in the center of the floor. In addition to the troopers in the back of the truck, most of the trucks had an M-60 machine gun setting on the top of the cab for extra protection.

It was impressive to see this number of trucks all in the same place. This was a massive display of the U.S. Army's power and the 1st Cavalry Division's assets. We rolled out of Camp Radcliff on Hwy 19 and drove through An Khe towards Bong Son. We drove all night and I stood with my rifle at the ready the entire trip, expecting we might be ambushed at any time. The lights on the trucks hardly put out any light. I noticed as we approached Highway 1 (which followed the coast) and got closer to Qui Nhon that there were Korean troops guarding the road for us. At first it was unsettling to see the Koreans on the road because their outward

Some of our platoon traveling by truck on Highway 19 heading to Bong Son.

appearance and uniforms were very similar to NVA soldiers. But the remainder of our trip to Bong Son was uneventful.

What we didn't know was that the 7th Cavalry was about to be involved in a multi-day battle with VC and fresh NVA troops. This five-day campaign proved to be the biggest battle of my entire year in Vietnam.

On May 5, 1966, we were alerted because another unit had set off a major ambush in the foothills above the Bong Son plains during the night. I later learned this ambush had resulted in many enemy soldiers being killed. I don't know to this day which of our units was involved, nor how many NVA they eliminated with their ambush.

The morning of May 6 we air assaulted into an LZ close to A Company 2/7 Cavalry; at the time they were engaged in combat with a large NVA force. This was one of the rare, truly hot LZs I air assaulted into during my year in Vietnam. This assault was right out of the movies, with bullets kicking up dirt all around us. The sound of the bullets striking the helicopters was one I'll never forget. I saw some soldiers fall while running from the helicopters; at the time I presumed they had been hit by enemy fire. Thinking back, it's possible many of them simply stumbled and fell, but I wasn't close enough to any of them to tell what really happened.

As we landed, one of the covering ARA ships banked over just behind the rear guard. The door gunner was leaning out by a strap and opened fire with his M-60 machine gun. I could see the Viet Cong soldiers, dressed in all black, running like hell. When the dust settled, I looked around and felt very lucky to have survived this air assault, still standing and undamaged.

The second platoon now had become the rear guard for Bravo Company and my squad was in the rear. I positioned myself as the very last soldier in the platoon. Somehow, I thought I could do a better job of protecting our rear. Who knows?

The first night we dug in and just at dusk a volley of white phosphorous mortar rounds exploded in the middle of the 2nd platoon's command post where our platoon leader, platoon sergeant, squad leader and two riflemen had been having a meeting. They all sustained severe torso and leg wounds, but thankfully none were killed. A medevac chopper came in quickly and transported them out to a field hospital for treatment.

As it turns out, this had been a sad case of friendly fire: an American mortar squad from another company had launched the mortars accidentally. This mortar platoon had no idea friendly troops were operating in their test-target area. After this incident it was crystal clear to me that when you were in combat it was just too easy to be in the wrong place at the wrong time.

I had been digging my foxhole with my entrenching tool and my foxhole buddy was watching me dig while he was resting against one of the many raised graves in the area. When the mortars hit, he suddenly dove into the foxhole with me and began bailing dirt out of it with his steel pot like his life depended on it, and it did. He was later wounded on May 6 and like many others I encountered during this battle, I don't know what happened to him after he left the field. I do know I looked him up on *The Wall* and never found his name, so I guess he survived. Another member of my squad was hit in the hip with a piece of mortar shrapnel. I know this because he dropped his pants and showed me. I told him to go see the medic, but he declined.

This accident resulted in the 2nd platoon losing our new platoon leader and new platoon sergeant. They were both new to us, and I never even got a chance to speak with either of them. Our fireteam leader then told us we needed to stay sharp and to continue with our mission.

The following morning we became the attacking force, while our sister battalion, the 2nd of the 7th, became a blocking force. I understand that the 2nd of the 7th was beat up in this battle and sustained more KIA's than we did. They were the blocking force, while we were pushing the NVA, who were desperately trying to escape, in their direction.

Many years after the war I saw a casualty list showing my platoon had sustained a stunning loss during this battle, on the 6th of May 1966; our platoon had gone from 34 to 6 troopers.

The first night of the battle puff-the-magic-dragon dropped flares all night long. These flares cast an eerie shadow across the fields where we were dug into our foxholes and as they floated down, they made a weird whirling sound. It's surprising how much light these flares put out; they illuminated the entire area and made us grunts feel ill at ease. Most of us had little sleep, if any, during that terrible night.

At one point during the night a sergeant had ordered me to fill in at another position on the other side of our company perimeter. From there 15 or so troopers were sent out on a recon patrol in front of the position I was baby-sitting. They were to return at the exact same place, so that no one would be accidentally shot. The signal they were to use when they were coming back in was a green hand-fired flare. After they had been gone about 15 minutes, a flurry of rifle fire and explosions began. I immediately prepared myself mentally for a fight; then, thankfully, came a flare of the proper color. The troopers came on the run towards the position I was covering. One of the guys dove into the prone-shelter I was in and we talked a little. He told me the squad had run into an enemy machine gun squad who were digging in and apparently planning to ambush us the next morning as we started to move. Someone had been smart sending out this recon patrol and this patrol had no doubt saved us from sustaining many more casualties. Luckily none of the guys on this recon were injured during this excursion that night. The soldier I was talking with told me he was certain they had wounded or killed some of the enemy.

The 2nd platoon was operating without a lieutenant, so we acted as rear guard for the rest of the company on May 6. I knew from the beginning we were in big trouble; a trooper had been sent back to the rear with his arm heavily bandaged. He appeared to have sustained a bullet wound in either his arm or shoulder and I could see by the number of bandages it must have been bad. The head medic then asked the captain if a medevac should be called in for this wounded soldier; the captain's response was "NO." He then said, "We'll have plenty more needing medevacs before this day is done." We found out soon enough that this captain knew what he was talking about. As we were moving forward, we engaged an unknown number of enemy troops. Our firepower was superior to theirs and the NVA troops soon broke contact. This tactic foretold what we could expect the rest of the day.

I was firing across a small stream and we stopped a moment. When we began moving forward again, I reached for my rifle and stupidly grabbed the red-hot barrel. The pain was excruciating, but there was no stopping here to seek medical treatment. I suffered with a scalded stripe across the palm of my right hand and this made a very bad day even more miserable.

Being behind the main fighting force once again, we couldn't fire our weapons because we had friendly troops to our front. We had stopped for a while and I was using a bomb crater as a ready-made foxhole. Word came down from the chain of command: "Blessing to the front." Not good! The message said to leave everything but your rifle and move forward. I was to report to the top sergeant; this was usually bad news when we were engaged in active combat. I wondered what kind of suicide mission the top sergeant wanted to send me on. I began carefully working my way forward and found the top sergeant. He was behind a huge bush with radios all around him, talking very seriously. When he paused, he told me he wanted me to carry a wounded little boy to the rear for medical evacuation. The kid was badly burned all over, most likely from napalm. Bullets were still hissing through the air, some uncomfortably close. When you can hear them hissing, they are always too close.

After trying to decide how the heck I was going to pick the boy up without doing further damage to him, a medic who was also headed to the rear and had been watching me said, "You carry my bags and I'll carry the kid." So, he grabbed the boy and I grabbed his three medical bags and we headed towards the rear.

Soon, driven by hissing bullets, we dove into a drainage ditch and landed in the middle of the company XO and his troops. While we were waiting for the firing to let up so that I could get back to my platoon and the medic could get the injured boy onto a helicopter, I was fascinated by the radio work of these Headquarters troopers. The XO seemed to be able to talk on three radios at practically the same time. He began talking angrily and suddenly turned to me and said with a bit of temper, "The medevac won't come in because they're not sure just where we are." He then ordered me to "take this orange panel into the open-area over there," pointing to a close by area, and hold it up facing northwest. I couldn't believe the pilots would not land when they knew the company had wounded on the ground and some were dying.

I did as I was ordered and got out of the ditch and held the panel high in the air. So, there I stood with this brightly colored panel in the air listening to the bullets hissing around me. I finally got down on my knees, hoping to be less of a target for the enemy bullets. But as the firing continued, I just awaited a bullet to find me. I could tell the rounds were coming from a long way away and lucky for me, whoever was shooting was a piss-poor marksman.

The reason for this dangerous assignment was clear to me; I knew the radio operator's job was to pop a smoke canister and then radio the pilots "smoke popped"; the pilot would then confirm the color. The pilots then used the smoke color as a ground reference point. This day, the pilots reported more than one popped smoke of the same color coming from more than one location. You couldn't blame the pilots; they were responsible for those expensive machines they flew along with everyone else on their choppers. These NVA had been smart by trying to get a medevac chopper to land near them so they could shoot the hell out of them and kill or capture the crew members. This subversive action, meant to undermine our procedures, told us we were probably dealing with a large, well-equipped NVA unit.

Finally, the XO yelled. "Leave the panel and come on in, the medevacs are on their way." Two medevacs landed, and we began loading the wounded. The injured were a mix of civilians, NVA or VC and 7th Cavalry troopers; some had already died or appeared close to death. I watched as one trooper died in the arms of a medic. After loading as many as we could onto the choppers, they just sat there and continued to idle on the ground. They couldn't take off because we were experiencing a heavy volume of rifle fire coming our way. Once there was a pause in enemy fire, the choppers lifted off. Just as they were lifting off, I headed back to my squad.

While trying to avoid an abundance of bullets peppering the air around me, I plunged headfirst into the crater my squad was using as a foxhole. I found my squad deep into a debate on how they were going to live better lives when they returned to the world. They talked about how they would go to church every Sunday without fail and promised to do many other things I doubted they would in fact do when they went home. I vowed at that time not to make any promises I probably wouldn't keep when I got back to the world. I found it interesting though, how bullets heading their way had changed their perspective on how they had been living their lives back at home.

At the platoon's location, I was fascinated watching the jets streak across our front dropping their bombs and was glad I wasn't on the other side. Even as far away as we were you could feel the concussion as the bombs exploded. Watching the jets drop napalm that exploded into walls of flame as it hit, without regard for whatever or whoever was in their path, was frightening. This is one thing that has always weighed on my mind; what the heck happened to all those civilians who couldn't get out of their village? The fact is visions of the horrific damage caused by these bombs and napalm only adds to the baggage combat soldiers are forced to carry with them the rest of their lives.

One F-5 Freedom Fighter came directly over the top of me. I happened to be lying on my back leaning against a bunker, looking up, and I saw him before I heard him. As he came into view between the palm trees, I saw a 750-pound bomb he was carrying release from his under side. I thought *oh no this is it, we're all dead.* But the bomb was going the same speed as the jet and angled down, hitting somewhere in front of us. I estimate it hit about 100 feet or so from us. When it hit, I bounced a foot off the ground because of this explosion and couldn't hear a thing; in fact, I was sure I was deaf. After a short time, my hearing returned but I still had ringing in my ears.

While I was still recovering from the bomb blast, a mama-san (older women) came out of one of the bunkers 10 feet in front of me and scared me half to death. I had no idea that anyone was in this bunker/bomb shelter. As it turned out she was just trying to get a breath of fresh air.

The 2nd platoon was ordered to move. We had to cross a long/narrow dike running between two dry rice paddies. We had taken so much rifle fire, we waited a long time before sending the next man. I'm not sure if the rest of the platoon was following our route at the time. The 1st and 3rd platoons were badly beat up and were leaderless, so the 2nd platoon was put up front. We hadn't gone far at all when a Viet Cong soldier jumped out of a hole 100 feet to our front, then tried to run out of the dry rice paddy we were about to cross. The three of us up front opened fire and this VC scout dove back into the same hole he had come from. My sometimes-not-too-trusty M-16 jammed after just three rounds. Here I was under heavy rifle fire, trying to knock a shell casing out of the firing chamber with a cleaning rod.

My M-16's jamming when I needed it most caused me to question whether I would ever be able to stop it from jamming. When the firing subsided, it got very quiet. I took advantage of the brief break in the action and repositioned myself feet first towards the enemy, thinking it would be far better to be shot in my foot, rather than my head. Then while lying prone on my back, I took the weapon apart and spread the pieces out on my chest then quickly put the weapon back together and prayed I had remedied the jamming issue.

Then all hell broke loose. Bullets flew so thick, they were clattering in the trees. The enemy was trying to break out through the 2nd platoon and the noise was deafening. It was like it was snowing with all the bits and pieces of the chewed-up trees falling on us.

We didn't know for sure how many enemy soldiers we had engaged, but I thought it could have been a large NVA unit trying to break through our platoon.

The enemy fire appeared to be high and most of it was above my head.

I looked ahead of me and lying about 10 to 12 feet in front of me was a buddy. He looked as though he was asleep, his head was down, and his nose was in the dirt. Upon further inspection I saw he still had his rifle braced against his shoulder and pointed straight ahead. Looking closer, I could see he had been shot in the neck and appeared to have died instantly. As fate would have it, a couple of minutes before, I had been standing in about the same place where he had lost his life. When you're in the infantry, you know being injured or killed in a fire fight is a very real possibility, but his death really hit me hard. We had discovered we both were from California and that we had attended rival high schools in San Leandro. He told me he wanted to become a minister when he got out of the service and it saddened me to know he would never be able to achieve his desire to serve those in need of spiritual guidance.

On the other side of the platoon's position, the machine gun squad was in a fight to the death. The enemy was trying very hard to overrun their side of the platoon. The machine gun squad was anchoring the right side of our position against a human wave assault. Lucky for all of us, they had been able to throw the assault back. We soon discovered many lifeless NVA bodies littering the area in front of our positions. During this assault, the assistant machine gunner was shot in the chest. Things had quieted down for a couple of minutes and our medic was able to start treating him right away. The medevacs were landing way behind our position and someone carried the injured gunner back to be transported out of the field.

Once the gunfire subsided our platoon began moving again. During this lull in action, I noticed a young girl standing near us. She was standing with her arms held straight down and out away from her body, her hair was completely singed off and she was naked. Our medic had just patched up the last of our wounded and all were headed to the rear for transport. I asked him if he could go see what he could do for her; he went over to her and gave her a drink of water from his canteen. When he returned, I asked how she was doing and he said she wasn't going to live. I looked back where she had been standing and she was gone. This sad tragedy stuck with me and was just one more terrible memory of this day during the battle of Bong Son. The saddest part of it all was the fact that our use of napalm had caused these awful injuries to this innocent child.

Suddenly, firing broke out once again and then stopped just as quickly. As we were holding the front, another platoon moved forward around to our left and led out across an open space towards another tree line. Once they were out of sight, a tremendous amount of automatic gun fire began and then the other platoon came running back. Upon their return they told us they had run headfirst into a group of NVA. Luckily, no one was injured during this brief encounter with the enemy.

We remained in place and occasionally the enemy would take pot shots at us. After a brief exchange of fire, our new fire team leader (who had only been in the field two days) asked me, "Do you see a mark on my neck?" I replied, "Yeah, a big red streak." He told me a bullet had hit a tree he was trying to squeeze behind, and it had ricocheted and creased his neck. I told him he was one lucky guy not to have been more seriously injured. Shortly after this exchange our machine gunner and his crew had slipped between us and I hadn't even noticed them. I was so busy at that point firing down range, I wasn't paying much attention to who was next to me or even 10 feet away. During the heat of a fire fight it's hard not to have tunnel vision, not noticing anything other than the attacking enemy.

A short 15 minutes later a rocket came roaring in, exploded and instantly killed our new fire team leader. I didn't remember hearing any helicopters at the time, but then again I was in a full-on fire fight and not aware of everything happening around me. Later, many of the guys in the 2nd platoon told me the rocket had come from one of our helicopters. Our new fire team leader's luck had run out, and after only two days in the field he lost his life to friendly fire.

When things calmed down a little, a trooper from the 2nd platoon we called Frenchy asked me to check his ass-end after the rocket had hit; he thought he had been wounded. I pulled a still smoking red-hot piece of metal out from under his pack and I'm sure it was from the rocket. Frenchy was one lucky trooper that day. He hadn't even been cut by the piece of sharp metal. I handed him the piece of rocket and told him it would make a great souvenir to take home. I reassured him he was uninjured and that nothing had penetrated his pack.

The rocket had wounded many others in the 2nd platoon. Since I was one of the few left untouched by the rocket, I soon found a line of injured soldiers forming behind me waiting to be patched up. What I had learned from my first aid classes in basic training kicked in and I began trying my best to help my injured buddies. We all carried a bandage with us that was to be reserved for our own injuries, however, I soon used my own bandage and even resorted to using the toilet paper packs we got in our sundries just trying to stop the bleeding. Some of these guys had multiple injuries and were carried off to the awaiting medevac choppers as quickly as possible. Many years after the war, one of the soldiers in my platoon wrote and thanked me for patching up his leg and helping him back to the helicopter to be evacuated. I remembered helping someone back for evacuation, but the entire incident had been so traumatic, and I had been so involved, I was unable to remember just who I helped that day.

It is impossible to explain how I felt during combat; only someone who has experienced it can truly understand. The adrenaline flows and brings on a high, I am told, much like someone taking drugs; but soon this feeling of euphoria leaves and your adrenaline takes a deep dive and you're left feeling like a deflated balloon. Combat stimulates every one of your senses. It's easy to perceive the visual, what with tracers floating around, orange (ours) going in their direction and green (theirs) coming our way. I found the sounds and smells overwhelmed me while engaging in combat. The pungent odors of the 2.75 rockets being fired by our ARA and the sounds of M-16s being fired on full-automatic along with the roar of the M-60 machine guns will stay with me the rest of my life.

All in all, it was a sleepless two nights and two very tough days. I have since learned that during this three-day battle, 335 NVA were killed and 22 more were captured by Bravo Company.

Historians have described this battle as a "classic air assault operation." From my perspective as a combat soldier, I didn't see anything classic about that mess. All I know is, I saw far too much death and devastation during those three days in May.

The last night we spent in this area wasn't far from where all the fighting took place. We pulled into what I understood was a battalion perimeter. Once settled, I took an inventory of what I had policed up after the battle. The RTO had been shot and wounded so I had his PRC 25 radio, an M-79 and three M-16s and my shirt was stuffed with around 40 empty M-16 magazines. In combat you tried to retrieve everything you went in with, not leaving anything for the enemy to pick up and use against you later.

That morning after the battle I looked around and there were six including me from the 2nd platoon still standing. I knew several of those remaining troopers, but I can't with any confidence give a complete listing of all the members of the 2nd platoon. When you're on a combat mission, there is little talking and most of us never had the chance to get to know one another in the field. As with any grunt, I didn't know the names of everyone in my platoon. The only troopers I really got to know were those in my squad and guys I interacted with when we were back in base camp.

On May 7 a grizzled old sergeant was near me and I started talking with him about the battle. I asked him, "What the heck were they shooting at us?" He asked me what I meant, and I told him some of the rounds made a weird sound as they went by. It sounded like a cross between a snap and a pop, but very loud. I asked him if it could have been the NVA .51 caliber anti-aircraft ammo. He replied "no" and that I probably wouldn't like his answer. He told me what I had heard were bullets passing very close to my ear. He said it was much like a jet breaking the sound barrier; the bullet pierces a cone in the air near your ear and makes a popping and cracking sound. Wow, his explanation shook me up, because I had heard a lot of those popping and cracking sounds all day.

I had a chance to see the weapons that had been gathered from the battlefield the day after the battle. I talked with a couple of troopers from another battalion. They showed me three .51 caliber machine guns, a huge stack of rifles and an odd little machine gun on wheels that looked more like a toy than a weapon.

Just before we departed the area on May 7, a soldier from another unit was moving through the area on patrol and asked where I was the day before and I pointed to the general area. He told me they had gathered a lot of enemy weapons out in front of that area. He said they counted 98 enemy dead and there were lots of drag marks where the enemy themselves had pulled off wounded and dead fellow NVA soldiers. A few of the dead they found had ropes tied around their ankles to make it easier to drag them away. One of the dead had something like a meat hook in his shoulder, to make it easier to drag the body away. What a gruesome scene that must have been, I'm glad I wasn't there when they were recovering the bodies because I didn't need another horrific memory of this war. The NVA once again proved how brutal they could be; even while trying to recover their dead and injured they seemed to care very little about their fallen comrades.

For the first time since embarking on our air assault into to the Bong Son Valley, I was able to write my wife a letter.

MAY 8, 1966. I got a letter from you yesterday, but they brought the mail out today and I didn't have any. I can't understand why I can't get more mail. It must be this darn army. We had a sergeant who had only been in Vietnam eight days (when our squad leader was hit, he took over), he was killed instantly when a rocket hit next to him. We hardly knew his name! War is hell. You would have been proud of me. We were fighting a heavy weapons company of NVA troops and we had a lot of wounded. Me, Dennis Blessing, the one guy that can't stand the sight of blood, patched up three wounded troopers and then went back to fighting. These people are weird. We give them lots of warning to get out, yet all they do is get into their bomb shelters (every hooch has a bomb shelter) and you wouldn't believe how many woman and children are messed up by our ARA and airstrikes….

The water there was more than just undrinkable, it was unhealthy. The local villagers used human excrement as fertilizer in their rice paddies. In addition to that, the Vietnamese simply go to the side of a trail or on a dike and squat down and go. Then they use whatever is lying around to wipe themselves. I pondered over how they took care of this problem, though not much, because I noticed when we gave out our C-rations they would take everything except the toilet paper and salt and pepper. All the water in these canals sooner or later went through the rice paddies. We did our best not to drink this water, but sometimes it was impossible. Let's face it, at times we were so thirsty, we'd rather take a chance on getting dysentery. Until Vietnam, I never experienced what it felt like to be so thirsty that I was willing to drink just about any water, from any source.

Generally, after a major battle it was common to need replacement equipment. The Army had a hard and fast rule at the time: if you wanted to get a piece of equipment replaced you had to turn in the same type of worn or damaged equipment. If it was reported as lost, the soldier was charged for the replaced equipment. There was one exception to this rule: after a battle a soldier could declare a combat loss and get a new issue of equipment without charge. So, of course, once a battle was over everyone in the company would put in for whatever they wanted and called it a combat loss. That was how I ended up with extra canteens; I really needed them and many times I was more than thankful to have them. The extra weight didn't bother me, as just knowing I had decent water to drink eased my mind.

> MAY 11, 1966. I just got a letter from you with a picture of J.R., thanks a million I sure did want a picture of him. We're on stand-by and man have we been living it up. I must have had 15 cokes today and at least 5 beers. We're right on the north outskirts of Bong Son. We went down to the Bong Son River to wash and really had a ball, the whole platoon (not me), bought "gook" hats and now you couldn't get them off their heads. I met a little girl named Lau and I made her some of my Kool Aid, she tried to take a drink, but said it was too sweet and she couldn't drink it. She speaks English better than most, and a little French. No telling what's up for the next few days. I sure hope we stay here. You can't imagine the feeling of pride I felt, when we walked into the brigade area and the G.I.s lining the road, were taking pictures and movies of us. You could hear them saying "there they are, the 1st of the 7th," we are a proud outfit and for good reason.

Someone sent one of the troopers a Monopoly set. But no one I knew was going to play Monopoly while we were here in Bong Son. Then one of the troopers pointed out an interesting detail: the Monopoly money looked a lot like the official MPC (script) that the Army issued us in Vietnam that we used instead of greenbacks. In Vietnam soldiers were not allowed to have American money; in fact, American dollars were considered contraband. I don't know why or even how the Vietnamese used our script, but they accepted it just as readily as P's. I think they might have used it by getting an American soldier to go to one of our PXs and buy something they wanted.

What happened next was no surprise. Once they discovered they could pass off the Monopoly money as MPC some of the guys began using it for Boom Boom girls. I admit this didn't bother me much, since I found Sin City and its military sanctioned prostitution less than legal. But these guys began using the Monopoly money in any way they could. It just wasn't right when they began cheating the little coke girls and boys—they worked hard for their money. They iced the cokes for us, then shook them up because the coloring settled to the bottom and after they opened them, then they would hang around until you were finished and collect the bottles. I found out later, they had to turn in an empty in order to get a new full bottle. Most of the merchants the troops dealt with, including the young ones, caught on very quickly that this Monopoly money could not be used at our PXs. Once this happened it ended this sad con game some of the troopers were trying to put over on our Vietnamese allies who were just trying to make a living.

While we were still at Bong Son, a tragic accident happened. After a group of soldiers had off-loaded from a Huey, they began taking off the tremendous amount of gear they were wearing. One of the troopers got his gear tangled on something and a pin from one of his hand grenades pulled out and then released the spoon. Once the spoon pops off, you have exactly 4.7 seconds until the hand grenade makes a very loud boom and sprays metal in all directions. The resulting explosion killed three and I understand eight or nine were wounded. I saw the wall that was near where the explosion took place and it was splattered with bits and pieces of various materials, some human I'm sure.

> MAY 12, 1966. Well, I still don't believe it, but they left me back today to guard the equipment. I wish I could do this every day. I even got a chance to shave for the first time in about four days. They really worked us out the last couple of days and I'm glad I'm not going with them today. I am going to sit back here and take it easy today. They passed out C-Rations and of course everyone got rid of the ones they don't want. A couple of us rounded up all the thrown

Hueys landing at Bong Son battle May 1966.

away cans, we found about 60. We traded 15 cans for three cokes. I just opened a can of cookies and later I'll make some co-co. Well, still no word when we're going back into base camp. I'll bet my package is waiting for me back in base camp. I can't wait to get it. Remember the one set of jungle pants I had. Well their gone. During the big battle I tore the seams between the legs, and they didn't give me a replacement pair until yesterday. You should see the pants they gave me, they're old and used with lots of holes in them and to top it off, they have a tag hanging off one of the belt loops. It's the same type of tag they use for wounded and dead, so you figure it out (what cheap bastards!).

I told you we went back to the same area the other day and you should have seen the mess. It was awful, there were all kinds of fresh graves. It looked like a lot of civilians had died after being caught in the middle of our big battle. They bury their dead, on top of the ground, right in their yards.

Later we were told not to give away or trade our C-rations, but occasionally some C's would end up in the mountains or jungles supporting our enemies. We found a way to solve this major problem and still be able to give away our extra C-rations to the local needy. We simply punched a hole in the cans with our trusty beer can openers, so the C-rations would have to be used right away and not eventually end up in the hands of our enemies.

Hungry Vietnamese kids running after C-rations I threw.

Trooper Yeomans sharing C-rations with Vietnamese kids.

Being assigned to guard equipment was great duty. The equipment was lined up in a square formation, with each of the four platoon's equipment on each side of the square. All I had to do was to lie around all day and make sure nothing was stolen. I was there alone, but I wasn't afraid. There were ARVN troops in the area, who could be called on if needed.

The entire company was out looking for a soldier who had rented a moped the day before. He then drove through an ARVN check point, even though they tried to flag him down. He just kept going until he was shot off the moped by the NVA or VC. According to the local villagers, the VC shot and wounded this guy. After shooting him off the moped, they picked him up and were parading him from village to village. Though the company searched all day, they never did find him. After I wrote and told my wife about this incident, she wrote back and told me that one of her friends had come to church the previous Sunday and said her boyfriend was reported missing in Vietnam. She said he had rented a moped and drove off into the jungle, and they couldn't find him. Small world isn't it!

When the troopers returned from looking for the missing soldier they were worn out. It was an extra hot day, way over 100 degrees, and they pushed them harder than usual. Looking at how exhausted they were made me even more grateful I didn't have to go out with them. When I was told they were never able to find this injured and missing soldier, I quickly drew my own conclusion and decided his fate had been in his hands the minute he drove off on that moped into enemy territory.

Normally, when a soldier left the field either sick or injured and never returned to the company, we rarely knew what happened to them. I never thought much about this before writing this book, but I guess I was forced to just put them out of my mind. Grunts in Vietnam were usually left to wonder if their buddies ever made it home. Being unable to have some type of closure was a major problem. You need to be able to get closure, just to keep your sanity and to grieve the loss of a friend or even that of soldiers you barely knew. When you're in combat together you can get very close to each other, very quickly. If one of you leaves the field and never returns, it's like losing a family member and never knowing what happened to them. Many soldiers found it hard to move on and were left with a hollow feeling that would continue to haunt them the rest of their lives. I did my best to just move on. I knew thinking about our losses and being unable to do anything about it would only increase my anxiety.

> MAY 12, 1966. Here we are back in base camp. Isn't it amazing how fast we can go from the field to base camp. This place looks better every time I come back to it. Pretty soon this hole is going to look like home (heaven help me). Well lover, I'm in high spirits, feel great even though I haven't gotten a letter from you yet today. Hey, they're giving out free beer tonight, uh-oh that's good news….

Whenever we arrived at the An Khe airport our weapons were always unloaded and double checked before we boarded trucks to take us to the Seventh Cavalry area inside basecamp. This time, as we were returning it was a surprise to see we were on a new road, one that wasn't even built when we left a couple of weeks earlier.

Suddenly, as we were entering base camp there was a big commotion and you could hear magazines being loaded into rifles and bullets being chambered and readied for combat. Looking up at the hillside in front of us there appeared to be Vietnamese covering the entire area. We were so far away; all we could see were tiny figures in black pajamas and conical hats spread across the hillside. They looked to most of us to be an attacking force who had already succeeded in breaching our base camp perimeter. Luckily, someone yelled "don't fire" just in time and averted a possible tragedy.

Huey returning to An Khe after Bong Son battle.

As far as our group knew, no Vietnamese were permitted inside our base camp perimeter. It would have been great if someone had given us a heads-up about the change in the rules. We found out later that the local Vietnamese had been hired to cut the brush on the hillside just inside the base camp perimeter.

When we finally got back to the company area, the First Cavalry Division band was playing the old cavalry songs "Gary Owen" and "The Girl I Left Behind." It felt great to be

"Garry Owen" B Company 1/7 Cavalry's Unit patch.

back out of the field and hear the band welcome us home. Their recognition of our part in the hard-fought battle at Bong Son filled me with pride and their renditions of these songs long associated with the 7th Cavalry made me feel good.

The battle of Bong Son had been as bad as it can get in Vietnam and my platoon had been right in the thick of this huge battle. Our platoon began with 34 troopers and only 6 of us were left standing at the end.

> MAY 12, 1966. I just got a letter from you and you sounded concerned about me; well don't be, I can take care of myself. When they show the 7th Cav on T.V. was it at Bong Son when we were in a rice paddy with kind of hedges around? If it was, I was there. I forgot to tell you, but we got a hero's welcome when we got in this morning. They had the band playing and two American girls from the Red Cross served our chow. Well better sign off. I want you to be a real good girl because I worry about you.

It appears there may be letters missing during this period after Bong Son, ones that I had written but decided not to send. I was truly sorry I had been so open and honest with my wife. Her letter to me after Bong Son made me aware just how much she worried about me. I decided it was best not to be so candid about what was happening and what I was feeling and thinking at the time. This was war and people were going to get hurt and die. I didn't think she could take hearing about some of the things that had happened to me; hell, I could hardly bear to think about them.

> MAY 13, 1966. I still didn't get the package or even a letter from you today. I did get a letter from cousin Steve today and he's got it made, he's the company XO and doesn't have to go into the field anymore. Well, all kinds of rumors are going around about when the First Cavalry is going to rotate home. It now looks like it's going to start the first part of July. It doesn't mean I'm going anywhere; it just means those who came over with the Cavalry will get to go home. The weather has been hot lately. We still aren't in the monsoon season yet, but it will be here soon.

Around this time, everyone began to worry about what was going to happen to the First Cavalry Division once the original troops rotated home. Those of us who came over as the initial replacement troops for those who were injured and killed during the big battle of the Ia Drang realized we had only been in country a couple of months ourselves and still could be considered as on-the-job trainees. Though we were fortunate to have been trained by some of the seasoned veterans of the battle at LZ X-Ray. Now these valuable troopers were rotating home and we could expect a huge number of greenhorns being sent to the field as their replacements.

Since our platoon had already experienced huge losses during the Bong Son battle, the impending influx of newcomers was scary. I guess in a way we felt as though the Army didn't see the big picture when it came to replacement of large numbers of battle tested combat soldiers with relatively untested troopers.

> MAY 14, 1966. The 2nd platoon came back and all they hit were snipers. I guess they really did some humping. Remember the other day when I said it was hot! Well it was 124 degrees and that's warm. I forgot to tell you but on our last mission our medic couldn't make it, so guess who acted as medic. Isn't that unbelievable! It's sure great to get a letter from you every day, keep up the good work!

> MAY 16, 1966. Well no mail has come yet today. I was mad this morning because I was on guard duty last night and I was supposed to be able to sleep till one o'clock. They called an alert and got me up at eight. You should have heard me raising hell. Now they say I can sleep this afternoon, but I'm still pissed off. Well lover, the days

are passing by. I'd like to get malaria just to get a little rest. It's terrible to say such a thing, but after a couple of months of this you have to get some rest. This place could drive you batty, but all I have to do is think of you and going home and get out your pictures and it helps.

My mention of malaria reminded me how the U.S. Army attempted to protect us from contracting malaria. They had us take two types of pills, a huge orange pill that we took every Sunday and a little white pill we took every day but Sunday. We asked our medic about the pills and he said they were originally a treatment for leprosy. Somehow the Army discovered that the pills suppressed the malaria bug. Many of the guys I knew seldom took the pills with hope they could get some time out of the field; I took them as prescribed and they apparently did stave off my getting malaria while I was in Vietnam.

MAY 19, 1966. Well I finally got a letter from you this morning. You said you hadn't gotten any letters for six days and I can't imagine why. I write to you every day except when I can't. We're out guarding the green line now, it's the defense barrier around base camp. It's not too bad, but they sure have been feeding us crap for meals....

I was truly surprised when my wife said she hadn't received any letters for six days. It took a lot of dedication on my part to write as often as I did. Many times, as we stopped on a trail, I would pull out my writing paper that I kept safe and dry inside my helmet liner; often the only dry place on me was under my helmet liner. Then, sitting down in the middle of the trail, I would begin writing. If we began moving again, I'd put my letter back away and continue writing when we stopped again. The only time I couldn't write was when there was no cover and it was pouring rain. None of the pens I was able to liberate would work when the paper got wet. I finally figured out why she hadn't received any letters for six days: the timing of her letter coincided with the battle at Bong Son. I still didn't understand why it took the mail so long to get home.

MAY 19, 1966. Gee, I'm glad that you got lots of mail. I know how I feel when I don't get a letter for even a couple of days. ... We're sitting here eating the popcorn you sent, and does it taste good! Last night I popped one and it was windy, and two thirds of the popcorn didn't pop, we still ate it anyway.

Don't know if anyone remembers those ready-made popcorn poppers. The ones that came in disposable aluminum foil pans that you shook over a heat source, and voilà, you popped a full bowl of buttered popcorn. Since we were on a continual camping trip with few pleasures of home, there was something very special about having hot buttered popcorn in the jungles of Vietnam.

> MAY 20, 1966. How are you and your new car coming along? I bet you're really having fun driving it; I just wish I could be there to drive it.
> We are still on the green line. It's nice here because we just sit, and I'm finally getting some much-needed rest from the daily humping through the jungle. I guess the Cav is in a battle not too far from here. There were quite a few NVA troops trying to get to our base camp to start a big attack, but our guys slowed them down. It's nice being this close to base camp because every other day or so we can go in and take a shower. I'm going in as soon as I finish this letter and I'll check to see if I got that package from you....

My wife had written and told me all about her new car. The guys teased me unmercifully about her going out and buying a new car with my combat pay. Her car purchase didn't bother me much because I knew she needed the car; she had a 60-mile round trip to her job. Her dad helped her buy the car and she did well. We had that car until 1980.

My buddies continued to razz me about my wife's new car for weeks on end. Guys in the Army were great at getting on you about something and pestering you without mercy. I discovered the best defense was just going along with them and they eventually left me alone.

I found I could get along in Vietnam with very little money. The only things I spent money on were personal items, beer and the occasional poker game. Since I was able to forgo the charms of the boom boom girls, there was little I needed. I know many will not believe me about going the year without female entertainment, but I never swayed from the commitment I had made to myself and my wife.

> MAY 23, 1966. Well, I spent my most miserable night in Vietnam yet. We went out on patrol yesterday afternoon and were out all afternoon. It rained the whole time and I had to try and sleep cold and wet. So, what happens? We had to go out on patrol again today and it rained all afternoon, looks like I'm in for another wonderful night. One thing I can say for sure, the chow can't get any worse. You wouldn't believe how bad it has been the last couple of days.

I'm told the "Supremes" were here at base camp today and of course I didn't get to see them. I'm in a line outfit and shows like that are for truck drivers and administration types, grunts guarding the perimeter seldom got included in seeing the entertainment provided at base camp. One reason I was so miserable yesterday was they used us for a damned test. A full bird colonel arrived by jeep and handed out some gas masks. He explained we were going to participate in a test and that they were going to spray tear gas on us from a helicopter. Our squad went in without gas masks to see the effect. We had gas masks with us, and it got so bad I finally had to put mine on. One thing I will say about this surprise torture, the colonel stayed and endured the spraying of the tear gas with us. So yesterday was a bad day and today's not much better. Oh well, I'm just glad to have the peace of mind that you're safe at home and don't have to go through things like this.

Can you imagine being wet all the time? This was how we lived, wet all the time, and it was miserable. If we weren't wet from rain, we were covered with sweat, so we were still wet. I can remember having to wring out my wet shirt as if it had just come out of the wash. When we stopped for the night, if we weren't assigned to an ambush or a listening post, we would immediately begin to dig our foxhole. I almost always started dinner and digging at the same time. If it was raining, we would put up a hooch first. The hooch usually went right behind the foxhole, and we would use two ponchos for a roof and one on the ground to sleep on. Most nights we were in two-man positions. This meant each soldier had to pull guard duty half of the night. Three man or more positions were considered a luxury. Guarding was boring and could be a dangerous job. Our lives depended upon at least one trooper awake on guard in each foxhole position all night long. Guards needed to be awake and alert; one sleeping guard in our defensive positions could prove to be very costly to us all.

During the dry season a lot of soldiers carried a poncho liner because they were comfortable to sleep on, but once they got wet, they were useless and were so heavy you couldn't carry them. In some areas we would set up overhead cover to protect us from mortars and rockets. It wasn't much cover since each foxhole I dug resembled a shallow grave. The most foxholes I ever dug in one night was four, they kept moving us all night and that got old very fast. The brass reasoned with us and told us it had to be this way, although no one ever told us why.

When we went out on an ambush no foxholes were dug, but at times we could dig what was known as a *prone shelter*; basically we'd dig individual foot deep areas to lie in. In an ambush the idea was to hit the enemy hard as you could with everything you had and run like hell. We didn't stick around since there was no telling what or who we had just ambushed; this was especially true during nighttime ambushes. I know for a fact we didn't stay to see how many enemies we killed or wounded. Our main concern after setting off an ambush was the hope that someone was aware of us coming back inside our lines and that some overzealous trooper didn't pop off a couple of shots at us as we were returning.

> MAY 24, 1966. Gee, I got three letters today, all from you. Wow, those pictures of J.R. are really cute, thanks a million; they're just what I needed. I've been hearing a lot about Watts and I think it's a shame. I want you to be extra careful in case something does happen there again. Glad to hear your using the dispensary, I can imagine how different it is from the one at Fort Gordon.

When I mentioned Watts, it was the area in Los Angeles where the riots had taken place in August of 1965. My wife was pregnant at the time and worked downtown at the main police headquarters, Parker Center. She worked 12-hour shifts and had to have an armed police escort to and from where she parked her car. That had been a scary time for everyone in Los Angeles. Apparently in reading my letter home to her, there must have been some mention of Watts in the sketchy news we were receiving, and I wanted to let her know I was concerned.

> MAY 26, 1966. Well, right now we're sitting here waiting to find out where we're going. We came off the green line yesterday and last night they told us we were going to Happy Valley early this morning, but we're not gone yet. The old guard of the Cavalry is getting ready to rotate. Things are going to be a mess when all the old timers leave, and the greenhorns start rolling in…. I want to thank you again for the pictures of J.R. there's nothing in the world I would rather get than a picture of him, well, maybe one of you too.

Waiting to go somewhere in Vietnam was weird because you rarely knew where you were going, nor what was in store for you. This uncertainty made the waiting almost intolerable. Many times I felt it would have been better to just get there and get whatever was going to happen over and done.

> MAY 27, 1966. Well, yesterday we went back out to the green line and built bunkers and dug foxholes. I'll tell you what, they could

leave me out there digging for the rest of my time here, at least Charlie isn't shooting at you. They pulled a good one on us yesterday evening. They called an alert and we fell out in the ditches. Of course, it started raining and I was sitting in the rain about 30 feet from our tent and did I ever get soaked, for no reason at all! Looks like we're heading back to the green line to build more bunkers today and that's fine with me. ...

I must say my wife did a very good job of sending letters and packages to me. When I made a special request, I knew I could expect to get whatever I requested in the next one or two packages. I didn't smoke, but I did enjoy a cigar now and then and she would send me some whenever I asked for them.

MAY 27, 1966. Wow, cold beer tonight for the first time since we've been back in base camp. I'm in seventh heaven because they are serving smoked beef sausages and I just love them with cold beer.... Well we worked on the green line today and built two bunkers. I still say I'd do this for the rest of the time I'm over here, but they don't see it my way. Well, it's too dark and I'm too drunk so I guess I'll go.

When we were assigned to the green line it was a great duty. Building bunkers and filling sandbags may not seem to some to be great duty, but it sure beats humping through the jungles and jumping out of helicopters. I did get a nice picture of my squad that day, shirts off and hard at work. I keep a copy of that picture above my desk to remind me of these guys, some didn't make it home and a couple of them were severely wounded. This one picture of the guys I got to know the best brings back mixed memories, some good and some are unbearably sad.

MAY 28, 1966. You know what! I almost believe I'd rather be back in the field than here in base camp. I tell you it's dangerous here in base camp. There is always a weapon going off or a knife fight just because these guys are kids and don't know how to drink and act. Last night a sergeant in our platoon was jumped and five guys kicked the you know what out of him. It seems they're not sending the best troops over here; they're using Vietnam as punishment. I don't know if I told you, there are a couple of guys from the Fort Gordon stockade that I had guarded while I was there. If a guy returns to duty from a stockade, they are sure to be sent over here.

We were on duty 24 hours a day, seven days a week in Vietnam. In base camp sometimes troopers drank too much beer, that's why most of the time we were in the field. We did have a lot of trouble in base camp. I would go have a few beers at the 7th Cavalry Club (they were usually 10 cents each and sometimes they were free), then I'd head back to my tent to write a letter. Many of the guys would drink until they passed out. It was a shame and a very dangerous thing to do in a combat zone. I'm certain the easy access to alcohol eventually contributed to the long-term problems some of guys experienced once they went back home.

5

Not So Happy, Happy Valley

MAY 30, 1966. Well, the typical thing happened this morning, something I'm always afraid might happen, our ambush got ambushed. We went out yesterday; but we were still short of the place where all the fighting was going on last week. When we landed at this LZ someone yelled to watch out for punji stakes and you should have seen them, they were all over. We're about six miles northeast of base camp. Occasionally we could hear firing and bombing. Last night our platoon was out on ambush about 600 meters away from the Company. We didn't hit anything, so we waited until this morning to start back. We got about halfway back to the Company and walked right into an ambush. Luckily, no one in our platoon was hit. The VC had set up between us and the Company and were firing on each of us hoping to get us firing at one another. One man was hit in the knee, but not from friendly fire. We didn't fire on one another as the VC wished and we foiled their plan to make us engage in combat with our own troopers. Yesterday our fire team of six had to go on a short patrol and three were wounded by punji stakes, once again I really do believe someone is looking out for me.

We were near base camp and having trouble with snipers. The snipers would shoot at our re-supply helicopters as they were landing. There's a picture of me standing in elephant grass firing my M-16 in a futile attempt to kill any of those snipers during a mad minute.

The Company had been in a loose perimeter waiting and observing when three shots cracked off near me. Within seconds I jumped through the bushes across the clearing where a trooper we all called Frenchy was lying on the ground holding his upper right leg and appeared to be in a lot of pain. I asked him which way the sniper went, he pointed and so I fired a 20-round magazine and sprayed the bushes down range in the general direction where he pointed. Our medic was there in an instant and started

Me firing my M-16 during "Mad Minute" in waist-high elephant grass.

working on Frenchy's wounds. I immediately began gathering a squad together to chase what I thought was a lone sniper. The VC we were chasing led us into a punji stake trail and five of us including me were injured. Once this happened, we abandoned the chase.

Setting up a punji stake trail and then attempting to lead us into it was a favorite ploy of the VC. The VC knew the punji stakes were virtually impossible to see when approached from one direction. They would stick them into the ground at an angle, with the point about knee high. These stakes were fashioned out of bamboo spikes and I'm told they were then dipped into human excrement to exact maximum damage to their victims. The VC would set up fields of these razor sharp, camouflaged weapons and they took their toll on soldiers all over Vietnam. These low-tech weapons often were the cause of severe infections and at times were the direct cause of amputations.

When we returned to Bravo Company the five of us were discussing our chase after the sniper who had severely injured Frenchy. We discovered not one of us knew Frenchy's real name. When our medic was patching up my punji stake wound, I asked if he knew Frenchy's real name and he said he didn't know. I then asked what name he had written on his medical evacuation tag and he replied Frenchy. This only proved to me that you could become very close to other troopers in the field and yet still know little about them, not even their real name.

Many years later in 2003 while attending a Cavalry reunion at Fort Hood, Texas I met up with Frenchy again and found out his real first name is Donald. After discussing the sniper incident with him, I was shocked to hear he spent a year and a half in the hospital recovering from his very serious wounds. He really surprised me when he said there were several VCs trying to attack us that day, not just a single sniper. Frenchy told me he was hit by a burst of point-blank AK-47 rifle fire that tore up right leg and thigh, leaving him with seven bullet wounds. He also suffered wounds from an explosion, possibly from a grenade. The explosion left him with over 50 pieces of shrapnel, many of which the doctors at the hospital were unable to remove.

I was stunned when he told me about the explosion that injured him. Although I was standing around 15 feet from Frenchy in thick tall bushes, I never heard the explosion that left him with such extensive injuries. There was an interesting side note to Frenchy's medevac ride to the rear. He told me the medic on board treating him was his uncle. What are the chances that could happen?

MAY 31, 1966. Guess what your bright husband did yesterday;
I was wounded in action in the Republic of South Vietnam. I hit a
punji stake and it's not that bad, it got me in the left leg just below
the knee and it sure smarted for a while. I guess I'll get a purple heart for it. If they do give me a purple heart, I'll send it home
to you. I'm enclosing what the business end of what a punji stake
looks like. The whole thing is about three feet long and both ends
are sharp. It's got about a foot in the ground and that leaves two
feet sticking out and that's what gets you. I was point man yesterday and we were going along this trail just covered in punji stakes. I
was pulling them out left and right and I had just pulled one out and
stepped forward when I felt a sharp pain and couldn't believe I had
hit one, but I did.

We have been having all kinds of trouble with this one sniper.
Every morning and every evening he's here to help us with our
meals; he makes them more interesting anyway, we have learned
just how low to the ground we can eat. We shoot at him, call in
artillery and mortars and ARA, but he always returns. Oh well, I
guess he lives a charmed life.

In this last letter I sent home the tip of a punji stake, just like the one
that wounded me. Luckily it was weathered because the enemy was known
to smear dung on the tips of the stakes to contaminate them.

I limped around for a few days, but never had to go to the hospital.
The others who were wounded that day later received their Purple Hearts
in base camp. My Purple Heart was awarded 32 years later, when an Army
review board found a mention of my punji stake wound.

The match-up between the artillery and the infantry was an important concept employed by the First Cavalry Division. Our artillery moved
constantly, sometimes as often as every 24 hours. They did this in order to
avoid becoming sitting targets for the enemy. Mutual support was the key.
The artillery supported the ground-pounders with their massive firepower,
and we guarded their perimeters just in case they were attacked.

Our artillery did a tremendous amount of damage to the VC/NVA
troops and let's face it, the enemy was just being smart in their attempts to
take out our forward artillery bases.

Later in the war, the artillery began establishing permanent sites.
Luckily most of the time enemy scouts were fruitless in their efforts to
locate our artillery sites. You see, the North Vietnamese were big on planning and this often proved to be their downfall when trying to locate and
plan an attack on our artillery. Their leaders had decided after their huge

losses at X-Ray that it would be difficult, if not impossible to overrun us. It took the NVA a lot of time to amass enough troop strength for a successful attack, and by the time they were ready, often our artillery had already moved on.

I understand that the NVA leaders believed there were spies among their soldiers because of all the air power and artillery we were able to accurately bring down on them wherever they were operating.

The howitzer M-102 the First Cavalry artillery used was new. It was lighter, and consequently easier to air-lift and move around. The gun's ability to fire a 35-pound 105mm shell 13,752 meters, swing around in a circle and fire at a much higher angle than the previous model of howitzer was a big improvement. This weapon's size and portability made it an ideal weapon for use in the Vietnamese jungles. Because of its ability to clear the triple canopy trees with ease, it proved to be a great addition to our fire power.

We usually enjoyed guarding the artillery because we didn't have to hump as much. As grunts used to eating C's, we really appreciated getting the hot chow that was provided to the artillery.

There were downsides to guarding the artillery. First and foremost, we knew the artillery was a giant target to the enemy and that the noise the guns made often gave away our location. Secondly, it was nearly impossible to get used to the H&I fire that went on all night long. You either learned to live with it or you didn't get any sleep.

We did local patrols or set up ambushes, OP's in the day and LP's at night, but guarding the perimeter was probably our most important job with the artillery.

The NVA eventually found a way to defeat the advantage the artillery firepower brought us. They developed a maneuver called *hugging the belt.* When they were able to locate one of our artillery bases, they would travel as quickly as they could and move in as close as possible trying to avoid detection. This plan by the enemy often defeated our ability to successfully mount a counterattack on the NVA. Sometimes they would get so close to the artillery base that it made it impossible to call in additional fire power for fear of sustaining American casualties. Our counter move was to have the artillery FO on the radio *walk* the rounds in until the shells were exploding nearly on top of our foxholes. From time to time there were American casualties because of this close support and the proximity of the NVA.

Once the NVA inflicted as much damage as they could, they would retreat to a safe area that had already been prepared for them and they would lie in wait for us to come and find them. The NVA would then attack when we went looking for them and inflict as much damage as possible to our troops. Once they were successful in killing and wounding as many Americans as possible, they would retreat across the closest border to a safe area to rest, refit and replace lost troops.

While at a reunion at Fort Hood, Texas, in 2003, I had a chance to talk with one of our first lieutenants about some of our operations. This lieutenant was the FO from the artillery for B Company and served in Vietnam in almost the same time period as I did. He really surprised me when he said he remembered me well as the platoon leader for the 2nd Platoon. I guess I was a takeover kind of guy and used to throw orders around, giving the impression I was in charge; someone had to be. Being a little older and more mature, I often stepped up and directed the squad on what I thought needed to be done. Making quick decisions is necessary when you're in active combat. There's no time for discussion, you just have to go for it and hope for the best.

> JUNE 1, 1966. We moved today to an artillery site near Pleiku. Looks like we've got it made, but not for long because I guess we'll be going in very shortly. I got three letters from you yesterday and it sure made me feel good. We made an air assault today (21 for me) right on the highway from An Khe to Pleiku this morning. What would you think if you were driving along and a bunch of helicopters set down in a road in front of your car? I can imagine what some of the people were saying there, here come those damn G.I.s again. I saw a helicopter knock itself down today. I was going to take ship number three, so the first two set down and the troops all climbed on and the first one took off and went between these two trees and it didn't look like he could make it, but he did. The second ship took off and tried to go between the same two trees, but it didn't make it and the rotor blade hit some limbs, the helicopter went up on its side and almost crashed, but the pilot regained control and landed in a field.

I have two pictures of this incident. I was in the third chopper when the second chopper hit the trees and I took pictures of guys bailing out of the Huey. Unfortunately, the pictures I took with my little Minolta camera were so blurry they didn't show the downed bird well enough to see the troops bailing out of the smoking chopper. Usually at these artillery sites about two-thirds of the company would pull guard duty and the rest of them would go out in squad or platoon size ambushes. The artillery liked having us there to help guard and we thought it was great duty, pretty much a win-win situation most of the time.

> JUNE 2, 1966. Well, we moved again today with the artillery. Chow has been extra good, as usual and we don't have it too bad. A friend of mine here is from L.A. and he wants to join the police department when he gets out of the Army in about six months. He asked me if you could get him an application, so I told him I would see what you could do. If you could I would appreciate it if you could send me some information and possibly an application. We're sixteen miles east of Pleiku and all they have around here is this damn red clay. I sure do hate this ground because we're red from head to foot and it takes at least a week to wash all the red dirt off. You know sometimes I feel sorry for these people and the way they live. It's really a shame anyone has got to live like they do....

While waiting for an airlift out to our next mission, our new FO (don't know his name), began calling in artillery support for practice. Four rounds at a time came crashing in. We knew it was just practice and didn't pay much attention to how close the exploding shells were coming to us. Suddenly, a volley came in very close to my squad and we all hit the ground. As we got up off the ground, you could hear angry comments about our new FO's ancestral lineage. Just then someone noticed one of the HQ group's RTO's didn't get up. He was about 30 feet beyond us, where the artillery rounds hit. Someone rolled him over and found a piece of shrapnel the size of a half dollar had hit him in the side of his head. He must have died instantly. Once again this was a needless loss from friendly fire.

On June 3, 1966, we were airlifted to our next mission, Operation Hawthorne. This mission involved the entire First Cavalry Division. This operation took place within Kon Tum Province in support of the First Brigade of the 101st Airborne Division. This was a search and destroy mission that took place from June 3, 1966, to June 20, 1966.

Around this time Alpha battery, 1st of the 21st Artillery, was attacked in Happy Valley. The VC left 54 dead in front of the four guns in their position. Our intelligence unit (S2) was estimating anywhere from a regimental size to two divisions were operating in our own backyard in Happy Valley. In addition to the expected VC contact, we were told that five to ten NVA battalions were just across the border waiting for the monsoon season to begin in August and September before crossing into Vietnam. The NVA leadership was aware of the anticipated VC onslaught and figured the First Cavalry was about to lose a huge number of their experienced personnel who had arrived in-country the previous August. Luckily there were many troopers who came in after August 1965. Those of us who at this point felt like seasoned veterans were ready to help the transition between the new personnel and the old.

> JUNE 5, 1966. I'm really happy for you getting your new job. I hope you are very happy working there. I can't understand why you haven't gotten a letter for six days. I write you almost every day with a few exceptions…. Good news, we probably will be out here two weeks. At least this place isn't too bad and we're getting half way decent chow….

I really got discouraged when I didn't get a letter for a few days, since it required a tremendous effort on my part to write to my wife nearly every day. Sometimes I got in a funk and began thinking my wife wasn't making as much effort writing me letters. During this time, I just couldn't seem to escape the effects of this war's negative environment. I can see now that when there was good food and good duty, I was far more tolerant of my surreal surroundings and at my highest high. When we were humping for days, sitting in the cold rain, drinking nasty water and eating C-rations it was hard to be positive about anything, and that feeling of hopelessness brought me to some of the lowest points in my life.

> JUNE 6, 1966. Well, I got a real sweet letter from you today…. This Army is really bugging me and so is this Vietnam. I really got pissed off earlier today. Oh well, not too much longer and I'll be out of this damn Army and be back with you.

The stress we were under at times made me wonder why more grunts didn't crack. I think every infantry soldier coming out of that place couldn't help but have some form of PTSD. How could you not have repercussions from what you saw, what you heard and what you did during the year you were trapped in that Godforsaken country? Yes, we were trapped, and it was very clear to all of us that we were stuck in Vietnam for one very long year. This was true for many of us, unless God forbid, we were severely injured or even lost our lives to this questionable war.

Even when we were in good areas and not too concerned about being attacked or contacting the enemy we had to contend with the constant boredom. These times of limbo brought out the worst in some of the troopers. During the down time the many personalities in a platoon would come into conflict. While in rest areas some of the soldiers would go out of their way to annoy other troopers and occasionally someone would wind up getting injured. I guess this type of thing was an inevitable side effect of the strain we all were under.

When our unit was out in dangerous territory most everyone tried to work together. We knew that failure to work as a well-oiled unit could result in disaster. I know that personally I was always on edge and thought I might be going mad; it was easy to become depressed and discouraged. The highs were really high, and the lows were really low. To keep my sanity, I lived for getting a letter from my wife. At times I had to go a few days before one would arrive and I tried to remain positive saying to myself, *maybe I'll get two tomorrow.*

> JUNE 7, 1966. Well, no letter today so they should haul one in tomorrow. This Vietnam and the Army are really getting on my nerves. I've just got to get out of this outfit. At least the time seems to be moving faster now. We're still in the same spot and these artillery guys don't have it as good as the last group we were with, although tonight they did bring out some beer and pop and had it ice cold.

About this time, we were notified the C-ration meals of beans with meatballs were bad and we were instructed to throw them away. Sure enough when I looked, I had picked the beans and meatballs for my one real meal that day. I only ate two C-ration meals, one was beans and meatballs and the other was beans and franks. Since I only ate one real meal each day, when they told us to throw away my only meal that day, I decided to go ahead and eat it anyway. I reasoned, what would be the worst thing that could happen to me? Getting sick or even dying in the field was always a real possibility. This mindset had become my attitude, as it was for most of the grunts who served with me. We were beginning to see just how cheap life could be in Vietnam and how it could be taken away in an instant.

> JUNE 8, 1966. Well, no mail yet today, but it might come in later on this evening…. We're still in the same spot outside Pleiku, but they're saying we're going back to base camp tomorrow. I hope I get a chance to get into town I'd like to get something for you and Tina.

> JUNE 9, 1966. Say, I got this guy to take a picture of your war hero with his swinger camera. We're back in base camp. We might even stay here a day or two. I'm hoping we do, so I can get the things I want to get for you. Gee, thanks again for sending the pictures, it's really fun to look at them with the guys. Oh, how do you like

what I'm growing on my upper lip? I'm hoping that I can wear it the whole time I'm over here and come home with it so I can hug you.

All the troopers in the second platoon had decided to grow handle-bar mustaches. It was a resolution which almost caused a revolution. The officers and NCOs determined these mustaches were not in keeping with the proper uniform and we were told they did not comply with the sharp appearance expected of a cavalry soldier.

We argued this look took us back to the Old West. We told them that these historical links to the old cavalry would build better unit cohesion, and ultimately bring us closer together. All this was of course a crock of bull, but we really wanted to keep those mustaches. I tried to hang on to my mustache as long as possible, but unfortunately, it was a lost cause and we were ordered to shave them off.

Me with my new mustache in early June 1966.

When we were in base camp and it was mortared or they called an alert, it was always unsettling. Just when you thought things were going to be quiet and you could relax a lit-tle, the war would raise its ugly head once again. They would either make us go into bunkers or trenches or put us on 100 percent alert and send us out on the green line. Every time we were put on alert it proved to be a waste of our time and energy. We never were attacked by a ground force. A couple of times sappers or snipers would get caught in the outer wire, but that was about all that hap-pened when I was on the green line. During my time in Vietnam none of these alerts resulted in any major

Me resting on some pierced steel planking—still sporting my mustache.

assault on base camp by the enemy. Often these alerts took the place of most of our base camp activities, such as sleep and the opportunity to just be alone on our own for a couple of days.

> JUNE 9, 1966 (evening). We had a battalion formation today and the other guys got purple hearts for being injured by punji stakes, but I wasn't on the list. Oh well, I did ask our medic and he said he would look into it.

There were four other soldiers, besides me, who had been injured by punji stakes at the end of May. All of them were in my platoon and everyone except me received Purple Hearts that day. I did ask our medic a few weeks later about the Purple Heart, but he had no answer for me. Then I completely forgot about the incident. (Eventually it was presented to me many years later at our local VFW's annual Veteran's Day ceremony.)

I have always had mixed feelings about receiving this medal, because of all the soldiers I saw torn up and those who never made it home alive. I believe there should be some type of delineation between minor injuries and those who got seriously injured or even killed. It's my hope that someday they can add a higher award for those who have been permanently disabled or killed in combat. The soldiers who gave their lives should fall under a category of their own, but it's clear *no medal* will ever serve to honor their lives being sacrificed to war.

> JUNE 12, 1966. Well, they pulled a fast one on me and we pulled out a couple of days ago with hardly any notice. So that's why I haven't been able to write. We're back for at least today and I hope longer. We were really moving out there in an area called Happy Valley. It's where all the fighting was last week. I did get a really nice souvenir out there and I'm going to try and send it home to you as soon as … [*rest of the letter missing*].

Happy Valley was not one of our favorite places. This trip out we made lots of contact with small groups of fleeing enemy troops. Whoever had gone there before us had hurt them badly and they were in no mood for more fighting. I did get a great souvenir, an almost pristine mahogany crossbow with arrows. I sent it home and still have it to this day.

> JUNE 13, 1966. Well, we're still out here in Happy Valley and we're supposed to go in tomorrow. Then there's a rumor that we might go on the green line, that's good news! I can't wait to get in and see if I got your package yet….

> JUNE 14, 1966. Well, no green line or base camp today. It looks like we might be out here awhile; which is bad news because there's nothing worse than Happy Valley. Other things I'm going to need soon are some more pens, you really go through pens over here and they're hard to get. I'm writing this letter lying down so that's why it's so bad. It's really hot today and I just don't even have the energy to sit up, besides that, we have a couple of persistent snipers that are trying to make life just a little more miserable and that's a good reason to stay lying down. Boy, they're terrible shots. If I was that bad, I think I would pack up and go home. We just pretend that they're not there.

I rarely said anything about anybody shooting at us in any of my letters. I'm not sure why I did in this letter. What I didn't relay to my wife was the fact that some of the snipers had special rifles with scopes and we had to be on guard when we ran into them.

Over the year I was in Vietnam I don't think I ever lost any of the pictures I had taken, and I tried to send home anything I could get my hands on that would fit in an envelope. By the time I came home, I'd gathered a huge amount of memorabilia. These were some of the items I picked up:

safe conduct passes, propaganda flyers, foreign currency, coins, and a tip of a punji stake.

> JUNE 15, 1966. Wow, I got four letters from you today ... guess I'll try to get that transfer to the MPs when I get back to base camp, right now we're on the bottom tear of the pecking order and it's bad....

The First Cavalry Division tested every soldier's personal mettle. We had a high degree of esprit de corps and were expected to go above and beyond on every mission. Although we didn't always agree with some of the decisions made by our leaders, in most cases we followed their orders.

In the First Cavalry Division, as with most American units in Vietnam, no one person or unit would stand alone. When someone yelled for help, we went. We never abandoned anyone. After a fight it was SOP to count noses and be certain we had accounted for everyone before we left the area.

> JUNE 16, 1966. Wow, I got three letters.... I see you have got on the Garry Owen crest. I've got a nice 1st Cavalry crest for you to wear, it will be in my next package home. I went downtown today and got some nice clothes for you and J.R. to wear. I hope you like them, but you've got to be careful of the weak stitching. I hope they fit. Well, it's almost dark so I better sign off.

> JUNE 17, 1966. Well, we're going out this morning, so I guess I better write, because it's a two-day mission and that means I might not be able to write....

My next operation, dubbed Nathan Hale, was conducted in the vicinity of Tuy Hoa and Dong Tre by the third brigade and the first brigade of the First Cavalry and some CIDG units from June 19, 1966, till July 1, 1966.

We were there in support of the 101st Airborne Division. They had engaged a huge number of enemy forces and asked the First Cavalry for help. Our A Company was involved, and I'm told it was a hairy situation, but little information about this mission filtered back to us. Following this operation, we headed into base camp. During this time our main missions were guarding Highway 19 or the green line around base camp. All First Cavalry battalions would rotate in and out of these two jobs.

JUNE 20, 1966. Well, we're going back in shortly, so I guess I'll write this then mail it when we get in.... We killed a Montagnard woman and I felt bad about that.... They're just pushing us too hard. What we need is a little rest, but they don't see it that way. I guess it's because we raise such hell when we do get back into base camp. Maybe if they let us back for a while the troopers would settle down a little.

This last incident was tough on all of us. One soldier was point man and he was in heavy brush and he shot a Montagnard woman. I was behind him with my fire team and I'd just bent over to fill my canteen from a stream, when I heard the familiar crack of an M-16 on full-automatic. Believe me this rifle fire caught my full attention. Our point man said he heard some scrambling next to the trail and figured he was caught at the beginning of an ambush; he automatically opened fire and sprayed the bushes with bullets. He said he knew there were no friendlies out in front of us because we were the first platoon into that area.

When the firing stopped, we found this Montagnard woman who had been hit in the arm. The others with her had disappeared into the jungle. This sad incident was yet another demonstration of the power of the M-16. Although, she had only been hit in the elbow, her arm was almost severed. We called for a medevac and our medic did what he could, but she died before the helicopter got there. I was surprised that she died, because she'd only been hit once. We buried her on the spot, under a tree in a shallow grave.

No one blamed our point man for shooting what he believed was the enemy; I think any of us may have done the same. Our policy was never to shoot at civilians or non-combatants, but while in combat there were times when this occurred, and we all felt the weight of taking an innocent person's life.

A major problem in Vietnam was distinguishing the friendly or neutral villager from the VC. Those hostile villagers could just serve as agents or couriers or they could be an armed soldier who would shoot you in the back if given the chance. It was impossible for a grunt to be sure of just who they were dealing with most of the time. This area was considered a free-fire zone because few civilians were in the area and when you did encounter someone, it was most likely going to be the enemy.

JUNE 21, 1966. Well, guess where we are at now, on the green line. That's good! We're on a tower right behind the company area, which makes it nice.... On our last little operation I got myself a pair of jungle boots. They are the old type, they're brown and they're very comfortable. They had been used a little when I got them, but they were still good. Well I'm back at the tent right now and I'm heading for Post Office, so I guess I better close for now.

The green line was a 150-foot-wide barrier, bulldozed and free of any grass or other foliage. This barrier extended 25 miles around the perimeter of the First Cavalry's base camp at An Khe. A part of this barrier had mines and all of it was covered by rows of barbed concertina wire. The barrier also had lots of bunkers and foxholes and there were towers erected in strategic places all around the green line.

The green line was considered some of the best duty a grunt could have. Someone told me it had only been breached a few times by sappers on a suicide mission, who were killed on sight before they could detonate any explosives they brought with them.

One of the stories relayed to me was a tragic event that occurred on the green line in September 1965, when Maggie the mule was shot and killed. She was the mascot of the 1st of the 9th Cavalry and I'm told was just trying to get back into base camp after dark.

Maggie the mule has an interesting back story. The story goes that she was a gift for the battalion commander. I was told that as a prank his soldiers pooled some money together and rented Maggie from a local farmer. They presented her to the commander on his birthday and I guess the commander loved her and decided to make her his unit mascot. Their prank had backfired on them and they all had to pony up the extra money to buy Maggie so their commander wouldn't find out they had only rented her. Poor Maggie, she just became another casualty of friendly fire.

Although at the time it was much too early to start talking about going home, I had made it through the first three months and was lucky enough to still be alive and kicking. Though I still had the ever-present prospect that I could be shot or even killed, for the first time I began to think I just might make it home in one piece.

JUNE 22, 1966. Well, I got a letter today. I sure enjoyed reading it and don't worry. Gee lover, I'm missing you more and more with every passing day (not that I didn't miss you two minutes after that plane took off from Oakland).

It was always nice to be near or in base camp because you could take showers, mail packages, go to the PX or even if you chose, go get a beer. Sometimes some of the guys went wild and really got out of hand, so much so that the officers and NCOs began taking ammo and grenades away from us. There had been a couple incidents with these lethal weapons but taking them away didn't completely stop the stupidity. Of course, these boneheads always had their fists and the mixture of alcohol and bravado resulted in many of these troopers heading for the medical tent.

6

Bailing Out the 101st Airborne

JUNE 24, 1966. Well, sorry I haven't been able to write but we're out in the field again. Remember the 101st Airborne that was hit so hard last week, well the battle is still going. Our A company was hit hard last night, but we were very lucky. We're down here kicking ass and taking names for the 101st, I just hope we stick to taking names. I don't know just where we are except that we're close to the South China Sea and at a Special Forces camp called Dong Tre. This place is miserable, and I'll be glad to give it back to the 101st. Lifeline our supply and mail copter just came in.... They are talking about staying down here for a long time, I certainly hope not.

JUNE 25, 1966. Hi sweetheart, well, we're at an artillery site now so I'll be able to mail this letter. We air assaulted from the Dong Tre Special Forces Camp yesterday and we are still just north of Tuy Hoa. Somehow, we didn't hit anything, but everyone around us was hitting something. I guess the 101st got battered badly.... I just got a letter from you, so they're not saying anything about the 1st Cavalry being down here helping out the 101st.... Well lover got to go now. A battery of big guns from the 101st is moving in so we have to move our foxholes.

A tragic accident occurred here just outside of Tuy Hoa. A medevac was trying to land at a medical aid station loaded with wounded and at the same time an ARA ship was taking off heading to the battle area, fully loaded for bear. This ARA ship was returning to support a fighting force who were in contact with the enemy. According to witnesses, at least one of the Hueys was flying without running lights. There was a horrific crash, and everyone on both aircraft were killed. This sad event was especially upsetting to a grunt. We were transported on Hueys when going into battle and relied on them to evacuate us if we were injured. Since this accident involved both types of assignments, ARA and Medevac, it proved to us just how dangerous this place was. Many times it was just being in the wrong place at the wrong time.

> JUNE 27, 1966. I have been reading and re-reading your letters, they sure are nice. That tall guy in those pictures is one of the survivors for the first Ia Drang and he lives near Oakland in California.... How did you like the war souvenirs? I found that on a sweeping operation in Happy Valley.

> JUNE 28, 1966. Well, got two letters from you and one from your mom. Your mom sent some pictures of you and J.R. ... I'm glad you got the crossbow. They don't really fight us with those, but sometimes they do use them as booby traps and they also use them to hunt game so they can save their ammo. Yesterday, because of all the walking we did, I could take my shirt off and just give it a little squeeze and the sweat would just pour out. Man, it's hot. I'd be afraid to look at a thermometer. Say lover, let me know how you like the clothes I sent and how they fit when you get them.

While we were in this valley at about 3:30 in the morning, an NCO came around and told us we were moving and to get ready and get packed. We rarely were asked to pack up in the middle of the night. Everyone was bitching, it was very dark and none of us were moving too fast. Then a sergeant showed up and said, "All right guys, we're much too close to a B-52 strike and the company must be moved by daylight." If the first NCO clown had told us just why we needed to move, we would have all been ready to go. We all picked up the pace after the sergeant gave us the heads up on just why we needed to move out in the middle of the night.

A little after daylight while we were moving, we began hearing these weird and very loud whirling noises. The noises we were hearing were the 2000-pound bombs being dropped from the B-52s. This Air Force bombing was what is aptly referred to as being "danger close" by the military. Being anywhere near a B-52 carpet bombing was downright frightening.

The noise from these B-52 bombs hitting the ground was deafening. I'm certain every one of us were glad we had moved further away from the impact area. As it was, the reverberating sounds of these bombs made it feel like it was the end of the earth. We were at least 2000 meters away from the impact area and this was the minimum distance an American unit could be during these bombing missions. I can't imagine being any closer than we were. This was one of the many terrifying experiences I had in Vietnam. This death out of the clear blue sky was something I'll never forget. I can still remember the concussions, one right after the other, and it seemed as though it might never end.

After the bombing ended, we were told to go back to the impact area and assess the damage. When we returned, we could see huge craters everywhere and they had already begun filling up with rainwater, making them look like a series of swimming holes. We didn't find any VC or NVA, but we did find signs that someone had been in the area in the recent past.

> JULY 1, 1966. Well, we're getting ready to leave to Dong Tre, but we're not going back to base camp. We're going near there, but not all the way back. I just had a guy take a picture of me and Shelby writing letters home. I can't wait to see those pictures. I hope they come pretty soon.

The next operation, Henry Clay, was conducted in the vicinity of Dong Tre and Cung Son in the Phu Yen Province. We were acting as a reconnaissance force. This operation took place from July 2 through July 30, 1966. The Third Brigade and First Brigade from the First Cavalry and some CIDG companies participated with us on this mission.

In my last letter home, I was apparently wrong again. I know we didn't

My best friend Shelby and I writing letters home.

Here I am sharing my C-rations with a young Vietnamese boy.

leave the Dong Tre area during this time period. The platoon was in a tight marching formation just outside of Dong Tre and my ankle twisted and I fell. I must have looked like I'd been shot by a sniper, because the sergeant came running back to me to see what happened. I picked myself up and we were moving again; just then an M-79 being carried by a soldier in front of me was accidently fired. He said he had his finger on the trigger and he tripped, and the grenade had been fired. Luckily, the grenade hit the soldier right in front of him and it ricocheted straight up in the air. Everyone in the platoon stampeded in all directions, not knowing just where this live grenade would land. When something like this happens, what do you do? Go left, go right, who knows. As luck would have it, the grenade did not explode. We were told that the grenades had a safety mechanism built in and the grenades had to make 33 revolutions before they are armed. This was yet another lucky break for our platoon: had this grenade not been deflected by hitting this guy in the shoulder, this might have resulted in many serious injuries.

Around this time some of our forward observers (usually officers in the artillery) had at least four wounded and one of their RTOs killed near Tuy Hoa. Things were beginning to heat up again. One of these officers was wounded while flying as an air observer in an H-13 Bell helicopter (known as Snoopy Scout). The others were on the ground doing their jobs as forward observers.

"Snoopy Scout"—H-13 Bell two-person helicopter used for recon.

JULY 3, 1966. Well, I'm sitting here on the LZ waiting for a lift out. I'm the only one going because I caught a bug. So, I'm getting out of the field for a while, goodie, goodie! I wish it could be Malaria so I could be out for a month or so; wouldn't that be great. I might get back to base camp and if I do, I'll be in good shape....

I had been so sick I couldn't keep up with the others in the platoon. My temperature was hovering around 101 degrees and although I was close to being unable to walk, it had to be 102 degrees before you could be sent out of the field. This hard and fast rule was tough on grunts because there was no consideration given to individual ailments that might render a guy unable to perform his job. Let's face it, no soldier would want to rely on a buddy who was too sick to have his back.

My condition caused a drain on our unit. Two soldiers had to stay back with me and plod along at my speed. They both helped me carry my gear, except for my rifle and that never left my side. The guy carrying my pack said it weighed a ton, and asked what the heck was in it. When I told him ammo, he couldn't believe how much I carried on a regular basis. After Bong Son I realized just how important it was to be prepared for the possibility of another major conflict with the enemy and carried as much extra ammo as I possibly could.

Eventually my temperature rose to 102 degrees and I was sent to the rear for treatment. They took me to the 71st evac hospital at Pleiku; at the time it was a lot like the MASH unit from the TV show. I think there were three tents and they put me in a large tent that was set up with cots that could house 30 patients. At the beginning I was the only guy in the tent. Each day they made me prick my own finger and smear it on a slide before I could get breakfast. I had been there one day when they carried in a guy with malaria and he was very sick. Then they brought in a tub filled with ice water and towels and began draping the wet towels over his body. I could see he was miserable, and I began to regret the flippant remark I made in my last letter home about wanting to get malaria. After seeing this guy suffering, I decided maybe being in the field wasn't so bad after all.

After a couple of days, I felt much better and my temperature went down. I spent three days in this primitive medical unit and then returned to the field. I didn't write a letter home for the five days I was out of the field recovering from my illness. When I returned to my platoon, we were humping all day trying to catch up with the rest of the company.

> JULY 8, 1966. Wow, have we been going. It's not raining right now, and I guess that's the only reason I'm able to write this. We have been going day and night. We're now with the rest of the company and at least will stay here tonight....

> JULY 10, 1966. Well, you know I kept saying things couldn't get any worse, well don't believe it, they can. I just spent a few of the most miserable days of my life. We have been going all day long, up mountains then down them, and to top it off every time we stopped, leeches would come after us.... Gee, last night on guard it was cold and raining and you know what keeps me warm? It's when I'm thinking of you most of the time. I thought of all the things we're going to do, and I was off guard in no time.

We had stopped for the night and after a B-52 strike, our platoon pulled into a tight perimeter. The next morning as everyone was beginning to get up, one of the guys cursed and yelled the dreaded word *leeches*. I checked myself immediately and counted 20 of them on me. One of the leeches had found its way beneath the belt of my pants and this creepy blood sucker had grown huge on my blood. These things couldn't be pulled off and trying to squash them was useless. As I a mentioned earlier in the book, the best way to rid yourself of a leech once it attached itself to you was to use mosquito repellent. As grunts we rarely were supplied with mosquito repellent and most of the time, we resorted to taking a lit match to the leech. This barbaric method of removing the leeches could and did result in a lot of pain from the burning match. There were of course times when a leech was attached to an inaccessible area of the body and help was needed from another soldier to remove it. One thing I know for sure, this attack of the leeches was a terrible way to start the day.

As far as I know there were two types of leeches in Vietnam. One type crawls on the ground and the other swims in water and for all I know they may be the same. For those of you who don't know what a leech is, read on. The leech is a type of blood-sucking or carnivorous worm with a flattened body, who exists by engorging itself with its host's blood. To this day, even the mention of these disgusting little creatures makes my skin crawl.

> JULY 11, 1966. Well, we're still here in the same spot but we've just been lying around so I guess it isn't too bad. We're test firing and I'm sitting right behind the firing line. My turn is almost up so I'll tell you how I do when I'm through. I sure have been missing you. I guess I'll just have to get used to it because I guess I'm still going to have a long wait. … I did pretty good, twenty hits out of twenty. It's starting to get dark, so I better sign off.

Our company commander at the time had a mean streak, along with a bad temper. Luckily, he had one saving grace that any grunt could appreciate: he knew how to keep us out of trouble. Sometimes he was overly cautious, but this only endeared him to his men. Most of the guys I knew had become comfortable with his combat decisions as he seemed to know just where and when to engage and often kept us from disaster.

> JULY 12, 1966. Well, we moved and right now we're sitting right on the edge of Cheo Reo. I sure was glad to leave that Tuy Hoa area…. Say lover, guess what your little boy did, he wrote a song and it's getting popular over here. As soon as I get back to base camp, I'll sing it on the recorder for you, it's sung to the tune of *The Green Beret.*

> JULY 12, 1966 (early evening). Well, it's almost dark so it's going to have to be a fast letter. Here's a nice map of Vietnam. I knew you would enjoy it. We're still at Cheo Reo and guess what, I've got a new job. I'm RTO for the platoon leader which means I'm the radio operator. The radio is heavy but it's a good job. Only problem is Charlie always likes to shoot at radio operators! Well, it's almost impossible to see so I'll write tomorrow.

JULY 14, 1966. I just got three letters from you. Gee, it sure makes me feel good.... I'm still the platoon radio operator and I like the job. Let me tell a little about it. My platoon leader's call number is jolly rings 2–6 and my call number is jolly rings 2–6 India. The radio is kind of heavy but it's not bad at all. About 200 meters away is a real big river and we go swimming every day. It has all kinds of stuff floating in it but it's cool and a relief from this lovely hot weather.... You were talking about it raining, well, it rained last night (nothing unusual) and I got all wet (nothing too unusual either). I bet you don't really understand how we live here or how it is to be wringing wet all the time. I could never put into words the misery and pain I am going through over here. This is a living hell. As I said before there are better days.

They made me a radio operator, and this was a real surprise to me at the time. I knew this job was one of the more dangerous assignments you could have in Vietnam. Charlie was always looking to take out the radio operators. After all, it was our job to call in the ARAs and artillery who could bring down such death and destruction on them.

I must admit until I re-read my letters home, I had little memory of my time serving as my platoon leader's radio operator. Reading about it jogged my memories. I instantly recognized my call sign "jolly rings," and I remembered carrying the PRC-25 radio that had been accurately nicknamed the *Prick 25* for its unwieldy weight.

I found that carrying the radio did have one advantage: the two back-up batteries that you needed to carry for the radio came in heavy duty plastic bags that, once emptied, could be used to keep my stuff dry. I wrapped my wallet in one of these bags and because of this my wallet and everything I carried inside of it survived my year in Vietnam. I found these plastic bags made me very popular when it came to battery changing time; grunts constantly looked to scrounge anything that might help them keep things dry in the field.

There's an interesting story about the call signs we were using for our radio communications. I am told that when the Seventh Cavalry came to Vietnam, all radio call signs started with a name of an Indian tribe, such as, Sioux, Comanche or Apache. This practice was quickly changed after the major battles that took place in November 1965. During the two battles that took place in the Ia Drang Valley, the platoons lost a huge number of their radios. Unfortunately, these radios had radio code books attached that revealed the call signs for various units in the Seventh Cavalry. The captured radios were then used by the NVA to eavesdrop on our communications. To eliminate the possibility of the NVA being able to hear what our plans were and where we were going next, an order was immediately sent down to change their individual call signs.

Our call signs were delineated by rank. The B Company 1st of the Seventh Cavalry battalion commander was simply known as *six*. B company's commander was *jolly rings six*. The second platoon leader was *jolly rings two six*. His RTO (me) was *jolly rings two six India*. The platoon sergeant, *jolly rings two six mike* and his RTO *jolly rings two six mike India*. This call sign system was very helpful when you were talking with someone on the radio; you knew just who you were talking with and knowing that had its advantages. If a call came in from *six*, which never happened to me, you knew you really needed to listen up. Not that you didn't listen to every call, but let's face it this was the Army and rank was everything.

When I said in my last letter that I could not put into words the misery and pain I was going through and that it was a living hell, I meant every word. As a grunt at the bottom of the chain of command, we went where we were told and for the most part did what we were ordered to do. As with grunts in other wars, we were often forced to endure unbelievable misery. Unlike the guys in the rear, we humped through the jungles and jumped out of choppers (sometimes these jumps were made into places no one in their right mind would want to go). Occasionally we engaged the enemy in a firefight, and these memories are hardest to get out of your mind. Seeing your buddies get injured and killed leaves you with a permanent invisible scar that never leaves your mind. I believe these things alone are the reasons Vietnam combat veterans feel such a close bond with one another.

> JULY 14, 1966. Yippie guess what? We're going back in tomorrow.... Wow, we have been out too long this time....

> JULY 15, 1966. Well lover, good morning. I'm sitting by the Cheo Reo airport right now and we're all waiting to catch our plane back to base camp. Boy, this radio is really a bitch. I'm still RTO and looks like I got the job permanently; but this damn thing is really heavy.... I think I'll have some C's. How about me eating a Pecan Cake Roll, it's my favorite cake in the C-rations. I wonder what the surprise is that you sent me and what my Father's Day gift could be. Gee honey I hope you understand about those days I wasn't able to write to you, but sometimes it's just impossible....

Upon returning to base camp on July 15, 1966, I had a surprise waiting for me. I was awarded one of the most coveted medals a grunt can be given, the Combat Infantryman Badge. The soldiers who are awarded the CIB are in an exclusive club. To be eligible for the CIB you must have an Infantry MOS and have served 30 days in combat.

In order to show the true importance of the CIB, the Army ordered that this badge was to be worn above all other medals (with one exception: the Medal of Honor was the only award that could be placed above the CIB).

> JULY 16, 1966 (morning). Say, how is this paper? I was over at the PX and they had some so I thought I would send you letters on this. Here's hoping for the very best. It looks very good about transferring to the 545th MP Company. I wrote up my 1049 today and turned it in today. I hope everything goes all right. I know it's going to make you feel better to have me out of this line outfit. Well, got to go—give J.R. his usual.

> JULY 16, 1966 (evening). Wow, wow and also wow, guess what I got today? My daddy's day gift, oh honey, I just love that radio. You can really use a radio over here, and those pictures, Wow, they are great....

> JULY 17, 1966. Gee lover, I just can't stop looking at those pictures that you sent to me. I just love them. It really makes things go easier over here and they take my mind off of everything. My 1049 to the 545th is still pending and guess what they did to me. We moved out in the field early this morning so that means I'll not be able to keep track of my 1049. Oh well, I still have high hopes that it will go through. We're at Dak To now and we have really got it easy. We are guarding the airport here and it's the easiest job I have been on since being in the 7th Cav. I'm still RTO and I'm learning a lot about the radio....

As it turns out the 101st Airborne was in the process of moving to Tuy Hoa and the 1st of the 7th Cavalry was the only major combat unit within the Dak To area of operation. At the time I had no idea we were the only combat unit in the Dak To area. This area was known to be very dangerous: its proximity to the tri-borders of Laos, Cambodia and South Vietnam added an extra level apprehension. Luckily for the 1st of the 7th the eastern front was quiet while we were there. Clearly, this was not the best place for a lone battalion to be stationed.

Shortly after the 101st left Dak To, I noticed they left behind a 4.2 mortar company. I'd never seen a mortar that big before and went over to take a look and shoot the bull with the guys.

One of the mortar guys told me an almost unbelievable story about what had happened to one of their troopers. One night after being awakened from a sound sleep, he found himself looking into some big green eyes and felt a hot breath on his cheek. It turned out a full-grown tiger had decided to join him in his bunker. The tiger got away before the guy could get his act together and grab his rifle. How this tiger got through all the barbed wire, trip flares, booby traps and mines no one knows. Apparently, no one else saw the tiger, but they found tracks the next morning. So the soldier's story was true, and he wasn't just seeing things.

Operation Hayes, our next operation, was conducted in the vicinity of the town of Dak To in Kon Tum Province from July 18 till July 31, 1966. This was a search and destroy operation led by the 1st and 2nd of the Seventh Cavalry and CIDG Special Forces

Guarding the airport at Dak To turned out to be very good duty. We made short patrols around our base camp area every day. The bunkers were similar to the ones on the green line at An Khe, but minus the towers.

There was a machine gun crew next to my bunker. While they were cleaning their weapons, a shot went off. I grabbed my M-16 and ran over to see what had happened, arriving just as the gunner jumped off the top of the bunker roof. The assistant gunner was running in the direction of the command post yelling for a medic and the gunner told me he had been shot in the leg. I immediately told him to unbuckle his belt and drop his fatigue trousers. About this time the medic showed up and upon scanning his body he discovered a red streak inside his leg a few inches below his crotch. There was a bullet hole in his boxer shorts, but no blood. This guy was one lucky soldier as the bullet only grazed his leg and didn't hit anything he might need later. The bullet had apparently lodged itself somewhere in the bunker. As I was leaving the area, I noticed the gun crew begin to dig around in the sandbags looking for the offending slug from the .45, a war memento no doubt.

> JULY 20, 1966 (morning). We're still here at the air strip near Dak To and we're likely to be here awhile. No word on my 1049 yet, but I'm still hoping for the best…. All it seems I can do lately is dream of you….

Around this time, it seemed that everyone in the company would line up to put in 1049s to go anywhere and do anything. Personally, I had decided I'd done my time in the field and deserved a transfer out of the line of fire. Although officers and medics were only required to remain in the field for six months, grunts were lucky to get out of the field for any reason.

Unfortunately, I knew it would take a few months to have a request for a transfer go up the chain of command for approval, but I still had high hopes for a respite from the constant uncertainty of being a combat soldier.

I began to feel I had stretched my luck about as far as it could go and it seemed clear to me that it was only a matter of time till the 2nd Platoon of Bravo company would hit something big. Except for our one huge battle in Bong Son the beginning of May, we had been living charmed lives. Every grunt on the front lines in Vietnam knew there was no safe place for them in the entire country. If your unit happened to be in the wrong place at the wrong time, the possibility of you making it home in one piece was next to nil.

I believe it was about this time that one of the platoons got a new LT who decided it was a bright idea to carry an AK-47 as his weapon of choice. I'll admit that in some ways this weapon was superior to our M-16s. They were loose, fired sloppy and were just plain ugly, but unlike the M-16 they didn't jam even when they were filthy dirty and full of rust. The 2nd Platoon was guarding a mortar platoon and the other platoons were on butterfly sweeps. This new LT for some unknown reason fired a burst from his AK-47 and the other platoons were close enough to hear this.

One thing you learned to develop if you were going to survive in Vietnam was a tuned ear to the sounds of the different types of weapons being fired. An M-60 from another platoon opened fire and pinned the new LT's platoon down. Both the LT with the AK-47 now under fire and the M-60 gunner were desperately calling for artillery fire. Frantically trying to sort out what was happening the FO started yelling over the radio for both platoons to cease fire. He then told them they were trying to call in artillery on top of each other. Wow, two platoons attempting to call in artillery fire on each other could have resulted in an unbelievable tragedy.

7

Malaria or Not Malaria

JULY 20, 1966 (evening). I got two letters from you today and was so happy to hear from you. Well, I got some good news and some bad news today. First the good, the company commander signed and approved my 1049 for the 545st MP company, so it's only a matter of time. The bad, I'm pretty sure I have malaria. The last time the doc took my temperature it was 101.6 and I have all the symptoms, right now I don't feel so hot....

JULY 22, 1966. Gee, it sure is nice here at the hospital.... Wow, and guess what time I got up this morning, 10 minutes till 7 A.M., a Vietnam first. I didn't eat breakfast because I didn't feel like getting out of bed. Could I ever spend some time here! The hospital isn't much to talk about, but it's a lot better than what I'm used to. I should be through with this in just a few days....

This trip to the hospital is a bit of a blur to me. I was so sick and between my high temperature and chills I was completely out of it. I can remember feeling very weak and found keeping up with the platoon impossible, but don't remember when or how I got to the hospital. Fortunately, my letters home filled in some of the blanks.

Since my symptoms once again could be malaria, they began having me prick my own finger and turn a sample in for the necessary testing. I didn't want to worry my wife, so I didn't dwell on how miserable I was feeling. Malaria symptoms are generally the same for everyone. First your temperature begins to rise rapidly, sometimes to dangerous levels. You then begin to experience severe chills, shaking so badly you can hardly sit still, and as the temperature starts to decline you begin to feel somewhat better. This scenario repeats itself over and over until the symptoms disappear. This was my second trip to the field hospital with the same symptoms, and though they tested me over and over again they didn't identify the malaria bug in my blood. But each time I left the field with a high temperature I

99

experienced the exact same symptoms and question to this day what caused these malaria-like symptoms.

These malaria symptoms continued to plague me long after I returned to the states. Shortly after returning home I began experiencing the very same symptoms and was hospitalized at Fort Ord in California for a month. I was told at that time I probably had malaria and eventually the symptoms disappeared. Unfortunately, I have had several relapses of the same symptoms. Once I was hospitalized for 30 days at a Veterans Hospital and eventually the daily high fever and chills went away. My last relapse was in 2004 and since that time, I'm pleased to say, I have not had a recurrence of these debilitating symptoms.

> JULY 23, 1966. I'm still here at Pleiku and don't know when I am going back. The doctor didn't even come around this morning to check me out. I feel just fine today, and I am really able to enjoy the food. They took another (ouch) malaria smear this morning and my fingers are looking and feeling like a well-used pin cushion. Nothing shows, so I guess I don't have Malaria....

I do remember my last couple of days in the hospital. When I began feeling better, I got a chance to look around and although the place was kind of sad, the good food and rest made it feel like a palace to me. I don't know if you have ever watched the television show *M*A*S*H*, but this place looked just the same. This base sort of gave me the creeps and when I inspected the guard bunker, I quickly concluded this was not a safe place to be. These rear base areas were extremely vulnerable, and their security left a lot to be desired. I noticed the perimeter had one lonely roll of barbed wire around the place, as if this would deter anyone from breaching the base. Our own base camp at An Khe had ten rows of barbed wire securing its entire perimeter.

When I was in the field I knew if I was to survive in Vietnam it was imperative for me to remain aware of my surroundings, and this practice carried over to wherever I went while in-country. When I looked around this MASH unit's bunker and the M-60 machine gun meant to protect the unit I couldn't believe my eyes. That M-60 probably wouldn't have fired on a bet; the gun and the ammo were covered in red dust that was deposited daily by the trucks who were driving by on the nearby frontage road. About this time, I started to think that being in the field with Bravo Company was probably a safer place to be than in this unprotected MASH unit.

My time at this MASH unit was just about up: I wasn't running a fever anymore and the daily ups and downs of chills, fever and weakness were gone. While I was there the medical staff appeared to have little to do. But I knew the doctors and nurses stood at the ready, just in case a major battle ensued, and the wounded would begin to roll in needing immediate treatment. These MASH units and their medical staffs were often a godsend to the injured soldier—proof positive were the lives they were able to save. They kept guys alive who in previous wars would have been sent home in a body bag.

As a grunt I thought we were the only ones who experienced true stress during this god-awful war, but the doctors and nurses in these field hospitals had a far different type of stress. Like grunts on the front lines, they had to learn to go from 0 to 60 in a flash. The trauma of attending to soldiers with serious injuries, no doubt, left their caregivers with indelible memories that would continue to haunt them long after the war.

I know I was glad to have a place to go and get some rest and recuperate from the debilitating symptoms I experienced. Once I recovered, I was more than grateful to be back to normal, or as normal as a grunt can hope to be in Vietnam. Well one thing I knew for sure, I was heading back to a combat zone and my buddies.

JULY 24, 1966. Well, so how are you doing sweetheart? I'm still here at the hospital but I expect to be thrown out tomorrow sometime; Yeah!

JULY 25, 1966. Well, here I am at the Pleiku airport. I was discharged from the hospital at noon and now I'm trying to get back to An Khe. Is it ever miserable, rainy and wet. I hope the weather isn't this bad at An Khe. This is really an experience traveling around the country like this, it's very interesting…. Wow, they sure have a lot of air traffic here. Well lover, I better stay awake so I can hear my name, bye for now.

Going military stand-by was a chore even here in Vietnam. At the bigger airports a soldier would give a destination, name and rank and then wait until called. As a private first-class E-3 you were on the bottom of the list. If someone of higher rank wanted to travel, even if you had boarded the plane, you were told to get off and they would take your seat.

There was a way around this irritating stand-by issue. I discovered that at some of the smaller airports you could find a pilot who might be going your way and hitch a ride. If you were lucky enough to find a First Cavalry pilot who was going your way, you could pretty much count on being able to hitch a ride with them.

JULY 26, 1966. Well here I am back in base camp. It sure feels funny without anyone around. The place looks like a ghost town. I went over and saw the 1st Sgt. of the 545th M.P. Company today and told him the 1049 was on its way. I hope it doesn't take much longer....

JULY 26, 1966 (afternoon). Well, it's back out in the field for me tomorrow. But I shouldn't have to wait too long till I get word on my 1049 and then they will send me over to the 545th M.P. Company.... Well, all we can do is hope and pray that my transfer comes through all right.

Here in base camp they had a Mars station and I had heard you could call home. I walked over to see if I could try using this service, but once there I decided it was probably best for both of us if I didn't call. I knew I didn't want to break into tears when my wife answered the phone and cause her to do the same. Living as we did, stressed and never knowing what might happen next, was a real strain on my personal sanity. A call home at that time would not have solved anything and would no doubt have made me feel even more miserable. Looking back now I think I made the right decision in not making that call home; it would have only increased my loneliness and caused my wife to worry even more about me.

JULY 26, 1966 (evening). Well, I just got three letters from you and enjoyed them all.... So my son can say da-da now, huh. Well how about that! He sounds like he is really growing up. ... Oh well, our day will come.

Of course, the reason I could write three letters in one day was because I had little else to do in base camp. Nobody bothered with me and I just stayed out of everyone's way. On this evening I heard the 5th Cavalry club was having some sort of USO show. I found my way over to it and it turned out to be a Korean lady singer. The room was packed, so I watched the show through a window for a while and it only made me feel homesick.

JULY 27, 1966. Well, I just got three letters from you and one from Aunt Leola. How about that! I want to thank you again for the Kool Aid and still would love to have you find black cherry, it's my favorite.... Oh yea, I'm back out here at Dak To and the company is still just sitting here.

> JULY 28, 1966. We're still here at the Dak To airport, doing the same old thing. I sure like re-reading your letters. All the guys just raved about your cookies....

The terrain around Dak To was impossible to navigate. The mountains there were very steep and during the rainy season when you tried to climb them, you would go three steps forward then slide two steps backwards. The town itself reminded me of an Old West town because of its wooden boardwalks. I could visualize someone walking down the street wearing a cowboy hat. There was one major difference in these old boardwalks—they were stacked high with C-rations for sale and I've always wondered where they got them.

> JULY 30, 1966. Well, we're finally stopped for a while, so I'll try and write you a letter. We have been on the go since early yesterday morning. ... We are wet all the time, if it's not from sweat, then it's from rain. It's been raining almost all night long. Yesterday morning we went out after a downed helicopter. We air assaulted on to this hill and have been humping ever since. I bet I've pulled 10 leaches off of me, I hate those damn things! It sounds like J.R. is really getting into everything I bet he keeps his mama going.

I remember being extremely angry at this time and I really can't say why. I clearly recall that the terrain we were trudging through was some of the worst we had seen up to that point and the bad weather added an extra level of misery. I mentioned we went out looking for a downed helicopter, but what I didn't tell my wife was that this helicopter had landed in Laos. The copter was strange looking. It had two angled side-by-side main motor blades. Since that time, I have learned this chopper may have been a Kaman HH-43 Huskie.

We were ordered to secure the LZ, which turned out to be located very close to where the tri-borders of Cambodia, Laos and South Vietnam met. We were on this mission to recover some type of equipment out of the chopper. I have no idea exactly what we were recovering, but apparently it was important to someone.

While waiting to be picked up we saw a formation of copters approaching. It turned out this was a company of CIDG troopers with their Special Forces advisor. The advisor stood out like a sore thumb; he was at least a foot taller than any of the others and the green beret he wore looked like a beacon. These poor mercenaries were carrying old World War II surplus army equipment. They even had a .30-caliber water-cooled World

War II machine gun. I had empathy for them having to hump in some of the toughest terrain in Vietnam; it seemed as though there was just one hill after another and no flat land anywhere near.

As we were leaving this area the helicopters took us to a bare ridge a few klicks away, inside South Vietnam. Only one helicopter at a time could land and I jumped off as the chopper settled onto the ridge. The guy behind me was a brand-new sergeant and as he was jumping off, he caught his gear on the door gunner's machine gun mount. The helicopter then took off with this sergeant hanging upside down and dangling half in and half out of the helicopter. He was being held by his pistol belt and the door gunner. Luckily the door gunner had been able to grab hold of the sergeant's pack straps and that along with being hooked onto the gun mount saved him from falling. The helicopter made a circle and when they landed the second time the gunner and I were able to get the sergeant untangled. I'll never forget the looks on both of their faces as the Huey came in for a second landing. To say they looked relieved was an understatement.

This sergeant was only with us a short time and I imagine this harrowing experience sped up his departure. Many sergeants were career soldiers and they seemed to come and go after having spent very little time in the field. These NCOs knew the ropes and quickly figured out how to get away from the dangers of daily combat exposure. Those of us in the lower ranks were forced to stick it out and accept our apparent destiny. We just plodded along, doing our best to keep one another alive.

Our next operation, Operation Paul Revere II, involved the Second and Third Brigades of the First Cavalry and the Third Brigade of the 25th Infantry Division. In addition, there were ARVN forces and the 3/1 ROK. This was a search and destroy mission that took place from August 1 till August 25, 1966, in the Pleiku Province.

Our adversaries were the 32nd, 22nd, 66th, and 88th NVA regiments and all of them were itching for a fight. Who knows what their intentions were, but I suspect conquering the large city of Pleiku was high on their list.

The 1st of the Seventh Cavalry jumped off from LZ Oasis on August 1, 1966, in support of A company 2nd of the Seventh Cavalry who were already on the ground. Each had one platoon who were overrun by the NVA and both sustained heavy losses. I am told some survivors played dead while being stripped of their weapons and ammunition, along with their wallets, watches and anything else of value. These molesting scavengers even removed their boots.

On August 9, one day after the two Alpha company battles and subsequent losses, an element of the 3rd Battalion of the Republic of Korea

(ROK) Capital Division contacted what was estimated to be a battalion of NVA troops. After the action the NVA retreated, littering the battlefield with 170 of their dead. They also left behind most of their equipment. Historically the NVA went to great lengths to police up their equipment and their dead, not wanting to let us know how badly we had hurt them. But that didn't happen this time; they just engaged the Koreans and once things got hot, they retreated, leaving most everything behind them on the battlefield.

This was the time period when the original First Cavalry troopers were rotating home and the new team were stepping up in their wake. Even though there had been a lot of unwarranted anxiety about this changing of the guard, the transition went well. The Airmobile concept was a winner and when deployed properly brought the all-important element of surprise to the enemy. Although we were still learning on the job, our leadership was top notch and forged ahead with the concept's original strategy.

AUGUST 2, 1966. I got a letter from you the other day, but I wasn't able to write because we were moving all day long. Guess what, yippee my 1049 went all the way up and all the way down and the first sergeant told me yesterday they were cutting orders for me. So, for sure this is my last mission with the 7th Cav.... We moved from Dak To yesterday evening to Pleiku. I guess we are going back out to Ia Drang and the Plei Me area. They won't be able to write any hero articles about me in the M.P.'s but at least I know I'll be coming home. The other day I got a *Newsweek* through the mail. Is it from you? My name and address were on it so someone must have bought it for me.

This *Newsweek* I began getting became a big deal in the company. When it came in the mail, within a matter of minutes the captain's orderly would show up and say, "Blessing, the captain would like to borrow your *Newsweek*." Then the platoon leader would stroll by and ask to borrow it and the requests kept coming. Of course, my squad always got first shot at this onion-skinned bonanza, and now that I was getting it weekly, I became very popular when it was delivered.

I know it appears by my letters that I was more than unhappy being in the 7th Cavalry, but in fact I was very proud to serve in this respected combat unit. At the time I was actively seeking a transfer out to the MPs my survival instinct had kicked in and I wanted with all my heart to make it back home in one piece.

Most of my buddies were beginning to see the handwriting on the wall and every time we got back to base camp after a few days of humping over steep mountains and slogging through deep mud, there was a new flood of 1049 requests. There was a huge divide in the lives of grunts in the field and those who were lucky enough to serve in just about any other capacity in Vietnam. We truly knew as a grunt we were on the bottom rung of a very tall ladder. After all, anyone who screwed up in a rear area job was sent out into the field as punishment. This absurd practice proved to us that the Army believed there was nothing worse than sending a guy to a combat line unit to punish him for his failure to do his job. The practice of sending screw-ups, drunks and losers to a combat line unit just didn't seem logical. Forcing us to become a form of adult babysitters for these guys only slowed us down and put our lives in more danger. Very few of these transplanted REMFs could keep up with us and many of them just disappeared after a very short time.

I believe it was around this time when we got word about a disastrous battle that decimated the 3rd platoon of Alpha Company 7th Cavalry. They had dropped 27 men in by Hueys to the unsecured LZ Pink in the Ia Drang. Very soon after they arrived the weather closed in and they found themselves under attack by NVA troops.

The sad thing about this attack was a decision made by the officer in charge of the lift company who refused to send in more Hueys or even try to retrieve the wounded.

This attack resulted in 18 KIA, 5 WIA, 2 missing and 2 who were able to hide. The two who had hidden were an NCO and the company interpreter. The (*#%*!*#) Major in charge of this lift company obviously never made it to our dinner invitation list.

During their mop-up operation our intelligence discovered that these NVA had been traveling with women. They had dug in, eaten C-rations and later searched the bodies of American soldiers more than just a few times. The big surprise here, they didn't execute the wounded. They did take their radios, weapons and anything else of value that they could carry.

AUGUST 3, 1966. Well, no word on the cutting of my orders but it's just a matter of time now. It has been hard trying to write you, for one it's raining all the time and secondly, we have been on the go most of the time. Between the two of those things I just haven't been able to write you every day. We are out in the Ia Drang Valley right now…. This should be my last mission with the 7th Cav. It will be great having a shower every once in a while and having good hot chow I don't have to cook…. You couldn't imagine how heavy this radio gets. But there are some advantages to carrying the damn thing, such as I do get more sleep at night.... Here I sit thinking about you and airing out my feet and it's the first time since I left the hospital they have been anywhere near dry.

AUGUST 4, 1966. No mail came and that's what I was waiting for. I figure my orders should be out by today and so it's just a matter of time and I'll no longer be with the 7th Cav., man you could get killed here. Has the time ever been flying by, but it can't go too fast for me.... I had planned on putting in for Ft. MacArthur when they ask me where I want to be assigned back in the states and as an M.P. I might have a good chance of getting this assignment. Wouldn't that be great! But don't count on it....

The terrible weather I mentioned in my letter was making life in the field even more depressing. Can you imagine trying to dig a foxhole when every shovel full is mud and each hole you dig instantly fills up with rainwater? It was beyond misery. There is something about constantly being soaked to the skin, in rain that doesn't let up, that takes away what little hope you have of life ever returning to normal.

We were sitting on the top of this hill and Bird Dog (our observation fixed-wing aircraft) had spotted something just across from us on the next hill over. The FO called in a flight of F-4 Phantoms and this one jet flew directly over our heads, so close I could see the pilot looking down at us. He had just fired his cannons as he flew over us, in fact the 20mm shelling was so close it seemed as if we were the ones doing the firing. We could see the explosions from the 20mm shells hitting on the next hillside and casings from this attack fell around us as we were lying prone in the grass. I had never been so close to a jet during this type of combat operation and it was both a scary and impressive experience.

Headquarters called on the radio and directed us to go over to assess the damage. My squad air assaulted across the valley and when we arrived at the next hill there were no LZs for the helicopter. It just hovered and the first soldier jumped out, falling through the limbs of trees and brush from about 10 feet off the ground. He hit the ground, rolled on his side and pointed to his ankle. The next guy out hurt his leg and his arm and now it was my turn to jump. Being this high off the ground and having to jump through tree branches seemed to me to be a sure-fire way to get injured or worse. I had no choice at this point; with two of my squad already hurt I knew I had to just throw caution to the wind and jump. The pilot tried to settle in a little lower in the trees and, thinking I needed another rest in the hospital, I jumped. Although I was jarred, I wasn't badly hurt.

No one else was hurt and we didn't make any enemy contact, although there were signs that the enemy had dug in and had been there in force. There were lots of bunkers and fighting positions located up and down the entire hillside. These enemy bunkers and fighting positions were interesting to me. The NVA would dig in and cover their bunkers with logs and dirt and cut slits in them for firing. The firing positions were often just deep holes dug into the ground. We called them spider holes because they were so small most American soldiers couldn't fit into them.

> AUGUST 5, 1966. Well, yesterday I got two letters and two packages from you…. The B-52 bombers have really been pounding the area around here and even though we are far away from where they are dropping the bombs they still shake the ground and rattle our brains a little, so you can imagine what it's doing to Charlie.

We we're back in the Ia Drang again. This area is a much different type of terrain than most parts of the central highlands. Most areas of the Ia Drang were not mountainous but rolling terrain with low, gently rising hills and seasonal streams running through the gullies. The one exception was Chu Pong Mountain, where the Ia Drang battle was fought during November of 1965. Hardwood trees were spaced about four to five feet apart and at maturity were about ten inches in diameter. The ground was covered with grass, some as tall as three feet. This type of grass could be walked through easily: it was just a matter of plowing through the grass. Occasionally, we would encounter the dreaded elephant grass and its razor-sharp edges could slice right through bare skin. This nasty stuff would slow our progress and no matter how careful you were, cuts were inevitable.

Giant termite and ant hills were everywhere. These big mounds were well suited for hiding and giving cover from grazing gun fire. This entire area was very deceptive: at a glance it looked as though you could see a long way, but because of the rolling terrain you could be a gorge away from a battalion and not know it until you were right on top of them. The rivers were not wide but were very swift and most of them could not be walked across. There were very few places where the rivers slowed enough so they could be easily crossed. Most of the well-trodden trails led to these river crossings and showed signs of many soldiers and heavy equipment traversing them.

In the Ia Drang you could take a compass heading and keep on course much better than in most areas of Vietnam. It was possible for a battle formation to spread out here much like what our officers had been taught in War College. This area made for easy walking in most places and would have been a great place to operate if it hadn't been for the large numbers of

NVA who populated the Ia Drang. The enemy preferred this area because of its proximity to Cambodia and the absence of nearby roads. Although some of the trails were wide enough to accommodate one-way vehicle traffic, the absence of actual roads made it easier for the NVA to operate in this area. Most military forces need roads to move their equipment and men, but the NVA were accustomed to operating without them and could rapidly navigate via these trails. Most U.S. Army units would have been impeded by the lack of roads in this area, but the First Cavalry Division and its airmobile concept provided the perfect answer to engaging the enemy in the Ia Drang.

The First Cavalry and its ability to swoop in with their helicopters and call in back-up air support gave the U.S. Army a leg up on the enemy and we were often able to outsmart the NVA forces. Though the helicopters were great, our need to rely on them and them alone sometimes proved to be our downfall. The one thing that could throw off the success of using helicopters was the possibility of bad weather. A perfect example of the weather restricting our ability to fight took place on August 8, 1966, when our 1st of 7th Cavalry found themselves locked in combat with the enemy. Unanticipated bad weather had set in and the Hueys were no longer able to fly. The helicopters' normal ability to re-supply and support the troopers on the ground was gone, leaving the guys on the ground without a back-up plan.

> AUGUST 7, 1966. Well, we're deep in the heart of the Ia Drang Valley and they have really been pushing us. I keep telling myself that things can't help but get better. Maybe we're going to get out of this place by tomorrow I hope so because this place gives me the creeps.... Not counting the time, I was in the hospital, I have only slept on a cot about six times. I can't even remember what a bed feels like. When I get home, I'll probably have to sleep out in the yard then work up to the floor, then the couch and in about two weeks I should be able to sleep in a bed.

They say that silence is golden, but for a soldier in a combat unit silence can make a difference between life or death. When on the move you needed to be as quiet as possible, as hushed talking and jingling dog tags could easily be heard by the enemy. To eliminate the constant jingling of the dog tags we taped them together and as far as the talking goes, we knew if we could hear each other that the enemy could hear us.

Our company had a few soldiers who snored and if they did, they didn't do it for long. The methods used to assure there was no snoring were simple; if you snored you were kicked or hit by clods of dirt until you learned a way not to snore. If you failed to find an answer to your snoring problem, you could count on getting little sleep. Silence while sleeping was one of those requirements enforced on grunts and by grunts in the field for their own safety.

Any noise at night was not tolerated. Myself, I could lie down just about anywhere and drop off to sleep. I found any little noise would wake me. Yet when the company was with the artillery the noise of the big guns firing at night usually didn't bother me at all.

After I returned home this sensitivity to unusual noises while I was asleep continued to bother me. I would be awakened by the smallest sound and get up and patrol the house to be sure everything was OK. I never found anything wrong and luckily my wife only found me on patrol a couple of times. When my wife discovered me awake, I just told her I couldn't sleep.

When we later bought our acreage in the mountains and I was staying there alone I would sit at night like I was on guard duty with my M-1 carbine across my lap. Please don't ask me why I did this, because I just don't have an answer. To this day I'm often startled awake and still roam around the house making sure everything is OK. Guess once you're a soldier, you're always a soldier.

8

Saving "A" Company
in the Ia Drang Valley

AUGUST 9, 1966. Well lover you might say we have really been going. I will get this mailed today. We have really been into it; I guess you have been reading about it in the papers. Right now, we're somewhere west of Pleiku and yesterday A Company just about got wiped out. We lost a lot of men and weapons yesterday, but the NVA troops lost quite a few also. It was a nasty night. We were the first company in to relieve them. We captured one, I imagine we could have taken a couple of more but all we needed was one for questioning. Well, let's just hope they've left the area. I'm not sure, but I think they're messing with my transfer. But nothing to worry about because when we get back to base camp and I can check on it.... Our first platoon messed up yesterday morning. It was early in the morning and the company was gathering to start on patrol from the night ambush. The first platoon had been on this trail and they went up the side of a hill to wait for the rest of the company. Then low and behold here comes about 30 NVA down the trail and so the first platoon opened up on them with unbelievable firepower and believe it or not they didn't hit a single one. We did get two packs, but not a single NVA. How about that!

The first platoon ambush, August 8, 1966. The S2 was estimating at least three NVA regiments were operating in the same area as we were, within the Ia Drang Valley. This would amount to 12 companies of soldiers or approximately 1,440 enemy troops.

Ambushes didn't require digging a foxhole, and digging those things was a dirty and tiring job, but having a foxhole at least gave me some sense of security. I must have dug 300+ foxholes in my year in Vietnam. But when setting off an ambush there was no such sense of security; most of the time you were on top of the ground where grazing enemy fire could wound or kill you.

We all knew ambushes required absolute quiet. Keeping quiet was one of the most difficult things for us to do. It's hard to remain still and not make any noise while you're setting up an ambush. Once the ambush has been set, it's a waiting game and you pray no one accidentally sets the sucker off before it's needed. When the time comes and the ambush is initiated, things happen quickly. Once the rifle firing stops, your central objective is to get back to the main body of your friendly forces as soon as possible. Remember, you're not dug in and do not know if you have ambushed a squad, a platoon, a company or worse. You run like hell and can't relax until you've returned to the safety of your own unit. Ambushes are scary, but they're a necessary element of combat. Surprising the enemy often resulted in the capturing or killing of high-ranking officers or scouts who could provide a bonanza of information about their own forces.

In the movies when the shooting starts, the soldiers all forge forward with little if any apparent concern for their own welfare. Let's just say this is not the way things happen in the real world. I guess the actors don't worry as much about dying as we did. Real grunts have many things to think about once the enemy bullets begin flying. My ever-present concern was whether my damn M-16 was going to fire. When setting up an ambush we often stayed in place overnight and I knew early mornings were the worst times to try and fire my M-16. There were times when overnight moisture would build up in the firing mechanism and my rifle wouldn't fire. Let me tell you, it's a sickening feeling when you try to fire your weapon during a firefight and nothing happens. You're left with one choice—get the hell out of there or die.

I can remember one night in August 1966 like it was yesterday. The second platoon lieutenant and his RTO were having a terrible argument accompanied by lots of yelling and cussing. The lieutenant's RTO suddenly threw his radio on to the ground and needless to say, this RTO was out of a job. The lieutenant then replaced his RTO with the platoon sergeant's RTO, and this left the platoon sergeant without an RTO.

Once again, my platoon sergeant asked, "Well, Blessing, how would you like to hump the radio for me?" My reply was not immediate; I'd already been an RTO and knew the ropes by that time. Then I started to weigh the pros and cons of being an RTO in the field. I thought well if I'm carrying the radio I won't have to go out on as many patrols. Ah, but the enemy targets the radio operator first during a firefight. Then I thought about the added advantage of no longer having to pull perimeter guard.

Oh, but there was still radio watch. You get the picture. As usual I was over-thinking this job offer, so I replied, "I'll do it, Sarge," as if I really had a choice in the first place.

Now came the adding of the extra gear needed by an RTO to my already overloaded pack. This radio weighed a ton and I knew carrying it meant something in my pack might have to go. The only extras I had in my pack were my supply of B-1 rations and since these were pretty much what I lived on, I decided I needed to find a way to keep them. They didn't weigh that much but they took up a lot of needed space. Then came the 300 rounds of ammo and the four hand grenades I always carried, and I considered them to be an absolute necessity if I was going to survive this war. In addition, I carried three canteens—water was often hard to come by and most of the time it was undrinkable when you were in the field. After having inventoried everything I already had in my pack, I decided I could handle the added weight of the radio, its extra battery and the three smoke grenades needed for communications. But boy was that radio a bitch to carry.

The ambush the night of August 7 was set up in a sort of a triangle on three small hills. The Headquarters Group which included the 4th platoon was in the small valley created by the three surrounding hills. Off to the west was the 3rd platoon, to the east overlooking a well-used trail was the 1st platoon and my 2nd platoon had the enviable job of guarding the Headquarters Group and the 4th platoon.

At daylight the 1st platoon had recovered their trip flares and claymores, then pulled back up off the trail on to the side of the hill that was behind them. Right then, the 1st platoon looked up the trail where they had just removed their trip flares and claymores and saw a platoon of soldiers and thought they were the 3rd platoon.

Right about then the new radio I had inherited is crackling over the company net asking if anyone was marbling (moving) and the response he received was negative on all fronts. He then responded, "Then who the hell is the platoon coming down the trail in front of us?" He then quickly identified them as NVA and the 1st platoon immediately was engaged in a full-on firefight. I'm sure the troopers in the 1st platoon probably wished they had left their trip flares and claymores out there just a little longer and saved us all from this nasty encounter with the NVA.

After the failed ambush the platoon sergeant described what occurred. He said they had their ambush set up on the well-traveled trail and decided to move away from the trail at first light. They then removed their trip flares and claymores and pulled back to have some breakfast.

Most of the ground-pounders took advantage of the break and were lying on their backs leaning against their packs. Luckily, they were lying in tall grass and were out of sight. The sergeant was eating some C's and was the only one standing. He spotted someone coming over a little rise in the trail and told his guys to get everything together because the 3rd platoon was coming. Upon further observation the sergeant realized his mistake and said "Shit, those aren't G.I.s!" That warning started some serious scrambling by everyone in the 1st platoon.

The sharp crack of rifle fire first thing in the morning is always a jarring experience for any infantry soldier. Rifle fire in a contested area usually meant something bad was happening to someone. The adrenaline begins to pump through your veins and your entire body goes into fight or flight mode. Of course, flight was not an option for an infantryman and your only choice was to hunker down and prepare for the worst. Any trooper who has been in a fire fight can tell you it's next to impossible to describe what it's like. The sounds and smells of a full-on fire fight, with the M-16s being fired fully on automatic, the M-60 machine guns blasting through their ammo and the distinct bloop sound of the M-79 grenade launchers stay with you forever. It's just one of those "you had to be there" moments. Looking back, I can tell you I remember most of the contact my squad had with the enemy and of course there are some battles I continue to try and forget. Being a participant in this war left me with a mental scar that will never go away. The visions of many of my friends and the innocent civilians who were killed by friendly fire still roam around in my nightmares.

Once the 1st platoon's contact with the NVA was relayed to our brass, we were then the ones who began scrambling around and preparing to assist in the fire fight. The captain took charge of the operation and started directing radio traffic. My own 2nd platoon was instructed to guard the 4th platoon and their 81mm mortar located behind a small hill in the valley below the action.

The 4th platoon was then ordered forward up the hill and brought us along to guard them. The captain then directed the 1st and 3rd platoons online. Their orders were to assault the tree line where the enemy had just seemed to disappear into thin air. Both the 1st and 3rd platoons were ordered to perform a tactic known as recon by fire. This common tactic required that you slowly move forward with all your rifles firing straight ahead in hopes of flushing out the enemy. Both platoons followed orders and while doing so, used up a tremendous amount of ammo while attempting to wound, kill or capture the enemy they had been seeking to find. Results were paramount to our brass and the captain in charge was furious when he discovered so much of our precious ammunition had been expended and there was not a single enemy dead or alive to show for this tactic.

Once the dust had cleared, the captain was beyond angry. He couldn't believe what he saw as a clear-cut mission could have been so royally screwed up. These had been hard core NVA and the 1st platoon's field of fire was clear—no trees, a slight decline down a small hill and only grass obstructing the view of the trail where the NVA were.

The captain's fury over what he considered to be a massive error in judgment by one platoon leader resulted in their entire platoon having to suffer.

The captain ordered the company to form up into a battle march formation. Then we began to march in the direction where most of the NVA seemed to have fled. Every couple of hundred yards or so we stopped and the 1st platoon would do a loop, or what we called a butterfly sweep, to the left. Then when they got back the captain would have them go to the right. This type of butterfly sweep was normally conducted by two platoons, but it was evident the captain wanted to make a point with the 1st platoon's sergeant. This area wasn't difficult to navigate, but the heat was overbearing and the 1st platoon suffered dearly. Yup, this proved to all of us you never ever want to make your captain that angry. We spent the morning seeking to find the escaping enemy with no results, but the 1st platoon took the brunt of the captain's ire. I'm certain the guys in the 1st platoon have a vivid memory of that miserable morning.

Noon was approaching and there was no additional contact with the NVA. Suddenly there was a large increase in radio traffic over Bravo Company's channel. This heavy radio traffic could only mean one thing: someone, somewhere was into something.

It wasn't long before we knew what was happening. It turned out that our Alpha Company 1/7 Cavalry had stepped into a hornet's nest. It was hard to believe, but in a matter of minutes one platoon was nearly wiped out and only a few soldiers survived.

Alpha Company had stumbled upon a much larger group of NVA, estimated to be as large as a regiment. These NVA were operating in the same area as the group of NVA our own 1st platoon had waylaid that morning and apparently our troops had merely inconvenienced the enemy during their brief firefight. This group of NVA were able to continue and had joined up with a much larger NVA unit.

Urgent orders were received from the 1/7 HQ to march as fast as possible overland to LZ Juliet for a Huey lift into the area Alpha company had been patrolling. The 102 howitzers were the first indication we were getting close to the LZ. Their familiar rapid fire, boom, boom, boom let us know we were getting close to the LZ. The infantry who were guarding the LZ had been running to where the chinook helicopters were bringing in more ammo in cargo nets. These guys were running back to the guns with as much ammo as they could carry and there seemed to be a beehive of activity all over the LZ.

A squadron of Hueys soon arrived to pick us up and then settled down into a long line, preparing for the anticipated enemy activity we were most likely about to encounter. Suddenly I realized that my new assignment as the RTO for the platoon sergeant probably wasn't such a bad deal after all. The platoon sergeant generally remained at the rear of the platoon and I would be right there with him, less of a target than I originally thought.

I was assigned to the #12 copter. I always found the arrival of an airlift to be chaotic and the loud, turbulent chopper blades quickly would get your attention. I was halfway walking and halfway running, heading towards the Huey when I was surprised to see a one-star general coming towards me. This was the one and only time I had seen a general out in the field, and I was so stunned I didn't know if I should stop and salute him or not. I wound up not saluting and just ran past him and boarded the copter. Once loaded, we took off in a 12-ship formation. It was a short time before I heard the chopper throttling back and could see where we would be setting down. It was a huge field of damn elephant grass, I hated this stuff. Its razor-sharp edges could cut you to pieces in no time. Things like having to jump into this perilous elephant grass stay with you; like all the other miseries of combat this was just another reason to hate Vietnam.

Just before we were preparing to jump an F-4d Phantom jet came across in front of us dropping napalm. If I had any reason to doubt how bad things really were, this fire from the sky removed any uncertainty. Believe me, the Air Force doesn't drop napalm just to clear the jungle.

As our chopper began to slow and started to hover above the 5-foot-tall elephant grass below, a young trooper jumped off in front of me. This guy bagged the prize of the day. He reached down in the elephant grass that had been bent over from the rotor wash and yells back up to me, "I got one!" He then proceeded to pull an unarmed, khaki dressed NVA soldier out of the grass. I could hardly believe my eyes and when I made my way down to the young trooper who was holding the prisoner, he handed the guy off to me by his collar. As the last trooper in the company and having nothing better to do at the time, I was given the unenviable job of guarding prisoners. Talk about a thankless job and this was one that could go bad in a flat second.

We had no idea how important this prisoner might be to the NVA or if his capture might result in further enemy contact in an effort to retrieve him. We estimated him to be around 35 years old and he carried no identification. The combination of his age, dress and no ID led us to believe he may have been some type of ranking NVA officer. It was odd that he had nothing on him other than his khaki uniform—no shoes, no headgear or any other equipment. We may never know what his mission had been that day when he found himself being snatched from the elephant grass where he was hiding, but whatever it was he must have been in a serious hurry and left behind everything he may have been carrying.

The platoon sergeant told me if we hit the shit and got into heavy combat to shoot the prisoner and I'm sure I would have followed his orders. I took this job of guarding prisoners very seriously. I knew if I became distracted a prisoner could grab my rifle and kill or wound me, or god forbid, kill or injure one of my platoon members and for that I would have never forgiven myself. During the time I guarded this NVA soldier he never gave me any trouble, nor did he utter a word.

Later the captain had me turn the prisoner over to the weapons platoon sergeant. I was standing there when the captain told the sergeant that he wanted him kept alive. This order to keep the prisoner alive was a job the platoon sergeant must have taken on with some apprehension, as most of the Alpha Company survivors wanted this NVA prisoner dead and they would have been more than willing to do the job. The sergeant carefully guarded the prisoner until he was safely loaded onto a Huey and sent back to a POW holding area where I'm sure he endured many hours of interrogation. As usual no information about this prisoner ever filtered back to us and I'll always wonder who he was and what he was supposed to be doing when we captured him.

My 2nd platoon was given marching orders to air assault into a large LZ about 300 meters from where Alpha Company was making a stand. We were lucky: for some unknown reason the NVA were withdrawing, giving up their advantage and now were trying to disengage. There was no doubt in my mind that our overpowering artillery fire and massive air support had a lot to do with the NVA running for cover. The aircraft dropping their huge bombs and the gunships firing their rockets had resulted in a rapid de-escalation of the combat activity.

Our company was now moving towards the area Alpha company was occupying; the artillery was coming in close and loud booming and crashing noises permeated the air. We were moving slowly and deliberately as we approached where Alpha company was making its last stand. Being the RTO gave me a front row seat to the action. While listening to the radio traffic I could hear the FO of the lost platoon calling for artillery fire. As we got closer to the action, we could see the devastating results from our air strikes, rockets and artillery fire. The ground in front of us seemed to be smoking and a shocking and appalling sight came into our view. There were bodies of NVA soldiers littering the ground: all were in khaki uniforms and laying in various positions. We all remained on the trail moving carefully while passing these NVA bodies and looking for anyone who might be playing possum and ready to open fire on us. Although I was still guarding a prisoner at the time, I kept a close eye on these slumbering menaces as we passed.

All of the sudden off to our left, one of the supposedly deceased NVA soldiers sat straight up. Boy, talk about a shock. My platoon sergeant and I both jumped. The sergeant and I then swung our rifles around towards this enemy soldier, but for some reason neither of us fired our weapons. The sergeant then hopped down off the trail, got a couple of feet away from the wounded enemy soldier, and then quickly returned to the trail. I asked why he hadn't shot the guy and he tapped his finger to his forehead and answered in a matter of fact manner, "He's got a hole right about here." I then looked back and saw what looked like a birthmark in the center of the NVA's forehead. As the company began moving forward again, I saw this poor soul put his head forward into his hands and begin to slowly rock back and forth. He didn't know it yet, but he was dead.

We then moved into the perimeter of Alpha company and there was a tremendous amount of commotion; we could hear our comrades yelling and moaning. It was a very sad day: most of the killed and injured had been the result of the platoon sergeant calling in artillery fire on top of his platoon's position. This had appeared to be a last resort on his part, because the NVA were beginning to overrun his men and they were in a full-out battle for their lives.

I had a chance to talk with a couple of the Alpha company survivors and the stories of how they survived and what the NVA did to them were chilling. The one guy said he was blown head-first into a large bush and luckily was not found by the rummaging enemy soldiers. I was told by one of the guys that the NVA came through the first time and policed up all of the weapons and ammo, then they came back and stripped the bodies of our troopers, taking their boots and some clothing and anything else of value they could find. Their third trip they returned and fired their rifles into the bodies of some of the dead and wounded Americans.

Another survivor had an amazing story to tell. He said he wasn't wounded but while he was trying to help a seriously injured buddy who was losing a massive amount of blood; his own fatigues, face and arms had become soaked with blood. The NVA were now going from body to body trying to make sure no one was still alive, and he knew his only hope was to play dead. He said he froze in place when an NVA soldier came over to him, then the enemy soldier pointed his rifle directly at him and attempted to fire, but for some reason the rifle had jammed. The NVA soldier then laid his rifle on this trooper's chest and proceeded to take off the trooper's boots. I can't imagine having to play dead, while an enemy soldier is stripping your body of whatever he thought he could use. There's no doubt that his clothes being soaked with his buddy's blood made this trooper's demise much more believable to this NVA soldier. The trooper said after the NVA soldier took his boots, he then just picked up his rifle and moved on, searching for someone else to violate.

Listening to these guys who had survived this terrible battle and its aftermath, I thought back to when we had first arrived in the area and came across the field of dead NVA. We could see that the NVA tactic of hugging the belt had once again resulted in their soldiers being able to get very close to us and the ensuing battle had caused our troopers to call in artillery on top of themselves in an attempt to stop the overwhelming enemy forces. The bodies of the NVA soldiers were almost in a perfect half circle around what was left of Alpha company. The NVA were careful to make sure they didn't leave anything of value behind for us to find. The troopers in Alpha company had been stripped of their weapons, ammo and packs and they all were barefoot. I still have this picture in my mind to this very day. Witnessing such carnage on both sides of the battle is something I've tried to forget, but it just stays in the back of my mind. You would think after 54 years these memories would fade but seeing such a gruesome scene left a permanent imprint on my mind and when it surfaces, the fear and anxiety I felt that day returns in spades.

Once again, the NVA had attempted to slug it out with an American infantry unit, and no one had walked away a winner that day; both sides had been bloodied badly.

Seeing the horrendous results of this fierce battle left me with an empty feeling. Coming upon so many dead and injured comrades caused an enormous amount of survivor's guilt and I continued to question why I was still standing when so many of them would never see another sunrise. War is truly hell: every combat soldier in every battle, no matter what war, can't help but carry these agonizing memories.

While in Vietnam, the anguish I felt, seeing so many grievously wounded and dead Americans and hearing the stories of the brutality metered out by the NVA overshadowed any form of empathy I might have felt for our enemies. Now, looking back, I can't help but feel an odd form of kinship with the ordinary enemy soldier. Hindsight has brought on a kind of clarity that has helped to dissolve my out and out hatred towards them. Most of the ordinary NVA soldiers were much like us, just trying to live through the war and return home safe to their families. It was the hierarchy of our enemies that I will never forgive for the way they treated anyone they considered their foe. They were a brutal bunch who directed their men to kill everyone and they seldom took prisoners. Their cruelty and total lack of humanity towards their fellow man can never, ever, be forgiven!

We finally stopped for the night following our attempt to assist Alpha company after their disastrous attack by the NVA. The next morning began as usual with a Mad Minute: whenever we were in a contested area, we would all open fire at daybreak in hopes of surprising anyone who may have crept up close to our perimeter during the night.

Shortly after our morning Mad Minute, we heard the mortar platoon sergeant yell out "short round" and everyone knew a mortar had misfired and was probably heading in our direction. I had been resting in my hooch and our captain was in his hooch directly across from mine. When we heard the warning, we both bolted out of our hooches and headed for the same large tree. We were fighting for position around it and began doing a sort of crab dance around the tree not knowing where the errant mortar round would land. We both had the same idea and were doing our best to keep this tree between us and wherever this live round was going to explode.

After what seemed like a lifetime, the mortar round finally hit the ground; it hit like a bolt of lightning with a loud thud and it was less than 10 feet from us. Whoa, this misguided mortar was much too close for comfort. Thank God it didn't explode.

Our captain was fuming mad; he started marching down the hill yelling obscenities directed towards the mortar platoon sergeant. Since our captain had been resting in his hooch, he didn't have a chance to dress and to this day I can still see him in his boxer shorts, T-shirt and shower slippers angrily chewing out the mortar platoon sergeant. The captain's state of undress seemed somehow funny to me and since his anger wasn't directed my way, I just smiled.

Right at dusk that evening one of the troopers decided to go out in front to go to the bathroom. He notified the positions to his left and to his right, which was standard operating procedure. Sadly, when the guy returned it was practically dark and a position two foxholes away from him opened fire on him. Personally, I don't believe this would have occurred under normal conditions, but we were on edge from everything we had seen during this very long day. We expected we could be attacked at any moment and reacted to every little noise or movement. Fortunately, this trooper hadn't been killed and was still alive when they loaded him on the helicopter. Once again, we were responsible for one of our own being badly injured. Whoever did the shooting that night will never be the same; as usual we never got any word about the wounded soldier after he left us and so there never could be closure.

> AUGUST 10, 1966. Well we're still here where "A" company had all the trouble. I got a letter from you yesterday evening and was so glad to hear from you. The first sergeant came out yesterday and he has bad news. He said my orders had been cut and he was sending a messenger to the field to call me out and before the messenger left my orders were called back. The first sergeant promised to check and see just what had happened and see what he could do for me. The only thing we can do is continue to keep our fingers and every-thing else crossable crossed for the best....

This news about my transfer being denied had crushed me. I was so looking forward to getting out of a combat line unit. Our first sergeant did as he promised and checked on what had happened with my transfer to the MP company. I guess the first sergeant at the MP company thought I had been a regular MP at Fort Gordon and when he discovered I was only on a temporary duty assignment he cancelled my orders. Guess it just wasn't meant to be, but having my hopes trashed after waiting so long for a transfer really sucked.

We had marched overland and arrived on a PZ for a helicopter lift out. The door gunner of the helicopter I was getting on only permitted four of us to load up. Normally there would be eight or nine soldiers aboard. I noted the pilot and co-pilots were a full-bird colonel and a major, and this was strange. Our Huey revved up and headed for the tree line then at the last moment the pilot pulled back, changed pitch and in the same instant hit the trees. Then, rearing back, the chopper backed off the trees it had hit.

This contact was a little like riding a bucking horse. I could see both the pilot and co-pilot talking on their mikes and there was a shuffling of the copters who were still on the ground and we tried to take off again. This time we made it out of the PZ with tree branches dangling off the chopper skids. I guess the engine on this Huey was just tired and beginning to show the wear and tear of daily use.

> AUGUST 11, 1966. We're sitting down here on the landing zone waiting to be lifted out. We are going back to a rest area for a while which is good news. I forgot to tell you about the photographer that I met yesterday. He is from UPI and he is really a great guy, he took a couple pictures of me reading your letters so if you see me in the paper, you'll know what I'm reading.... Shelby and I are the only ones left in the platoon. It looks likes "A" company might have themselves a hero. The fellow's name is Hawthorne and he was a machine gunner. I guess they have put him in for the Medal of Honor, he was the one person everyone counted on to defend them and even though he was wounded he kept right on firing until his machine gun got shot up. They say that as they carried him to the LZ to be picked up by a medevac he was yelling he would kill them all because they had shot up his machine gun. I've said it before and I'll say it again, machine gunners are crazy.... We're just about ready to move out. So, give J.R. his usual and thanks again for the cute pictures.

> AUGUST 12, 1966. Well, mail came in and all's I got was a *News-week*. I'd sure like to know who got that subscription for me. Every-one sure likes to read that magazine.... We're still in this rest area, but we're on a 30-minute alert which means we could be on heli-copters within 30 minutes heading just about anywhere. It's still raining all the time, but not quite as much as it has been the last couple of weeks.... A good friend of mine named Shelby just came by and said to say howdy. Damn a helicopter just blew your letter off into the mud.

I mentioned my buddy Shelby in my letters of August 11 and 12. Shelby and I were the last ones remaining from our original platoon and we had become good friends. He was older than I and we often talked about our lives back home and how much we hated the war. We both had the same mindset: above all we just wanted to get home in one piece and go on with our lives. I think I knew from the day I met him we were destined to be friends for life.

The rest area I mentioned was known as the oasis. The oasis was a tea plantation and its owner had demanded that no foxholes be dug on his property. Although we were ordered not to dig foxholes, there were many dug back in the tree line. Our brass probably knew they were hidden there but I wonder if the property owner ever found them.

While we were at the oasis, I was making myself some stew when one of the troopers said, "look at that snake." Besides leeches, snakes were next on my list of least favorite things. This one was a huge cobra and the only one I ever saw in Vietnam. Someone quickly dispatched it with their M-16. Following the cobra's being shot our resident "snake lore expert" told us that cobras usually have a mate and if one is killed the other mate will tirelessly seek out whoever killed its mate. I didn't sleep much the next night after hearing this fine bit of snake lore and the next few days I was extra vigilant and kept an eye out for the mate of this cobra. Looking back now, I can see how easy it was to be psyched out by such preposterous fairy tales. We were constantly on edge and easily accepted such hogwash as gospel.

Snakebites were not a major problem in Vietnam. In fact, it appears there is only one recorded incidence of death caused by a snakebite and this was as a result of a Marine lieutenant who was bitten while jumping from a helicopter onto a coiled cobra. We were told there was another snake said to be even more dangerous than the cobra. It was described as a little green snake and they called it "a one-step snake." As the story goes, you could only take one step after you were bitten before you were dead. Don't know to this day if the "one-step snake" existed, but we were always on the lookout for one.

I'm told that most of the soldiers who were sent to our snakebite treatment center in Long Binn were found to have been bitten by scorpions or insects. Vietnam was full of annoying, vicious and poisonous insects and animals ready to make our lives in Vietnam even more miserable.

> AUGUST 16, 1966. Well, as you can see all my writing material got wet so I guess I will have to do with what I've got. Man, it really rained yesterday. Gee I really get pissed off at this army when I'm not able to write to you every day, but I do try…. I guess the NVA are in real bad shape after hitting "A" company because of what the prisoners have been saying. This Ia Drang is the worst area I have been in. I'm not sure we will ever find a worst area! Boy, do I ever need a rest….

Each time we returned to the Ia Drang area it reminded me what a terrible place it was. It seemed as if the ghosts of all of those lost there were still hanging around, waiting for us to join them.

One of my saddest days in Vietnam occurred during this trip back to the Ia Drang. We were sweeping through the area taking prisoners. I was still carrying the radio and heard that the 1st platoon and the Headquarters Group were about to cross a one-log bridge across the river. I followed our platoon sergeant down to the river and while he was talking with someone, I stayed by the log bridge. The river was moving scary fast below this log bridge. While I was waiting for my sergeant, the Headquarters Group began crossing the log. I met up with a young soldier who was really concerned about crossing the log bridge; he was the last in line to cross. I noted his name was Kemp and he was a private E2. He kept trying to get up onto the log but couldn't steady himself enough to take a couple of steps. Even though there was a rope stretched above the log that served as a kind of railing, the log was wet, and I saw why this trooper was having trouble. I noticed that Kemp was also a radio operator and was worried about being able to carry all the extra weight of his pack and the radio across this makeshift bridge. I could see the obvious fear in his eyes, and he told me he didn't know how to swim. I then tried to convince him he probably wasn't needed across the river, since five radios were already there. But he insisted he had to go. He then proceeded to hop up on the wet log and began shakily creeping forward. I saw he was really in trouble and called to him to unbuckle his web gear and just let it go. He had come to a full stop and I continued to try and coach him not to look down, but to keep moving forward. What happened next will forever haunt me; one second he was on the log bridge and then he slipped and bounced off the log into the river. That turbulent river was travelling at such a rapid rate he was gone the second he hit the water.

One of the Bravo platoons spent the rest of August 17 going down the river looking for Kemp's body. The Cavalry had a hard and fast rule that no matter what, we always tried to recover our fallen soldiers. The platoon had been unsuccessful in finding him and returned to the main force about dusk. The next day was the second platoons turn to search for Kemp, but we found no evidence of him or any of his equipment.

Though I had never set eyes on him before the day he died, witnessing his pointless accident left me with an unbelievable sense of regret. I've always second guessed what I might have been able to do to stop him from plunging to his death that day into that unforgiving river. I now realize I must accept the fact that his fate was in his own hands that day and there was nothing I could have done to save him.

You can find Freddie Kemp's name on the Vietnam Wall "registry" in Washington, D.C.: Panel 10E—Line 16 (the Wall itself has only his name).

FREDDIE KEMP
PVT–E2–Army—Selective Service
1st Cav Division (AMBL)
Length of service 1 years [*sic*]
His tour began on Aug 17, 1966
Casualty was on Aug 17, 1966 [*sic*]
In South Vietnam
Non-Hostile, died missing, ground casualty
drowned, suffocated
Body was not recovered

AUGUST 17, 1966. Gee, I got 6 (six) letters from you yesterday evening. Wow, I was squinting reading the last one, but I got it read…. We're still in the same location and I guess we're moving shortly to somewhere. Who knows where? We're northwest of Pleiku and close to the border for your map.

After "A" company's fight we policed up a lot of prisoners. The 2nd platoon was following the Ia Drang River when our point man suddenly stopped abruptly, and everything instantly became quiet. Instinctively you knew there must be some sort of problem up front and everyone just froze in place.

The point element found a rope bridge across a part of the river that would have been impossible to wade across. This was not too far downstream from where we lost Freddie Kemp into the river's swift current on August 17. The platoon then carefully crossed this makeshift rope bridge. What we found on the other side of the river were the remains of an abandoned and well camouflaged NVA hospital. Bloody bandages littered the area and although the bodies and equipment were gone, we could see this had been a big operation. The size of this hospital surprised all of us. It appeared it could have held as many as 200+ wounded and we were the ones who were probably responsible for those wounded. Seeing the evidence of what could only be called a massacre brought me back to the reality of how ugly this war had become.

It only took us a couple of minutes to re-cross the rope bridge and get back to more friendly ground. I don't know if anyone cut that rope bridge down after we crossed back, but someone should have.

We then began guarding the mortar platoon at the very spot where Kemp went into the river. The mortar crew was firing in support of our troopers on the other side of the Ia Drang River. Occasionally we could hear bursts of M-16 fire coming from the other side of the river and it sounded like some of the NVA soldiers had decided not to surrender and were putting up a bit of a fight.

The mortar platoon suddenly stopped firing and that got everyone's attention. Then one of the troopers yelled out "hang fire." I had missed mortar training in AIT and didn't know what that meant, but by the panic in the guy's voice I knew it couldn't mean anything good. I then watched in awe as they took the mortar tube loose from its base plate and tipped the top of the mortar down towards the ground. Then one of them caught the misfired round as it slid out of the mortar tube and immediately ran and dropped it in the river. I asked whether the misfired round could have exploded, and they all answered in unison "Yeah!" Well that was a real lesson for me and from then on, I kept my ears open when I was anywhere near the mortar platoon and made sure I got as far away as possible from them when I heard the words "hang fire."

We had been on alert and the 25th Infantry, who were new to Vietnam, called and said they needed help. They were just moving into the Ia Drang area and when we heard they would be taking over in this area we were more than ready to give it to them. We answered their call for help and began marching overland in a battalion battle march formation to relieve a platoon from the 25th that had been overrun. We learned that four choppers had dropped off most of the platoon, and before the choppers could get back with the rest of the platoon the soldiers on the ground had been wiped out. My second platoon was right in the middle of this battalion battle formation, with other platoons and companies on both sides and in front of us. We were in a very bad location and knew if we were attacked, we would have no way to fire in any direction because we had only friendly forces around us.

While we marched along, a helicopter gunship accidentally fired on us, but no one was hit and lucky for the gunner we didn't shoot back. We trapped one NVA in a bunker and he was the only one the 2nd platoon ran into that day. We weren't having any luck trying to talk him out of the bunker, so we tried firing our M-16s into the bunker and dropped in a couple of hand grenades but that didn't work. Finally, someone dropped in a smoke grenade and that did the trick. The enemy soldier couldn't breath and suffocated and when he was dragged from the bunker, he was already dead.

Although we continued to hear some rifle fire, the 2nd platoon never got involved because the fighting never came our way. Thankfully we weren't asked to go towards the sounds of the guns.

AUGUST 19, 1966. I got a letter from you last night and it was already getting dark. We're now at LZ Juliet in the Ia Drang valley and they're giving us a little bit of rest. They are giving us hot chow and everything. Guess what? They gave us all clean clothes and now I have a complete jungle outfit, boots, pants and shirt. How about that! …

AUGUST 20, 1966. Well, I wrote your mama a letter and told her happy birthday. What did you get her for her birthday? I wish we were someplace where I could get something for her, but out here there is nothing and nobody except people you don't want to meet.… We were out with the action the other day. I didn't want to say anything while I was out there so you wouldn't worry. We had those NVA really on the run. We chased them (on foot) for about five days. We found 19 dead one day and took 15 POW's. I picked up a lighter made in China and a wallet with Hanoi stamped on the front. The fad is to get a pistol belt buckle with a red star on it. Drat it, I never got one and I wanted one so bad. They were really on the run and you should have seen all the equipment they dropped, and these hardcore troops just about never do this because they must carry the stuff so far to get it to here. We found all kinds of ammo, some grenades and a few rockets. Well lover, got to go eat breakfast so I'll sign off.

During this time, North Vietnam was telling the world they were not in the south. The war, according to the North, was a Southern revolutionary fight and they were not participants. The fact that I had found a wallet with Hanoi stamped on it had dispelled the North's claims and finding that wallet was a real coup for me.

Apparently, and luckily for us, the battle with Alpha company had taken the fight out of most of the NVA. Except for the hardcore rear guard, the majority of those who were left standing just wanted to get out of our way. Even though most of the enemy had fled, it was still a very dangerous place to be and we took a few casualties.

Early on during my tour, our military intelligence had developed leaflets to be distributed by packing them into artillery shells and firing them into contested areas. These leaflets were known as safe conduct passes or Chieu Hoi. At least 220,000 of these leaflets were distributed during this campaign. The message on the safe conduct passes told the enemy if they handed it to the allied forces when surrendering they wouldn't be shot. Our intelligence had verified that this program was working; they were being picked up and read by the enemy and used when surrendering. During

SAFE-CONDUCT PASS TO BE HONORED BY ALL VIETNAMESE GOVERNMENT AGENCIES AND ALLIED FORCES

Đây là một tấm Giấy Thông Hành có giá trị với tất cả cơ quan Quân Chính Việt - Nam Cộng - Hòa và lực lượng Đồng - Minh.

Nọ 755860 AD

Safe Conduct Pass—these were distributed to VC/NVA in hopes of convincing them to surrender without fear.

interrogations of 550 suspects, about 70 percent of them had picked up and carried these safe conduct passes just in case. The prisoners also relayed to their interrogators that their superiors had warned them they would be shot if caught carrying these allied passes.

We policed up a lot of prisoners in this area, usually finding one or two at a time. Most of our captives were NVA stragglers who had the fight taken out of them. When we came across more than a couple, they would often open fire on us and then we would cut loose on them and capture them.

In the past when you found an NVA soldier in this area, you could find a safe conduct pass tucked away someplace. But now, even though these leaflets were littering the ground, they were no longer being picked up by the NVA. This told us the leaflet program was no longer having any success and we were now dealing with committed, hard core soldiers.

I was still guarding prisoners at that time and I witnessed our captain's method of extracting information from captured prisoners. Our captain spoke fluent Vietnamese and easily communicated with the prisoners. When we brought the prisoners back, most of them were starving, so the Captain used this fact to his advantage. He would open a can of C's then squat down in front of the prisoners and wave a spoon full of food under their noses. He would then begin slowly eating from the can while asking the prisoners questions. I wasn't close enough to hear anything they said, but it appeared the prisoners were answering him and not just telling him to fuck off.

We were back on patrol, and this is when my life changed forever and my nightmares began. We were still in the Ia Drang and making sweeps to see what we could find. What we found that day is almost indescribable. There were dead NVA lying everywhere. We could smell them before we could see them, and the stench was unbearable. The LT then sent me down a steep hillside to check out some of the bodies that were barely visible. I found the wallet and the lighter I mentioned earlier lying close by one of the dead NVA soldiers. He appeared to have been trying to burn some equipment he thought to be valuable before he died. Another enemy soldier was propped up against a tree and looked very alive with his eyes wide open. I almost shot him but as I got closer, I could see he was all puffed up and had been dead a while. Then I looked up the next ravine off to my right and saw several NVA lying there. Three of them were lying together and it looked like two of them had been carrying a wounded soldier on a stretcher. Both legs of the wounded NVA soldier had been amputated at the knees and were heavily bandaged. I saw the two guys who had been carrying the stretcher were obviously dead, but the guy on the stretcher looked like he was trying to say something to me. I carefully approached him, my rifle at the ready and pressure on the trigger. When I got closer, I could see there were maggots all around his lips and they were moving, making it appear he was talking. This scene comes back in my nightmares to this day and I doubt I'll ever be able to escape the torment of what I saw that terrible day.

Operation Paul Revere II officially ended on August 25, 1966, and had included part of the 2nd Brigade First Cavalry, plus the 3rd Brigade of the 25th Infantry Division, some ARVN forces and some forces from the Republic of Korea (ROK). The enemy body count for the whole campaign was 871. I don't know how many allied forces were listed as KIA, but I do know Bravo Company 1st of 7th Cavalry lost that one trooper, Freddie Kemp, to the swift waters of the Ia Drang River. He was eventually designated as MIA/BNR (missing in action, body never recovered).

9

Fiftieth Air Assault

We got a surprise delivery on August 20: HHQ had sent us out some special rations to divide up among ourselves. One item was a #10 can with no label on it and when it was opened, I saw it was sliced beets and I offered to share it, but there were no takers. Since I liked beets, I intended to eat the entire can by myself, but I couldn't eat more than a few bites. This was the first time I realized I couldn't eat like I used to. It was a waste, but I had to throw the rest of the beets away.

I had acquired a taste for the tropical candy bars (chocolate bars that didn't melt in the heat of Vietnam) and little cans of chocolate milk they had started sending us. At first, I could hardly choke them down, but their taste grew on me. Luckily for me most of the guys didn't like either of them, so I had a bounty of them all to myself. Unfortunately, we only got them for a few weeks and just as I had begun looking forward to their arrival, we never got them again.

Well, my little meal plan came to an end one night when the captain was checking the perimeter and discovered the troopers were throwing away a lot of C's. After he saw all the waste, he cut the whole company back to two meals a day. So, there went most of my extra cookies and cocoa and crackers and cheese, but I made do with whatever I could find.

> AUGUST 22, 1966. Say I got a package of candy yesterday. Wow, it sure was good. Thank you very much my lover. We went out on an air assault yesterday and then right back into Juliet yesterday evening. I just hit 50 air assaults. That's quite a few isn't it? It's back to raining but not near as much as it was about a week ago. Encouraging news is that we're not into the monsoon season yet so I guess I can look forward to lots more rain in the future. Right now, we're on alert and if anything comes up, out we go. Write soon!

We were still in the same area of the Ia Drang pursuing the NVA stragglers from the big battle with Alpha Company. Each evening we would pull into a company perimeter and our S-4 would send us out a hot meal. This night was a tough one: all around us were the dead bodies of NVA soldiers, some of them had been lying in the heat three or four days and the smell was overwhelming. The stench of the decaying enemy bodies cut down on the appetites of most of the troopers, but not my own. That night we had hamburgers and mashed potatoes; I think I had three hamburgers. There was plenty of food left, but I ate all I could. Normally nothing would be left, but most of the guys were a little green around the gills from stumbling upon these dead NVA and the mere mention of food sent them running.

That evening as we were beginning to wind down from this awful day, the sudden sounds of a weapon we all recognized got our immediate attention. Off in the distance we could hear the familiar sounds of a mortar being fired, but we didn't know if it was theirs or ours. Once we heard the bloop, bloop and then a delay and another bloop of a mortar being fired, I looked around after the first volley and no one seemed concerned. The second volley hit a little closer, then the third volley was closer yet. It appeared that someone was walking the rounds in and we must be their target. When the fourth barrage was fired, there was a mad scramble into foxholes or any deep hole where you could find cover. When these rounds finally hit, they were close, but not within our perimeter.

We were not sure if our Delta company was responsible or if the enemy was trying to wipe us out. But, let's face it, we knew it didn't really matter who was firing the mortar rounds; if they come your way they don't differentiate between friend or foe. Fortunately, no one was injured and the rest of the night was quiet, thank God, because we all needed a little quiet after the tough day we had endured.

AUGUST 24, 1966. Well, we just got back to Juliet from a company size ambush last night. Yesterday morning they told us to pack because we were going to the Oasis, but guess what, we didn't quite make it. Mail came in and all I got was another *Newsweek*. At least that's something. Guess what, there's a rumor about us going into the Oasis tomorrow and then into An Khe and base camp the next day. I can hardly believe it. After 40 days in the field you can get a little tired of the whole mess. This will give me a chance to go over to the 545th MP company and see what I can do about getting my orders reinstated. Just in the last month supplies have gotten a lot better. When "A" company got wiped out I saw more dead

Americans than I care to remember. It was really a mess and I'll never forget this place. Look at one of those leaflets that I sent home and you'll see a map and I have marked on it a few things of interest. Like Chu Pong Mountain and LZ X-Ray, which was where the 1st of the 7th's big battle took place last November. Also, where "A" company got wiped out and where we took the prisoners and found all the dead NVA. It's been a hectic couple of weeks and I'm glad as hell that it's all over for now…. Well, lover, better get down to the stream and take a bath while I still have a chance.

Company size ambushes suggest we were in a very bad area. Well, this was Ia Drang. The only time the whole company would stay together on an ambush is when HQ felt we were in danger of being attacked by a large enemy unit. This entire area was known to be saturated with the enemy and the daily stress of wondering just when you might make contact kept us on edge. Fortunately, the enemy we did encounter were only trying to escape back across the border and the prisoners we took were in very poor condition and just ready to give up.

We were a sad looking bunch of troopers after "A" company got wiped out and the aftermath of their battle left each of us with indescribable horrific memories. Luckily, very few of us would ever be more miserable than we were after this month in this place worse than hell, the Ia Drang Valley, Vietnam.

AUGUST 25, 1966. Well, we're now residing back at the Oasis and we are setting up here. Rumor has it that we'll be in base camp tomorrow. I hope so because I have so many things that I want to get done. Plus, I'll see if I can get a tape made for you. Well, lover, I'm hard core now, but I'm sure I'll be able to adjust back to civilian life. I'm so lonesome I could cry….

AUGUST 26, 1966. Well, were still here at the Oasis, but we still might make it in today. It really doesn't matter too much to me because this place is a real nice place. For your map the Oasis is about a third of the way to the border from Pleiku, due west. The 5th of the 7th is moving up here someplace close. There's a rumor out that B company will be the ones to train them as soon as they all get over here. Last night was the first beer I've had in a long time…. Man we have been out in the field a long time and it's bad in a lot of ways. The morale goes way down, and everyone has jungle rot now. I have just a touch of it on my feet and ankles but some of the guys really have got it bad and it's just from not being able to take a bath every once in a while. If they do what they're saying every-body should be able to get rid of everything. What do you think of the wallet stamped with Hanoi? I found it on a trail littered with clothes and ammo and grenades. Those NVA soldiers we were chas-ing were in a world of hurt. I think we have it rough, but those guys really have it tough, but of course they're used to living in the jun-gles and we are not....

It was about this time that I ran into a guy I hadn't seen in a while; he was an E-7 who had come into our platoon a few months before. He was a REMF from records or some other cushy job in the rear who was sent to the field for punishment. He seemed like a nice enough guy, but he had a major drinking problem. He was a pathetic soul when I saw him again: he had been stripped of his rank and busted down to E-4, and as a forty some-thing lifer this loss of rank, prestige and pay grade must have been dev-astating for him. They now had him humping mortar rounds, one of the tougher jobs in the Army. I had always felt sorry for the guys in the mortar platoons who had to carry those heavy mortar rounds, but I felt especially bad for him. He wasn't cut out to be a grunt, let alone a member of a mor-tar platoon.

I developed an appreciation for the mortar platoon troopers when I tried to pick up one of their mortar base plates and could hardly pick it up. Humping all their heavy equipment through the jungles of Vietnam seemed to be an almost impossible job and it was certainly one of the most thankless of assignments. On top of everything else, these guys often had to protect themselves with their personal weapons. When things really got hot, they sometimes found themselves jumping in where needed, acting as replacements for killed or injured troopers in other platoons.

AUGUST 26, 1966. Well, we're still here at the Oasis and I don't know when we're going back in. The 2nd of 7th Cav went way down south to the Mecon Delta about 40 miles from Saigon. Gee, I hope we don't have to go down there. The 1st Cav covers more area than any other unit over here in Vietnam…. Oh well, I got to go for now so give J.R. his usual XXX's.

As RTO I had been sent out on patrol with a squad to sweep out to our front. These operations were conducted from time to time to keep our defense posture and our combat proficiency at a high level and most importantly to deter any attempt by an enemy unit or sniper to get close to our positions and do some damage. Most of the time there wouldn't be any enemy contact, but if just one of these sweeps succeeded in locating the enemy, this would have made all these patrols worthwhile.

As we were returning, the other riflemen on the patrol were picking through the remainders of battle debris and equipment fragments. I was sure all the good stuff was already gone and didn't see anything that looked worthwhile. I saw our unit perimeter and I left the rest of the guys still scavenging through the battle debris and headed back in alone.

As I got close to our perimeter one shot rang out and I froze thinking they might have fired at me coming back in. I had called ahead and let them know we were out in front of the perimeter and returning, but sometimes this information didn't get relayed to where it needed to go. Many of our accidental injuries were the direct result of this failure to communicate.

After hearing the one shot a soldier came running across the front of the foxhole positions. Our medic came running from the other direction at full speed with his medical bag. I was close enough to hear their conversation and the medic asked if someone was shot. The soldier told him yes and the medic and I both told him to lay down. This trooper was an assistant gunner for the machine gun crew and wore a .45. Unlike most soldiers who wore their .45 on their sides with the butt of the pistol either facing forward or backwards, he had chosen to wear his holster in the front like an Indians loin cloth. He said he had just cleaned his .45 and was re-holstering it when the ejection slide hung up on his holster and jacked a round into the chamber. Because his finger was on the trigger the pistol went off and the bullet then traveled down his leg. His injury did enough damage to require a trip to Japan for treatment, but he healed quickly and returned to the second platoon after a couple of months.

AUGUST 28, 1966. Wow, I got three letters yesterday evening. … Well for sure we go in tomorrow and you know where I'm going to make a beeline for. I sure hope the first sergeant over there can do something for me. Oh well I'm getting used to this type of life so I guess I can get through the next seven months….

The company had set up in a very strong position on a hill: there were three sides and a long finger ridge pointing up the fourth side. My position was on the far side of the perimeter away from the finger. Every day at least one patrol would contact an NVA unit, but it was a rare event when an enemy patrol would want to start a fight with us. They either gave up or vanished into the jungle while being chased by our bullets. Frequently these enemy soldiers were unarmed and couldn't have fought back even if they wanted to.

The company dug in on a hilltop with a nice slope that provided more protection. One of the other platoons put an LP on this finger ridge, sort of a land bridge making it very hard for the enemy to get to any of our positions. This was done as an early warning for the rest of the company. After midnight while I was on radio watch, I heard the LP reporting enemy soldiers all around them and passing their position heading for the rest of the company. This is the very purpose of an LP; they were essentially cannon fodder if found by the enemy, but their existence was vital to ensuring the safety of the entire company. As soon as I had finished eavesdropping on the LP, I woke up the platoon leader and told him what I had heard. He immediately alerted all our platoon positions that it was very possible we were about to be attacked. Right about that time the NVA hit a trip wire and set off a trip flare and the position nearest that side of the perimeter set off a couple of claymores. This was scary stuff because this was what the enemy liked to do just before launching an attack. It was called probing and was meant to find weak points or locate where our machine guns were positioned. The machine gunners were told not to fire until they were certain the enemy was mounting a full-scale attack, trying to assure their positions would not be discovered until a full attack was underway.

The next morning nothing was found—no equipment, blood trails or anything. The troopers on this LP had been very lucky they were not located. A few times when there was no evidence of the enemy having been in the area, there were suspicions about whether the LP had seen or heard anything. I doubt this was a bogus sighting because I could hear the desperation in the LP leader's transmission, they were begging to come back into the safety of the company, but the captain told them to sit tight until the morning.

AUGUST 30, 1966. Well, we're back in base camp again. It sure feels good after being in the field so long. I got a letter from you last night from August 17, it had been missent to the 1st of the 5th Cav by mistake....

AUGUST 31, 1966. Well here I am up at the E.M. Club having a couple of buds thinking about my favorite lover. We're going on the green line on Monday whenever that is....

This last letter shows how little we cared about what day of the week it was. I was always aware of the date because my watch had a date display and I used this when writing my letters. I had discovered it was not practical to keep track of what day it was, one day just followed the next and it seemed as though I was on a never-ending dangerous carnival ride.

SEPTEMBER 1, 1966. Well, how have you been? You'll never guess where I'm at right now. I'm in the 85th Field Hospital at Qui Nhon and it's close to the ocean. Remember when they found the spot under my lung at Fort Gordon, well, the doctor told me to have a check-up every year to make sure everything is all right. So here I am at the 85th. It really is just like a vacation, lay in bed all day, good food, wow! What more could I ask for. This is really the good life; the only bad thing is that they don't have any beer for us. But this hospital is really nice. It's got regular buildings with cement floors (how about that!) and all kinds of nice things I've never seen any place else in Vietnam. It's great and I hope I'm able to stay here a while; it will be a nice treat. Guess I better go eat and you better not be wishing me out of this place like you did the last time. Oh yeah, keep writing to B company and I'll let you know if I stay here or not.

I remember when I heard we were about to go back on the green line after having so little rest, feeling as though I was just about ready to break. I knew I might come apart at the seams and desperately needed a respite from field duty. I decided my best chance of getting away from the field was to request a check-up of the spot on my lung. The doctor at Fort Gordon had been adamant about my need to get a check-up every year, so I went to the medic and explained the situation and he sent me to the Qui Nhon Army Hospital for a medical check-up and x-ray.

SEPTEMBER 3, 1966. Well, I'm still here at the 85th evac hospital enjoying myself. They ran a lot of tests on me yesterday and I guess I've got more to go through today, but it's not so bad at all. This type of torture I can take…. Give J.R. his usual.

At the hospital, life revolved around food. I can't say the food was that good, but at least it was cooked by someone other than me and it was always hot. While I was there, I asked for and received a pass to go downtown to the PX (post exchange). I took off to look around. Qui Nhon is a very large town for Vietnam and is located right on the ocean where Highway 19 to An Khe terminated into Highway 1.

When I got to the PX there was a long line standing in front, so I got into the line of about 35 soldiers and waited my turn to go inside. I kept noticing there were soldiers just walking by the line and entering the PX, when a soldier who was walking by grabbed me by the arm and asked why I was standing in that line. When I told him I was waiting my turn to get into the PX, he laughed and told me that line was for the Koreans. Guess the Koreans could only enter when another Korean was exiting. We went right to the door and entered immediately.

So here I was inside and saw they had new cars you could buy and pick up in the states; this was a great deal because there were no taxes on the purchase. I wanted to get a camera and I was looking in the camera case and it didn't have much of a selection. A PX employee asked me what I was looking for and I told him. He said to come with him, and around the counter we went. In the back room the employee showed me a huge selection of cameras. He explained that if they put them all out the Koreans snapped them up as fast as they could put them in the glass showcases. The ROKs were getting U.S. Army pay in Vietnam, much more pay than they received in Korea. So, with this extra pay they bought all they could get their hands on and sent it home to sell on the black market. The Koreans were tough fighters and I appreciated them because they protected our backs, so I guess I couldn't fault them for profiting on their purchases from our PX.

> SEPTEMBER 4, 1966. Well, I can't find a pen, so you'll have to put up with this. I got a chance to weigh myself and guess how much I weigh? I'm at 162 how about that and I have put on lots of weight the last couple of weeks ... and my year is just about half over.

> SEPTEMBER 5, 1966. Well, I'm still here at the 85th I'm really enjoying myself.... Well love, there's one thing I know for sure, when I leave Vietnam I'll either be a broken man or a pretty cotton picking tough guy! ...

While I was getting some much needed rest from field duty, I began to see there might be a light at the end of the tunnel after all. Spending so much time alone I found myself beginning to ponder what my future might hold after the war. I continued to wonder if I could ever leave Vietnam behind me once I went back home to the good old USA. Being a grunt out in the jungles looking for trouble and sometimes finding it had left me feeling uncertain about my safety, and I was afraid I might not be able to assimilate back into society when I went back into the world. I knew that veterans from all wars carry around a lot of baggage when they go home. The terrible things you see can't be unseen and to this very day I have the occasional nightmare reminding me that the Vietnam War is still there in the recesses of my mind.

> SEPTEMBER 6, 1966. Well, still here at Qui Nhon. I only have a couple of more days here and back to the miserable field. Let me

tell you what a day is like here at the hospital. They wake me up at
5:00 A.M. and the ward boy comes around and takes our temps.
I roll up my mosquito net and by this time it's time to go to chow
6–7 A.M. Then the doctor makes his rounds checking each patient.
I usually read in the morning. Then it's 11:30 A.M. and that means
it's time for my lunch. After lunch I stop at the coke shop for a 7-Up
and then off to the shower. Back from the shower a short trip to the
hospital P.X. (just to see what's new), and then a light nap, light
reading and a letter to you. By now it's time for dinner, then a trip
to the coke shop and back into bed and a little evening reading. At
7:00 P.M. it's lights out and so ends the day. It's really resting, and I
must say I was in need when I got here.

I found the mandatory use of mosquito netting humorous, as a grunt
carrying mosquito netting in the field was unheard of. There was no way
for us to carry this along with all our gear and ammo, let alone use it in the
field. Just try and envision a two-man foxhole covered with mosquito netting and you can see how silly the rule sounds. In base camp we were threat-
ened with a court-martial if we didn't use our mosquito netting. I'm sure
you can see the irony in this way of thinking: after all when we were in
the field and often covered with mosquito-attracting sweat we didn't use
it. Yet when we were just kicking back in base camp, we could be subject to
a court-martial if it was not used nightly. This didn't make sense then and
still doesn't make sense to this day.

Whether you used mosquito netting or not, you had a good chance of
getting the dreaded malaria. The disease-carrying mosquitos resulted in a
huge number of soldiers in Vietnam contracting malaria.

Shortly after writing this letter, the doctor came through and discharged me back to the field. I had been dreading it, but I was thankful for
the time I had away from combat. I was able to get my head screwed back
on straight and that alone made my return to the field easier to take.

When I returned to base camp from Qui Nhon I got the news that
we were heading out to the Bong Son area to be attached to the first of
the 9th Cav (our Recon Unit). The 1/9 Cavalry's method of operating was
somewhat unorthodox but working with them was almost fun. A platoon
in a recon unit worked with the same helicopters all the time, so we got to
know the crews and pilots and they got to know us.

The 1/9 seemed to work at warp-speed (yes, I know Star Wars didn't
exist yet, but I thought this term described them perfectly). In just one day
we made nine air assaults while we were attached to the 1/9 Cav. On one
of our air assaults we saw a VC running below us as we came roaring into

the landing zone. When the platoon went looking for him all we found were his Ho Chi Minh slippers (they looked just like flip flops); he had run out of his shoes. We called these sandals retreads, because they were fashioned out of truck tire treads and their soles had the grooves you would find on tires. Because I was on point, I found the sandals first and quickly tied them on to my pack, figuring they would be a great souvenir to send home. Unfortunately, the sandals were lost in the normal way I lost things; they were torn off my pack while I was humping through the dense jungle.

There were some pilots who liked to fool around by flying very low, sometimes as low as two feet above the rice paddies. One pilot enjoyed giving us E-ticket rides by rapidly taking the copter up and down, like riding a bull at the rodeo. These antics were a short release from the normal tension filled rides we often experienced and most of us had fun. This pilot's clowning around ended abruptly when he turned around looking very concerned and told us a scout chopper had spotted some NVA in the An Loa Valley. He said he had been ordered to air assault us into the LZ nearest where the NVA had been sighted. We came in hot right behind an ARA ship firing their rockets. We hit the ground in a field with a low rock wall surrounding it and believe it or not, although we were right behind the ARA ship flying at about 100 knots, the only people we saw were civilians already butchering the cow the ARA ship had killed with its rocket fire.

We immediately began a search for the NVA the scout chopper had reported being in the area. After searching for a while and not finding anyone, one of the troopers suggested that they might be in the water. We were walking next to the An Loa River so we dropped some grenades into the water but nothing happened. Then a sergeant went to the edge of the river with nothing but his .45 and found three dead VC who had been hiding under the overhanging riverbank.

As I have mentioned before, the civilians in Vietnam who just wanted to live peaceful lives were caught in the middle of this war. Sometimes they supported whoever was in the area just to keep alive and maintain their peaceful way of living. I felt bad for the non-combatants in these rural areas. They suffered terribly due to outrageous acts on both sides of the Vietnam War. This time we were responsible for the villagers losing a cow to our rocket fire. Losing their livestock was a big deal to them because these animals were an absolute necessity for the Vietnamese farmers who used them to plow their rice paddies.

I did my best not to think of every one of the Vietnamese I met as a possible VC. I remember that while we were near Bong Son I came across a mama-san who came out of a house and offered me a cup of tea and I felt

I couldn't refuse her offer as it would have been discourteous of me not to join her. So, I sat down on her front porch and sipped a cup of cold tea with her. Some of the guys looked at me like I was crazy, but to me this was one of the nicer moments I had in Vietnam.

> SEPTEMBER 8, 1966. Gee, I got a wonderful letter from you last evening. We're still in the south of Bong Son area and we're staying in villages that are built on dikes. These people sure live an unusual life.... I just found out the town we're near, it's Phu May.

We used several tactics on operations, but while we were attached to the 1st of the 9th Cavalry, we were using the hunter/killer approach. This approach had the hunters actively seek out the enemy and if contact was made with an enemy unit, a killer unit would then air assault in and try and finish them off.

Common hunter/killer operations usually had nine platoons from a battalion out hunting and three platoons were held in reserve to engage the enemy if contact was made. This method worked well because the reserve platoons would still be rested and ready to go when there was enemy contact, and should additional troops be needed the hunter platoons could be sent in as necessary. This type of warfare was known as piling on, when more units were sent in to engage the enemy. General Kinard had another way of describing this tactic: "First find the bastards and then pile on." I admit it was a great comfort to know if we were out beating the bush for the enemy and did hit something, someone was just waiting to air assault in to help us out.

> SEPTEMBER 10, 1966. Well, we're still out and it looks like they're going to keep us out a while. At least we're not humping all the time, but it would be nice to get back to the green line. What have they been saying about Vietnam lately? We haven't been in any action for a while except when they mortared base camp a few days back, good thing I wasn't there. It's hard to get used to these cotton-picking C-rations again. But really after you learn how to fix them, they really aren't too bad....

> SEPTEMBER 11, 1966. Well, here we are back on the green line and I got a letter from you plus two *Newsweeks*. I'm sending you a paper we get every once in a while. That one story on the front page about the guy fixing his machine gun with a ballpoint pen is in A company 1st of the 7th Cav and that happened out in the Ia Drang. ...

SEPTEMBER 12, 1966. Well, guess how many letters I got today. The total was 4 and all from you. I sure love getting letters from you.... I have not told you about this for fear of worrying you but remember in Bong Son when our platoon was wiped out; well some had been by our own doing. There were only a few that went down by Charlie's hand; most of our casualties were by our own hand. I'm more afraid of our own artillery and air support than of Charlie. Oh well, it's a sad story. You know I have found a new courage that I didn't have. I can go out and face Charlie with a new-found skill and a stability that I never knew I had. I'm not afraid of being wounded or even dying for my country. I want you to be brave with me and yours is just as hard of job as mine. Just think of the day we will be back together, and life will mean so much to us, more than it ever would have been if things had been different. I miss you and all the little things we had together.

SEPTEMBER 14, 1966. Well, no mail yet but I thought I'd drop you a line on what's happening, nothing.... Right now, I am watching some people herd their cows back towards town. Our tower is right on a river and in front of us is a footbridge that the people use to cross. We're on the country side of the main camp so there aren't too many people that go by....

When we were in the field on patrols everyone in the platoon was aware of and concerned about the number of casualties we were sustaining due to friendly fire. This was a scary situation that sadly seemed to increase during my year in Vietnam.

Because we were in such small groups in the field, I frequently lead a squad. While in charge I could determine what I believed was the best course of action to take in any given situation. Often, we would pow-wow among ourselves on what to do—it worked better this way. After all, what path we took could cost someone their life. There were times when we all decided the best course of action was to do nothing. I personally felt it was best to do nothing rather than stumble into a sketchy situation where there was no one to back us up.

About this time the Army was offering to give us six extra months of leave when we went home, if we would sign up for an extra six months of duty in Vietnam. I admit this offer enticed me, but my wife wasn't having any of it; she said she worried constantly about me and wasn't going to let me voluntarily extend my stay in Vietnam for even one more day.

SEPTEMBER 19, 1966. Wow, I got five letters from you and one from Aunt Esther. Four of your letters had gone to the hospital and then had come back to me, so they were very old. I went to the dentist today because a filling fell out and got an appointment on the 21st of the month…. Give J.R. his usual.

The constant uncertainty of being a grunt in Vietnam wears on you, but you must learn to live with it, or you might go bonkers. As time went on, I tried to envision what a normal day would be for me once I went *back to the world*. It had been just a little over six months since I was on American soil, but now trying to picture myself at home with my family still seemed like an unobtainable dream to me.

10

Seventh Cavalry's 100th Birthday

SEPTEMBER 23, 1966. Well, I got a letter from, of all people, Cousin Dan. I was so happy to hear from him. He is being commissioned into the Marine Corps as a 2nd Lieutenant. He says he expects to go to Vietnam about July of next year.... The 21st of September was the 7th Cav's 100th Anniversary. They had a big party and gave away all kinds of free beer, but of course being the line troops, we didn't get a single can or a minute off. I'm becoming more bitter towards the Army and I'm finding myself having trouble controlling my temper. I've never had that problem before.... Oh well there's just got to be better days ahead. Just think if I could catch malaria, that would be a 30-day rest and 30 days Charlie wouldn't be shooting at me....

As you know by now, I had already been sent to the rear two times with malaria symptoms, and I knew malaria was no walk in the park. It's clear by the above letter that I was once again being overwhelmed by my situation in Vietnam and looking for any way to escape and get away from the bullshit being meted out to us daily. I knew many troopers in B Company that got malaria and by reading this letter I hoped I'd get it soon so that I could get some rest and decent food. Although I knew first-hand how awful malaria was, I still had a warped thought that getting it would be better than humping through the jungles of Vietnam. Strange thoughts come to your mind when stress and desperation take over; you just begin to look for any way out of the misery you're being forced to endure.

SEPTEMBER 24, 1966. Well, I got three letters from you. I hope you're not getting sick or anything.... So J.R. is really a beautiful baby, huh. I'm glad to hear that he eats so well.... Speaking of food I've got the February *Playboy* and they have a recipe for lobster flambé and boy does it sound good. I'm going to have to try it when I get home.

143

When I read this letter I realized just how hungry I was for a decent hot meal. The fact that I got a new *Playboy* magazine and actually found the most important part of the magazine to be a recipe for lobster made me realize what life in Vietnam had done to me. Before arriving in Vietnam, I know the naked women in the *Playboy* magazine were the very reason I bought it, but now sad to say it appears my craving for good food had become my main interest.

> SEPTEMBER 25, 1966. Well I got a letter from you today. I just got back from mailing a package to you. It's got all kinds of junk in it. You might give your dad something for his birthday from me. I'm sending home a special forces soft cap, a set of fatigues and jungle boots, one flashlight, one wallet, one role of film, one recorded tape, one magazine of Vietnam and those pictures you sent me, and I guess that's it. The fatigues are my size and so are the boots....

I tried to send home meaningful things from my tour in Vietnam. Much of the clothing and personal items I sent were used or given to me by departing troopers. My wife put these things away for me and I still have most of them; although the fatigues no longer fit, I wore the boots for a couple of years and have replaced them twice since the war. The flashlight was an old World War II model with the colored lenses. It was a great find, but it was stolen in a burglary at my home in the late 70s.

I had been told many stories about guys sending home weapons, but I never even tried. There is a story about a colonel's driver who recently had been reassigned to our line outfit and had accumulated several .45 caliber grease guns he picked up during his travels. He decided he was going to try and send one home to his mother to keep for him, but he figured it best not to send it in one package. He disassembled the weapon and sent it in several packages, but the only thing that made it home was the barrel. After all the effort he had put into this covert project, he then opted to take an all or nothing approach and sent an entire grease gun home. This time he succeeded and managed to send the .45 home; I've often wondered if he still has it.

> SEPTEMBER 26, 1966. Well, I didn't get any mail today. I'm out on an O.P. still but it's really not too bad because there is no one near enough to bother us. I'm looking for that package and as far as I can see it should be here very soon. I'm a little hungry so I think I'll cook supper while I'm writing you. Let's see, I think I'll have some beans with frankfurter chunks in tomato sauce. Wow, I just got my favorite cheese flavored with caraway seeds....

We were guarding base camp and normally this would have been good duty, but our squad was out in front of the green line serving as an O.P. (outpost). My squad was beyond the barrier all the time, both day and night. Being in charge of a squad of nine, I reported directly to our superiors. We had a PRC-25 radio and an RTO and an M-16 with a starlight scope that was intended to help with the visibility at night. The starlight scope didn't work worth a damn for me. I'm color blind and green deficient so I couldn't see a thing through it; everything was just a big blur to me. The scope itself was supposedly meant to give us a leg up on the enemy, allowing us to see them at night before they could get near to us. Unfortunately, because everything looked green the guys told me nothing looked real to them. We didn't use it much, although looking back I'm sure most of the guys could have seen in the dark very well with this special scope.

I never really felt this job was too dangerous as it was considered by most of us to be good duty. At first this task was great. We were so close to base camp, I would rotate two or three soldiers in to take showers, go to the PX or have a beer. The guys always came back before dark and none of the troopers ever went AWOL or were even late. This duty did have its own special bonus: if we reported in, we were freed from the daily harassment the rest of the troopers in the company were having to put up with.

> SEPTEMBER 27, 1966. Well, I went in again today and went downtown. There just isn't anything worth buying down there, everything is made in Japan anyway. The first sergeant told me today that my R&R was coming up the middle of next month.... Give J.R. his usual and oh yeah, you can't fool me. Someone put him up to the da-da picture stuff. Who knows maybe he'll think his papa is a war hero when he gets home.

My wife told me she had been holding up a picture of me in my Class-A Uniform for our son to see, and telling him it was da-da, hoping he would be able to say it when I got home. This plan backfired on her one Sunday when she took him to church. A long-time friend of my wife came to church in his Army uniform and of course our little guy immediately pointed at him and said da-da. My wife said you could hear chuckles coming from the congregation who knew where I was at the time. My wife's friend immediately announced, "it wasn't me," and everyone had a good laugh.

About this time the USO was bringing Bob Hope to An Khe for a show, so the LT called me over the radio and asked me to come to the green line for a conference. He explained to me that we had to start patrolling at night. I argued with him, rationalizing that any night patrols would be much too dangerous. The grass was dry, and you could hear someone coming through it at least 50 feet away. Besides, when the heck would we sleep? He told me he didn't care what I thought and starting that night, a moving patrol was to be done all night long. I did understand his reasoning: if we hit anything that might be heading toward base camp, the guards on the barrier line would know something was up. But, come on, this type of patrolling is very dangerous and could quickly become a suicide mission if we were unlucky enough to bump into an enemy patrol. Just thinking about how the Army expected our little squad to wander around in the dark, seeking to find the enemy, with little or no sleep, was one of the most absurd ideas I had ever heard while I was in Vietnam.

When I got back out to the troopers, they unanimously said no way when I told them what we had to do. Trying to be a good soldier, I told them we had no choice, but then the fight was on. After a long and fruitless argument, the radio operator we had with us from Headquarters Group came up with an idea. He suggested that we begin patrolling as ordered and once we found a good place to stop, we would stay in place. He said it was foolproof, he could call in fake positions as if we were still patrolling and there was no way they could catch us; after all there were no friendlies out where we were. At first this ploy seemed to be working perfectly but it was nearly ended when on the second night someone guarding the green line thought they heard something and called in an ARA ship. Suddenly the ARA ship began firing very, very close to our position. I quickly called and asked for the ARA attack to be stopped, explaining that we must be lost because we seemed to be very near to the impact zone and the rocket fire ceased. Fortunately, no one ever asked about this incident.

The day came when Bob Hope's USO tour was due into base camp. I was having a meeting with the LT the day before the show and casually mentioned I was going to draw straws and see which three of the guys with me on the OP would go to the USO show. The LT went through the roof and in no uncertain terms told me I was to be 100 percent in the field the next day. He said if I had a problem with those orders and could not follow them, he would bust me down to Private E-Zero. I went nose to nose with him about this, but I knew I wasn't going to change his mind.

The LT was obviously just acting on orders from the higher-ups, but this order just pissed me off. Everyone knew the REMFs were first in line for these shows and few if any grunts would get to see the show. The grunts in the field who were expected to guard outside the green line rarely had the official opportunity to attend the USO shows. To this day, even thinking about how little concern our superiors had for those of us in the field leaves a bad taste in my mouth. I realize we truly needed the REMFs back in base camp, but it's sad to think that no one really seemed to care a rat's ass about our mental state and how much a brief break might have helped us to relax and wind down a little.

I was fuming all the way back and when I returned, I had already decided what I was going to do. I had the guys draw straws for a special OP assignment: they were to stay out all day, till way after the USO show was over and would be on an ambush assignment with just their rifles and some magazines. I told them they were to join back up with us just before dark. That was that. I'd made my decision and just sat back and waited to see what would happen. I was surprised when I got away with it and managed to keep my lousy two stripes. Oh yea, I told the lucky troopers who won the drawing that no matter what they did be sure to stay away from the LT.

I know I have made it more than clear that field troopers held a serious grudge against the REMFs. The truck drivers, cooks, supply, clerks, mechanics, etc., were there to provide everything we needed in the field and we certainly could not have done without them. Although we knew we needed them, at the time we just didn't like them. Most of them got to stay out of harm's way, got hot chow and could count on getting a good night's sleep most of the time without having to stand watch out in the pouring rain. Some of the REMFs even had jobs with regular hours, just like being back in the world.

Not being able to see USO shows when they came to An Khe made the divide between the REMFs and the grunts widen even further. It's just one of those things: you're naturally jealous when you see someone get something you believe should be given to you. It wasn't so much that their life was perfect, but they did have it so much better than any of us in the field.

Many grunts went out of their way when they were in base camp to intimidate REMFs by slapping a magazine into their weapon or pulling a pin on a hand grenade when they were refused something. Luckily, no one got hurt during these displays.

Well, enough about REMFs: they were after all just the lucky ones who never had to experience the horrors of combat. They were still in the military and in Vietnam, serving a year away from home in a war zone.

SEPTEMBER 30, 1966. Well, lover we're off the green line and are staying in base camp tonight. Then off to Bong Son. Oh boy, I just love that place....

The third brigade was sent by truck in the middle of the night to the Bong Son area. We traveled all night and arrived at LZ Hammond just before daylight. All night long helicopters flew by at tree top level and the line of trucks didn't seem to end. The ROKs were along the highway guarding for us. I got the impression the army brass was inviting an attack, but we made the trip unmolested and uninterrupted.

Our next operation, Operation Irving, took place in the vicinity of Phu Cat, east of Highway 1. It was a Search and Destroy Mission that began October 2, 1966, and lasted until October 24, 1966. Most of the field units of the First Cavalry Division participated, along with the 22nd ARVN Division, ROK Capitol Division, ARVN Airborne Division and the CIDG Special Forces.

> OCTOBER 2, 1966. Boy, have we ever been going. I got a package with nuts and stuff the other day and yesterday I got a nice letter. I'm glad your dad liked the letter I sent him. Right now, we're south of Bong Son near Phu Cat. Our platoon just took five VC prisoners and there's probably a lot more around here. Also, we captured a woman and two kids, I'll tell you this is a sorry war. They got us up at 4:30 this morning and we moved out and were going for an hour and a half before daylight. Normally this would be all right, but in the heart of VC controlled area? Of course we got sniper fire....

Bravo Company was coming to the aid of the 1st brigade. They were in contact with a large unit made up of both VC and NVA. A blue team from the 1st squadron of the 9th Cavalry had spotted the remnants of two North Vietnamese battalions. The 1st of the 12th along with two companies of the 1st of the 5th Cavalry had them surrounded. They were pounding them with everything they had available to them. Now and again we would see Puff the Magic Dragon fire those mini guns, a spectacular sight at night and just about as striking during the daytime. Watching Puff was like watching a fire hose spraying tracers and bullets back and forth.

While we were searching villages near the fighting, we kept an eye out for a fighting bunker and if we found one, we had the engineers blow them to bits. The difference between a bomb shelter and a fighting bunker were simple. A fighting bunker had at least two ways out, and in this area the one outlet came up from an underwater canal. Bomb shelters had only one entrance and exit.

Each of us carried a stick of C-4 explosive and often used small amounts of it to instantly heat our C's and water for cocoa or coffee. It was the end of a very long day and the engineers were preparing to blow up a fighting bunker. These C-4 sticks weighed 2.2 pounds and I was looking for a way to lighten my load, so after I kept just enough for personal use I asked the engineer on top of the bunker if he would use the rest of my C-4 to help blow up the bunker. The engineer told me to throw it up to him. A couple of other troopers must have thought this was a great idea and suddenly I noticed most of the guys were giving the engineer their extra C-4. As I watched huge amounts of C-4 being stuffed into the hole in the top of this bunker, I knew it was time to move away from the impending explosion. I began moving my fire team down the dike we were on; as we moved, we passed another fire team and told them they better move away because there was a lot of C-4 about to explode. They just waved me on. Sure enough, when the C-4 exploded, the concussion blew that whole fire team off the dike into the water. Chunks of dirt as big as soft balls began falling around my squad and we were at least a hundred feet away from the explosion. Thankfully no one was injured, but I'm certain the fire team that went swimming in the filthy dike water was sorry they had ignored my warning to them.

Some of the guys did stupid things during this operation. One fire team took a large clock and a multiband radio from a bomb shelter and the owner complained to someone and the captain found out. When he found out he made the entire fire team take them back and apologize. Another fire team stuck a pot-bellied pig with a spear and grievously wounded the poor animal. I had one of my fire team guys put it out of its misery. These actions did little to endear us to the locals and only added to the possibility of their making allegiances with our enemies.

Near the beginning of this operation the company dug in next to a fast-moving water canal and my fire team was picked to be the LP. I had two brand new troopers, one I didn't trust and the other was an Eskimo who didn't talk, he mostly grunted. It didn't take me long to realize these guys were going to be a problem: one was too independent, and it was clear the other didn't care about anyone but himself. He bitched and whined far too much about everything and was more afraid than he should have been, and it showed. The Eskimo just couldn't communicate and seemed unwilling to take any advice. I knew I wouldn't be able to count on either of these FNGs if the shit hit the fan.

As an LP we were expendable, and I knew it. Our job was to serve as early warning for the rest of the company. Now I was certain the 1st of the 12th Cav hadn't killed all of the NVA and VCs they had trapped, and some would escape after dark. During the day there was far too much contact with the enemy, so I expected action that night. I begged extra grenades from others in the squad. Then I checked out my M-16 as best I could. Before we left, I said my goodbyes like I might not return. Every seasoned grunt knew how dangerous LPs were and understood my situation.

As my fire team left, we crossed this broken-down bridge spanning over a channel of water that was about 15 feet below. The bridge only had a couple of mismatched boards still in place; the rest were missing, and it was obvious it would be nearly impossible to try and come back across it if we needed to return to the company after dark. I decided this could only be used as a last resort if something bad came our way. Two trails merged at the downed bridge, so I was looking for a vantage point where I could see both trails just before the merger. The village was deserted, and I found an abandoned house that fit the bill. The soldier I didn't trust kept saying he was about to shoot something, and the Eskimo just laid down and went to sleep on the floor of the house. I kicked the Eskimo hard, but is didn't faze him. As far as I was concerned, I might as well have been alone on that LP. I considered these guys as liabilities, and I was sure I couldn't count on either of them if we got into a fire fight. I accepted my fate and hunkered down for the night, keeping a watchful eye on both trails and on these idiots I had been saddled with. During the night I called the LT over the radio and gave him the most accurate information I could about our location. He assured me he knew right where we were. I wasn't at all certain he knew our LPs exact location, just the general area, and that kept me on edge throughout the night. When morning came, I was amazed we had survived. I could hear heavy gun fire during the night and for a while I thought there was little hope we would make it through the night. The Eskimo was still asleep, and Mr. Untrustworthy was just plain useless. This was life and death stuff and I'll never forget how helpless I felt without someone to have my back when I was on that LP.

It had rained all night long and the water in the channel we had crossed the day before was now roaring. Looking around I could see we had no choice now but to cross back over the broken-down bridge to B Company. I've got to admit I was more than a little relieved when we joined back up with the safety of our company.

A couple of days later our platoon leader sent my fire team up a trail to check it out. I'd put Mr. Untrustworthy on point and as usual he just didn't listen to anything I told him. I pointed out that I had noticed some punji stakes on the side of the trail and cautioned him to make sure to stay on the trail. The trail had a curve in it and as I came around the curve, I saw him immediately grabbing at a punji stake that had gone half-way through the calf of his right leg. I yelled at him to stay still and not try to pull the stake out of his leg. Once again, he ignored my advice and began ripping the punji stake back out of his leg—doing so only left toxic slivers inside the wound that could cause a severe infection. If he had waited like I told him, I could have helped him break off the end of the stake and pull it straight through, lessoning the chances of an infection. Later one of the guys who had been wounded went to the hospital in Japan for treatment, and while he was there he was in the same ward with Mr. Untrustworthy; he told me the punji stake infection had resulted in gangrene and the guy lost his leg below the knee. Even though it angered me that this guy appeared to have needlessly caused his own injury, I still can't help but feel empathy for him; his life was changed forever on that day.

> OCTOBER 10, 1966. Gee, I got a letter from you last night with two pictures.... It rained almost all night long. It has already rained once today but now the sky is clear. We completely leveled a village yesterday, and today we are in this same area blowing up bunkers, well there went another bunker or two....

We were encountering a lot of enemy at the time but only in small groups. We could usually get the drop on the enemy soldiers because they often carried their rifles over their shoulders or by the barrel. American soldiers were taught to carry our rifles at the ready slung and pointed to the front and we could get the drop on most enemy soldiers. Point in fact, the guy who took over my fire team was walking point and just as he rounded a curve, he came face to face with an NVA soldier. Because this trooper had his rifle at the ready, he just fired and blew the NVA away. As it turned out this NVA soldier was severely wounded but not dead. One of the other platoon members saw what had occurred and went up to the NVA soldier and finished him off with a bullet to the brain. It wasn't pretty; there was a tiny hole in his forehead and the entire back of his head was missing. I personally never felt the need to coup de grace anyone, but it happened. Most times it was simply a matter of ending a guy's pain that was going to die anyway, more or less a mercy killing.

Shortly after this incident my fire team was on point and stopped when we came to a T in the trail. I put security out in both directions and waited for the LT to come up and decide which way to go. The LT assigned the other fire team in the third squad to take point and we were discussing which way to go. I overheard the other fire team leader telling my good buddy Shelby to kneel down in the middle of the trail if he saw any enemy coming his way. He told him he would come up on his right and the other soldier would come up on his left, this way there would be more firepower going down this narrow jungle trail.

The trail was as narrow as they ever got, with nothing but thick jungle on each side and only room for one person at a time on the trail. My buddy Shelby rounded the first corner and immediately knelt down, and at first, I believed they were practicing and thought it was a great idea. It wasn't a practice and suddenly all hell broke loose. Lots of rifle fire caught us all off guard. Suddenly our guys were in a full-on fire fight. Apparently, Shelby saw three VC coming towards him and he knelt as ordered and opened fire; two VC were KIA and one got away. It was more than likely that these VC were looking to ambush our platoon.

During this skirmish I was involved in a bit of a fiasco. Our machine gunner and I tripped over one another trying to get to the front and his machine gun's barrel got buried in the mud, thus making it useless until the mud could be cleaned out. Because we got tangled up, neither of us participated in the fire fight that took place in front of us.

We captured two Thompson submachine guns and one M-1 rifle. The type of these weapons let us know these were VC and not NVA we had encountered. The VC captured most of their weapons from the South Vietnamese ARVN, who usually were armed with U.S. Army surplus World War II weapons.

Oh, how I wanted one of those Thompsons; I had been fed up with my M-16 for months and thought if I could "acquire" a Thompson it would be a superior weapon for me to use in the field. Sadly, our LT immediately notified HQ about the two Thompsons we'd captured, and they immediately responded and asked for the serial numbers on the weapons. I tried my best to have the LT say we only captured one Thompson, but he was straight arrow and told them two were captured. Whoever wanted them in the rear wanted them badly enough to immediately dispatch a Huey to pick them up. So off they went to some asshole in the rear, who probably has concocted a colorful story about how he personally captured these weapons in Vietnam.

During this operation I was heading up a fire team and the LT sent us to check out another jungle trail. I sent the Eskimo to the right and told him to go around the corner out of sight, step off the trail be alert and wait. So down the trail he went. About five minutes went by when we heard three quick shots that seemed to come from the Eskimos direction. I was pretty sure the shots were from an M-16. So down the trail I went to see what happened to the Eskimo. When I finally caught up with him, he was hot footing back towards to where he was supposed to be. He was three or four corners beyond where I had told him to go and out of breath. I asked what the shots were for and he said one word, "Gooks," and pointed down the trail. The LT came running up behind me, saying, "Can't you get anymore out of him?" All I could do was shrug my shoulders.

Then the LT spread the platoon out and we moved forward expecting trouble. We got to a clearing and the LT started a squad around each side of the clearing. I was trying to get the Eskimo to tell me what happened, but all he could say was Gooks, three and points up the trail. As we reached the other side of a clearing, we found a blood trail. The platoon began to follow the blood trail and sure enough we came across a body. The body had been dragged along for a while and abandoned. When we inspected the body there were two bullet holes in his chest just two inches apart. Everyone in the platoon was impressed by the Eskimo's shooting ability. We had only heard three shots and the Eskimo managed to hit this one VC with two of them from about 150 feet. The shocker here was the recovery of the weapon this VC had been carrying; it was an M-16 that looked as though it had just been taken out of a packing crate. This was the first time we had found a VC with one of our own weapons and we were all trying to guess where it had come from. It was only much later in my tour that I found out just how extensive of a black market existed in Vietnam and if you wanted anything, and I mean anything, it could be had for the right price.

11

Off to Rest and Relaxation in Hong Kong

My first two letters October 11 and 12 were generally just personal and continued to relay to my wife how lonely I was and how I missed her.

> OCTOBER 13, 1966. Well, I'm about to have another day and another dollar. We are moving into a secured area sometime today and we should have it made for a few days…. No mail came in but maybe tomorrow I'll get one….

The platoon had been going over the hill to the An Lao Valley and the Crows Foot almost every day. One night we would stay on one side, then the next we would stay on the other near Phu Cat. During this time, we became familiar with the An Lao Valley. The houses there were spread out because this was a rural countryside setting.

The squad was searching through a village. The new fire team's leader took over point and I heard a commotion. As I came around the corner prepared for whatever, I couldn't help but laugh a little. The fire team leader was apprehending a possible VC in black pajamas with a pistol belt slung around his waist and he, along with a woman and a young girl, were all standing with their hands in the air. For some reason seeing the group with their hands in the air struck me as funny: they all looked as if they were in a scene of a Western movie. I guess it was the rural setting we were in and I just didn't anticipate seeing any bad guys waiting around to ambush us. The new fire team leader wound up taking the VC into custody and let the woman and the girl go.

Near this village we were resting with a group of villagers, the ARVN were trying to get everyone to move out of this contested area. Their plan was to move them to a safer area that was now controlled by the ARVN. I noticed a bunch of coconuts up in a palm tree and asked one of the men in

154

the group if he would climb up and knock a few down to me. He looked at me and shook his head no, then he said, "Number Ten." I then noticed the leaves on the trees were brown. These trees had obviously been sprayed with Agent Orange.

As the people moved out of this area, we would burn their houses. I was given the unenviable job of lighting one of the houses on fire and found it to be more of a problem than you might think. It was a tough job because everything was damp all the time, and it was almost impossible to light a house on fire with a match. I had been carrying a white phosphorus grenade and was looking for a way to get rid of it and this seemed to be the perfect opportunity. So, I pulled the pin and popped the spoon and it made a funny popping noise as a trickle of smoke came out of it, so I quickly threw it as far as I could. I now think it must have been a dud that appeared to go off in my hand but had that been true I wouldn't be writing this right now. The fire finally caught, and I've always hoped that the fire destroyed the grenade. I carried that heavy, useless grenade for a very long time and never carried one again after this near miss.

> OCTOBER 15, 1966. Well, I got to watch T.V. last night and I saw the *Adams Family, Gunsmoke* and *The Danny Kaye Show*. It really felt funny watching T.V., I couldn't stay interested in it....

We were the palace guard near Phu Cat and it was great duty. I believe it was for the HQ of the 1st Cavalry Division, but I'm not certain. This was also an ARVN training camp and I found some time to visit with their soldiers. A couple of the soldiers invited me into their barracks at Phu Cat and we all had a good time checking out each other's weapons. They liked my M-16 and many of them offered to trade their weapons for it; one guy even handed over his Thompson to trade, but I handed it back and told him I couldn't do it. This time we had with the ARVN was a great escape from our day to day war zone activities.

The 2nd platoon was the first to get a day off here. The whole platoon was invited over to the airbase at Phu Cat for a hot meal. The Air Force was just beginning to build the base and security there left a lot to be desired; one lonely role of barbed wire surrounded the place and there were no bunkers or foxholes to be found. I couldn't imagine how they expected to protect the place if it had been overrun in the early days of construction. I guess they intended these guys to fight out of their jeeps or just run like hell.

One perk that came along with this duty assignment was a hot meal, one that didn't come out of a can that you had to cook yourself. Some of our second platoon guys were invited down to the airmen's whorehouse and I guess someone said something that some airman didn't like, and a fight ensued. I don't think anyone got into trouble for the fight, at least I never learned of any punishment being given to any of the combatants. I wasn't there for the fight, but the ruckus did end our stay that evening at the airbase.

> OCTOBER 18, 1966. Gee, I got three letters from you this morning. I'm glad you finally got some mail from me because I know how it feels to go without mail. Still in the same area but we should be moving sometime today to another area. I'm looking forward to that package; I should be getting it anytime now....

I constantly looked forward to my wife's packages; she usually sent along some goodies to eat. Eating almost nothing but C-rations was depressing: they could satisfy your hunger, but did little to satisfy your cravings for the food you enjoyed before coming to Vietnam. I constantly craved Bob's Big Boy hamburgers and I even dreamed I was with my wife enjoying a burger with a side of french fries and blue cheese dressing to dip them in. As a note, when I eventually made it home that was the first place I wanted to go and eat, but after a year of eating bland C-rations the hamburger tasted terrible to me.

Our next operation, Operation Thayer II, was a search and destroy mission and involved the following First Cavalry Units: 2/8, 2/12, 1/7, 5/7 of A and B Companies and the 1/9 recon, plus ARVN and CIDG Special Forces. The area of operation was in the vicinity of the Crows Foot and Bong Son. Dates of the operation were October 25 and continued through the remainder of 1966.

> OCTOBER 25, 1966. Gee, I got two wonderful letters from you yesterday.... Guess what? I go on R&R either the 9th, 13th or 18th of November and I'm going where I wanted to go, Hong Kong.... I just got word, Hong Kong on the 13th of November.... Oh well, not too much longer now.

I had still been trying to get my R&R in Hawaii so I could meet my wife there and enjoy some boom-boom, but the Army had put the brakes on Hawaii; I guess too many guys were too close to home and some just didn't return willingly. So, I settled for R&R in Hong Kong and I looked forward to escaping field duty for a week and getting back to some sort of civilization.

OCTOBER 27, 1966. Well, we're out on patrol right now and we're taking a long break so I thought I would drop you a short line....

While on patrol that afternoon some shots were fired to our front. My fire team was on point, so I cautiously moved forward. I looked ahead and could see what I believed to be some Popular Force (PF) soldiers shooting rifles into a pond. It looked like they were fishing with firepower, not exactly a fair fight. These guys were dressed in black pajamas just like the VC. But their demeanor was not that of our VC enemies as they didn't seem disturbed by our presence. We called HQ to verify these guys were what we called "ruff puffs" and they told us there were friendlies in the area. Even with HQ's verifying they were most likely friendlies, we still decided to take the long away around and circle away from them. We just never knew who was who in Vietnam and when we saw armed soldiers in black pajamas it was just common sense to stay away from them if we could.

We had a dog handler with us for a couple of days. When we came upon a bunker, we would call the dog forward. Then the dog would stick its head in the bunker and wag its tail. I asked the handler how he knew when there was someone in the bunker and he told me the dog would alert him. I asked if he was sure? He said he would stake his life on that dog. I liked having the dog around: he was always on alert and his ears were constantly moving. He provided an early warning system for us all. Unfortunately, we only got to keep the dog for a day and a half. The area we were traversing was full of thorns and sharp rocks that tore up the poor dog's feet and the handler and the dog were transported out on a medevac chopper.

OCTOBER 29, 1966. Well, I got a letter from you just the other day. We lucked out today, we are securing for the mortar platoon so that means no humping. I'm sending you this 500 yen note, I was saving it to take to Japan, but now I'm going to Hong Kong. It's worth about a dollar and a half, it's winnings from a poker game. I sure hope it doesn't rain in Hong Kong when I get there. I can't wait....

We were at LZ Bird in the An Loa Valley and my squad was going out on a night ambush. I led the squad out just a little before dark and found the ambush location just at dark, perfect timing for setting an ambush. The site was a very nice vacant house with a small stone wall around the home. We hadn't begun setting up when one of our squad members points up a path. We hit the dirt behind this low wall and this VC walks right up on top of us. A couple of troopers opened fire and quickly dispatched this VC soldier. He had been carrying a bag of all sorts of "funny money" in it and we immediately split it up amongst ourselves. As it turned out this was great betting money for poker games.

We had heard a trooper from A company was rumored to have found a huge pack of crisp, brand new U.S. fifty-dollar bills in a cave near this same area of the An Loa Valley. He turned it in because he was sure it had to be counterfeit, but to everyone's surprise it wasn't. When he turned it in the Army told him he could file a claim for it and if the true owner wasn't located, he could get it back. The last I'd heard he was going to sue the Army for the money. Don't know how any of that turned out.

> NOVEMBER 2, 1966. Well, got your package with the nuts in it today. I got a letter last night also. Man, those nuts were really good, and the whole squad chowed them down in no time. I'm squad leader again, we lost another one. These last few days have really been bad. Have I ever been miserable, it's raining just about all the time and we are out on an operation. We made an air assault the other day and right now we are very close to Bong Son (about three miles south and about a mile inland). We should be due for a rest here soon, I hope so anyway…. I've got to get going. I'll try and write more often but sometimes everything is just too wet.

Bravo company had air assaulted into another hot LZ. This time the LZ was not nearly as bad as my first Bong Son, but bad enough. The second platoon had been in the middle of this assault formation. This is a terrible place to be: there's not much you can do. You are forced to take whatever the enemy throws at you because you can't shoot back with friendlies in front of you.

> NOVEMBER 5, 1966. Gee, last night I got two letters plus two packages. Wow, what a haul. The package with the batteries and tape came just at the right time because I'll be going on R&R in about five days….

> NOVEMBER 6, 1966. Well, I got two letters and a Newsweek today. Guess what, I went back to the rear area today and you know what they did? They gave us all new clothes, new pants and shirt, jungle boots, socks and even new underwear. Only five of us went in, all because of our feet. We're at LZ Hammond which is just south of Bong Son….

Occasionally our medic asked to look at our feet. This time when he checked our feet, he sent five of us back to a rest area to be seen by another medic. Guess they felt we needed time to help our feet get dried out and heal a little.

> NOVEMBER 7, 1966. Well, I'm still here in the rear area. I wrote your mom and dad this morning. I forgot to tell you but yesterday before I came out of the field a photographer took a couple of pictures of me then asked where I was from. I said Los Angeles so watch the *Times*. Did I ever look the part of a warrior, unshaven and my pants were all ripped to hell. It would be funny if they did print that picture wouldn't it! I can't wait for R & R, it's one day closer ... boy do I ever need a rest.

While reading these letters back to back I noticed something that had never occurred to me before. I noted that prior to my trip to the rear for foot treatment a photographer had come by and taken my picture, one that showed the obvious poor condition of my clothing. My shirt had holes in it, and one leg of my fatigue pants was torn from the crotch all the way down to my ankle. Then miraculously, when I got to the rear, I was suddenly issued all new clothes all the way down to my underwear and boots. I now wonder if the photographer's picture of me might have had something to do with my being resupplied new clothes. Thinking back, I knew I had been living with my clothes in that condition for a couple of weeks and up to that point no one noticed or seemed to care. Whatever the reason I know I couldn't have been happier at the time; new clothes and boots really improved my outlook and made my life more comfortable.

When it came time for me to leave for R & R, the U.S. Army was in top form; they were sure to see to it that any stress I was already under was about to be increased two-fold. We were in a little valley between Bong Son and the An Loa Valley. Our 1st sergeant called me and said a helicopter was coming in for me and to grab my gear and get over to the CP. I thought, *isn't this just wonderful*. I waited for what seemed forever to take my R&R and now I was about to take off in a fog bank where I couldn't see ten feet. I thought at the time that they would probably call off the trip because of the fog but was I ever wrong. The CP talked the pilot down by listening to the sounds of the helicopter coming in lower and lower. I seriously began to question this trip altogether and wondered whether I'd ever make it to my R&R in Hong Kong.

The Huey landed and I hopped on, but the pilot sat on the ground for a while before we took off. A short time later we took off and quickly broke through the fog into a clear blue sky and soon we were flying over a sea of white clouds. I calmed down immediately and sat back and tried to enjoy my ride to temporary freedom.

> NOVEMBER 11, 1966. Well what they don't do to you just to let you go on R & R … they just don't give you enough time to get ready. Oh well, at least when I get to Hong Kong, they won't fool with me anymore for a little while. They pulled a fast one on me and said that I go on R & R on the 13th, true but I've got to be in Saigon by the 12th. Oh well let's just hope I make it.

> NOVEMBER 13, 1966. Well, here I am finally on my way to Hong Kong. I have already bought a suit for 20 dollars. One of the guys needed the money and the suit is worth 60 dollars in Hong Kong and over a hundred in the states…. I'm due to come back from R & R on the 18th in the morning. So well, it can't last forever. They say they have some really nice restaurants and I plan on visiting most of them. At the R & R Center in Nha Trang they had a club and they were selling; believe it or not, ice cream. I ate just about two dollars' worth. You know you can't just take a soldier out of the field and drop him some place where he can get all kinds of rich food and drink because he'll get sick. Oh well, maybe I will have learned by the time I get back home (although I doubt it).

> NOVEMBER 15, 1966. Kowloon, Hong Kong. Gee it sure was nice talking to you and hearing your voice. I just discovered something; I don't know what to say to you over the phone. My goodness what's going to happen when we come face to face? My guess is we will drink lots of beer….

As I explained earlier in the book, my wife had given me a Bulova Caravelle wristwatch before I left for Vietnam. When I began serving in the field, word got around about my wristwatch and soon you could find it being passed from soldier to soldier as they stood watch. There was one major downfall to lending it out—guys who smoked used their lit cigarettes to read the time. During the last few months they had burned some holes into the crystal. I took the watch with me to Hong Kong to see if I could get the damaged crystal replaced. I found a little watch repair place and the guy behind the counter told me he would fix it and in broken English told me to come back at 10 the next morning. When I returned the next morning, he proudly showed me my watch and it looked brand new: he had replaced the crystal and then he took the time to remove the back and show me how he had cleaned and oiled the watch from top to bottom.

So, I asked him how much and he said ten dollars and then I asked, "Hong Kong dollars?" He nodded his head yes. At that time the exchange rate was about 4.74 Hong Kong dollars to each American dollar, so I got this watch repaired like new for a little over two dollars American.

> NOVEMBER 16, 1966. Well, lots of doings yesterday and so far today I started off the morning with a cold beer (oh man Vietnam was never like this)… I just keep thinking of the fun we could be having in a city like this together.

I met a medic from the 5th Cavalry who was sitting in the same row as I was on the plane to Hong Kong. We got to talking and he told me he was married and so I thought he would be a good guy to pal around with while I was in Hong Kong. I figured we could try out some of the restaurants together and since we were both married, we could keep each other away from the ladies of the evening. Shortly after meeting him he hit me up for a loan; he said he didn't have much money and wondered if I could help him out. I myself had little money, but I told him I'd see if I could get my wife to wire some to me. The morning after we landed in Hong Kong, I called my wife and asked if she could wire me $100, but I didn't tell her I was going to lend most of it to a guy I didn't even know. All I needed to know was that this guy was a medic in the Cavalry and that was good enough for me. Back in those days an international wire transfer was a big deal. My wife went to two banks and had to wait most of the day to arrange to have the $100 wired to me. When I got the money, I lent him $75 of it and he told me his wife was wiring money to him the next day and he would pay me right back.

Well the next day came and my medic buddy was nowhere to be found, and now I was the one who was short on money. Luckily, I remembered that I had stuffed some of the "funny money" we had found on the body of a dead NVA soldier in the An Loa Valley into my bag. I doubted any of the money had value, in fact many of us had been carrying it in our packs to light on fire to heat up our coffee. I noticed a money changer on the street and handed him all the bills I had, and he quickly separated them into two piles. He gave me one pile back waving his hand and saying no good, and the other bills he exchanged for about 50 Hong Kong Dollars. I was amazed to discover how much spending money I got from what I had considered monopoly money.

I roamed around Hong Kong on my own the next couple of days. I drank a lot of beer, ate some interesting food and shopped a little for presents for my wife and my sister. There were signs all over Hong Kong advertising steam baths and massages and though that sounded great to me, after talking to some other troopers I found out these services included some extras that for sure would have violated my vow to keep faithful to my wife.

> NOVEMBER 17, 1966. Well here it is, the last night, and us G.I.s are going live it up … and do the town right…. Do I ever love you and miss you but our time will/is coming and we will be in one another's arms shortly and the letter writing will stop. That's what I like, action not words….

My last day in Hong Kong I came across the medic who'd borrowed the money from me and he was quick to tell me his wife never sent him the money he owed me, but he promised he would pay me back just as soon as we returned to Vietnam. As the old saying goes, "no good deed goes unpunished." This guy now had a young lady draped all over him and he was showing her the town on my money. I was more than a little irritated with him and for that matter, myself. We had made a pact on our trip to Hong Kong that since we were both married, we would stay away from the shady ladies in Hong Kong, but I guess once he could pay for one of them our pact went out the window.

I don't know exactly what the plan was, but the medic introduced me to his new friend and then his friend introduced me to her best friend Ping. They were going to see the movie *Nevada Smith* and asked if I wanted to tag along and I said sure. Ping was much older than me and said she had a 15-year-old daughter, and for some unknown reason she felt the need to explain she was a kept woman of a ship's captain.

When the movie was over, Ping asked if I would like to join her and her daughter at her apartment for dinner. This was my last night in Hong Kong and since I had little money left, a free authentic Chinese meal sounded great to me and I accepted her invitation. When I arrived at her apartment, I discovered she had ordered Chinese take-out food delivered and that was a disappointment. Once we ate, we were watching television and her daughter said she was tired and went off to bed, then Ping said she was tired and that I could keep watching T.V. if I wanted to. I think she thought I might follow her into her bedroom, but I didn't. I soon left and as I did, I left my last Hong Kong twenty dollar bill on her table to show my appreciation for her kindness.

These six days passed so fast and most of my R&R is a blur to me. I guess this trip just didn't live up to my high expectations. I missed my wife,

I missed home and having to return to the war in Vietnam only depressed me.

The incident with the medic left a bad taste in my mouth. To my wife and me $75 was a lot of money and I was just too trusting. Karma caught up with the medic though; on the trip back to Vietnam he told me the girl he was with had given him the clap. He told me that it wouldn't be a problem for him since he could treat it himself without ever reporting it to anyone. I've wiped his name from my memory, but if he's still around and reads this maybe he'll contact me and forward the $75 + 54 years of interest. I know this is a tongue-in cheek joke, but sometimes us old codgers do try to atone for stupid things we shouldn't have done to others in our youth.

> NOVEMBER 19, 1966. Well back from R & R today, there just wasn't enough time. I got nine letters from you, a letter from Sgt. Timmons and a letter from Aunt Esther. I had a wonderful time in Hong Kong but there was something missing—you, I would love to take you there even if it would cost me a fortune. Oh well, we do have 30 days to look forward to being together. That does sound like a good idea on paying off the car by using the allotment check, boy you're going to be a good budgeter I can tell.

At this point (around Thanksgiving 1966) I was one discouraged, depressed and anxious soldier. I was so lonely and so disheartened. I was back in Vietnam and once again had to come to terms with just how I was going to remain alive for my last three months of this god-awful war. The Vietnam War was an oddity: it came with an expiration date for most of the ordinary soldier as our tours were for one year. But when you were a grunt you were constantly questioning where that final bullet was going to come from, or what stupid accident was going to end your life. I know it's a morbid way to look at things but as time neared to the end of my deployment, I began believing in the short-timer's dread. I knew this was not the time to become too cautious, but as each day passed my anxiety grew. Caution can become a form of fear and constant fear is something no grunt should display; it only weakens your ability to make sound decisions.

> NOVEMBER 24, 1966. Well, we had a real nice Thanksgiving believe it or not. I got four letters from you, yay. I'm sending you the menu....

The Army did go out of its way to put on an excellent spread for Thanksgiving. I do know it was a memorable meal. It was hard to believe but we had Thanksgiving dinner with all the trimmings served to us on top of a mountain in the boonies.

The company had pulled into a perimeter in a very strong position, so if need be, we could defend ourselves. This wonderful meal is one of the few positive memories I have of being in the field in Vietnam. We had a true day off, without all the bullshit; just good hot food and a peaceful time with my buddies, it was great!

A short time after Thanksgiving a newly minted sergeant sought me out and asked if I would go out on a LRRP (long range reconnaissance patrol). I told him there was no way; I didn't volunteer for missions like that because I wanted to go home in one piece. He argued with me for a while and said this was an important mission and he only wanted guys who were well trained. I continued to be unyielding to his request, so he finally left. Later that day he returned with reinforcements and they all were trying to convince me to go out on this likely dangerous mission. The sergeant then showed me a list of troopers who had agreed to go on this recon patrol and said they had been picked because they were considered the very best in their individual specialties. He then tried to inflate my ego and said I was picked because I was the best point man in the platoon and he only wanted the best. He finally was able to convince me that I was truly needed, and I agreed to go.

Our hand-picked squad traveled as a unit back to Phu Cat where we were issued LRRP rations. They were great: all you had to do was heat some water, then pour it into a plastic bag that contained this freeze-dried stuff. Then you sealed the bag up and after a few seconds you had an instant meal.

We then prepared our gear to go out. I was issued a map of the area around LZ Bird. At the briefing we were told we would drop into a saddle above LZ Bird and move to the mountain top overlooking LZ Bird and report any enemy activity. We were told not to engage any enemy forces we might encounter. On the map LZ Bird showed as a military area. As is the Army's SOP, after all this planning, etc., the mission kept being put off and it was finally cancelled with no explanation. I think we were all relieved when we were directed to return to our own squads.

While I was at Phu Cat I noticed a big group of soldiers standing around the medical aid tent and wandered over to see what was happening. They were all there looking at a helmet that belonged to the point man for A Company. One of the guys told me it had a bullet hole right in the center front and indicated the trooper was dead before he hit the ground. Seeing this helmet, I immediately had a flashback to my first day in Vietnam when I saw a soldier carrying a helmet with a bullet hole in the center front that he was taking back home as a souvenir. My immediate thought was that the helmet I was looking at now would never be anyone's souvenir, only sad evidence of another young man's life having been abruptly ended in this terrible war.

Very soon after this planned LRRP was scratched, LZ Bird was overrun by an NVA regiment. This planned recon mission I had reluctantly volunteered for most likely would have been in the thick of things and who knows what would have happened to our little recon unit. *Man, that was a close call.*

> NOVEMBER 27, 1966. Well, I started this letter at 12:50 p.m. on the 25th and never got it finished. It has been raining ever since early in the morning of the 25th and all my writing paper and your incomplete letter got wet. These three days it has only stopped raining a few minutes at most. Has this ever been a miserable three days. The first day they couldn't get C's in, so we went without chow, the next day they only brought two meals apiece and finally today they brought in three meals. We were hungry and I never thought C-rations could taste so good....

I never said anything to my wife about my dumb decision to volunteer for an LRRP. She worried about me constantly and I didn't want her to think I would willingly seek out dangerous missions. This situation was just one of those times I felt I was needed, and I agreed to go on the spur of the moment. Once again fate or whatever intervened and the mission was called off and none of our newly formed recon unit found ourselves in the middle of a major battle, where many lives were lost.

What was on my mind while I was attempting to write this last letter was a little gruesome. For some reason I could picture some NVA soldier removing one of my wife's letters from my lifeless body and taking it as a war trophy. My letters often got wet while I was writing them, and I'd carry them around until they could be finished. But I cherished my wife's letters and didn't want them falling into the hands of the enemy, so I would read them over a few times and then burn them.

As I relayed in my last letter, we were suffering in the rain and it rained non-stop for days. Because of the bad weather it took time for us to get re-supplied with C-rations. I tried to think ahead most of the time, and in this case my foresight of collecting unwanted C's that other soldiers threw away made me hero for the day in my squad. I opened my pack and saw I had 15 to 20 cans of cocoa and cookies and crackers and cheese. When I began passing them out to my hungry squad, they couldn't believe

I was carrying that many cans of C's and everyone thanked me for them. I believe I may have given a few of the guys a new way of setting their priorities when it came to what they really needed to carry in their packs. Food, water, ammo and a working weapon were absolute necessities for a grunt.

The morning of November 30, 1966, in the Kim Son Valley close to the village of Phu Huu 2, the war returned to the 1st Cavalry in a big way. In the pre-dawn hours three battalions of NVA troops began their attack on firebase LZ Bird. This multiple day battle is well documented by many troopers who lived through it. This was a tremendous battle and it resulted in the award of Medals of Honor to two 1st Cavalry troopers.

During the battle of LZ Bird our platoon along with five helicopters were being held in reserve on a little hilltop out in the middle of the An Lao Valley, adjacent to the Kim Son Valley. Looking down the valley we could see a major battle raging below us and it was clear to see we would soon be thrown into the fray.

Standing there in the cold drenching rain I could feel the water running off my helmet and down my neck. I had my rain jacket on, but my rifle was upside down on my shoulder and I noticed it had a steady stream of water running out of the barrel. I couldn't cook a meal, write a letter or even sit down. We all just stood there on the side of that muddy hill, shivering and watching our comrades fighting for their lives below us. This moment in time is etched in my memory. I remember thinking that if I ever had a bad day once I was back in the world, I'd look back to this miserable day and my outlook on life couldn't help but improve.

Sure enough, our time had come to join the party; at dusk we were told we were moving and loaded onto the helicopters we had been guarding. We lifted off and headed towards the village where we could see the tracers and hear the rifle fire. We immediately drew some fire and it was unnerving to see those enemy green tracers floating up at us. Luckily our chopper didn't take any hits. After passing the village, we air assaulted across the An Loa River and dug into the muddy ground. Digging a foxhole under those conditions was darn right impossible; you know, each shovel of mud was met with a hole full of water. Not a fun job, but a foxhole was a must for a grunt. We spent that night hunkered down, wondering when or if the enemy would head our way.

The next morning the rain had stopped, and my squad was sent a short distance upriver and told to watch the other side and make sure no one tried to cross. After a while we saw three young males in black pajamas walking down to the edge of the river on the other side. The path they were taking was about eight feet lower than ground level. I called the captain and asked what he wanted to do. He asked if they were armed, and I replied negative. He then told me to keep them under observation and shortly after this they climbed the embankment behind them and disappeared into the village.

We could only see the roofs of the houses in the village across the river from our position. The entire squad kept a watchful eye and suddenly the same guys climbed back down the embankment, but now they were dressed in khakis and carrying AK's. I frantically called the captain and relayed our new problem and he told me to hold our fire; he said he would call in a fire mission from the howitzers at LZ Bird who were a short distance down the river. We argued about the map grids and the coordinates and so the captain said he would have the Bravo Company mortar platoon fire a WP marking round. I heard the mortar round when it was fired. The entire squad was lying on their bellies watching the other side of the river. I didn't see anything, and immediately asked "did you see it, did you see it?" No one replied until we turned around and saw the huge white cloud of smoke right behind us on our side of the river. I then yelled into the radio "it's on our side of the river!!!" and in a moment of panic I yelled cease fire three times. The captain was about to call in 155mm howitzers and if they hit where the marking round had hit on our side of the river those cannon shells would have made mincemeat of us all.

About this time the second platoon showed up and we all took the three enemy soldiers under fire. I don't think we got any of them, because they just seemed to disappear from our sight on the other side of the river. A squad from the 5th of the 7th showed up on the other side of the river looking for them but they found no sign of them or any bodies.

DECEMBER 5, 1966. Well, we are now at LZ Mead. We are going into LZ Hammond tomorrow and take showers and get cleaned up. We are securing artillery here which isn't too bad of a job. No word on if we are or are not going down south still. We sure had a ball today in the choppers. We flew at over one hundred miles an hour just a few feet off the ground . . Was it a thrill!…

DECEMBER 7, 1966. Well, you'll never believe this, but the sun came peeking through the clouds today. That old sun sure feels good. We haven't had any mail for a couple of days because we're not with the rest of the company. We are up guarding a battery of artillery on top of a hill. Yesterday, the platoon went out on a recon mission. It is different than how we work most of the time and was lots of fun. When recon goes in they don't prep with artillery or

A.R.A but instead everybody shoots their weapons out the door of the choppers…. Well let's hope the next couple of months go by fast.

I remember this time very well. This was what I thought Air Cavalry was all about, air assaults and wild maneuvers. No daily ground pounding and digging foxholes. We even had time to get acquainted with the chopper crews and learned some of their tactics. Sorry to say we only got to operate with this recon unit for a couple of days, but it was very interesting to see how they worked. They were kind of crazy, but we had a lot of fun with them.

Guarding the artillery was considered easy duty for us, but since they were often a main target of the NVA this wasn't exactly a safe place to be.

The artillery soldiers were cleaning their howitzer and one of them said, "Don't look, but there is a gook sitting in the grass directly across from us on the next hill." I glanced to my side and could see him, and he seemed to be watching our every move. This artillery site would have been next to impossible to overrun: it was situated on the top of a hill and the surrounding hillside was steep and couldn't be climbed easily. The NVA were doing their darndest to figure out how to hurt us, so this guy on the next hill was most likely an enemy observer on a recon mission.

The guys in the artillery said, "Don't look at him and we'll get this mother fucker." The artillery continued to clean their gun and the gunner loaded a round in the firing chamber as they moved the barrel of the gun up and down. When the gun came around and was pointing directly at this enemy scout, the gunner yanked the cord and boom, the guy was vaporized in a flash and all that was left was a pile of dirt clods where he had been sitting.

DECEMBER 9, 1966. I'm sending you the material for ordering me the *Newsweek*, it costs $12 for a year's subscription. I'm glad my letters make you feel that you are here with me but I'm glad you're not. Well we're heading out on patrol, so I've got to go.

DECEMBER 13, 1966. Well, we have moved. We are now at Phan Thiet. It is right on the ocean and about eighty miles north of Saigon. See if you can find me on a map. Bet you can't, but Phan Thiet is a very large town and I would think it would be on any big map of Vietnam. So far it seems like a real nice place. We came down here yesterday by C-130 from LZ Hammond….

Our company had been at Phan Thiet in late August: we were there at the time to assist C Company of the 1st of the Ninth with Operation Byrd. But we didn't stay long and returned to the Bong Son area shortly after our arrival.

This trip to Phan Thiet was different, I think we may have been used as guinea pigs this time. They were having us go out on patrols with the ARVN. When an ARVN company would go out, an American platoon would accompany them, and vice versa. Our 2nd Platoon was one of the first to go on one of these patrols.

We left from the airport area near Phan Thiet and moved inland; the ARVN's moved very fast and when we came upon anything like abandoned structures or whatever, they just plowed through not stopping or looking at anything. These were supposedly search missions. Things came to a head when it hit around noon and the 2nd Platoon leader said he wanted to stop so we could have lunch. They insisted we continue forward on patrol and try to get back as soon as possible. After thinking about this I couldn't blame them, because they were going back to their families and all we had to look forward to was maybe some hot chow. This day we stopped to have lunch and the ARVN left us behind and continued with their mission. I'm unsure just how many platoons had similar experiences with the ARVN, but I believe our core differences of how best to patrol was part of our inability to operate effectively together in the field.

> DECEMBER 16, 1966. Well, not too much is happening today. Guess what, they gave me a pass into Phan Thiet yesterday and we are way out in the field. I went into the airport by helicopter and then signed out and went by truck down to Phan Thiet. It is quite a town…. I've got to go, give J.R. his usual.

I enjoyed walking around Phan Thiet and seeing how the people lived. I thought about sitting down at one of the European style tables they had set up on the sidewalks and ordering a meal. But every time I got near one of the restaurants the smell of the fish sauce they poured over everything turned my stomach.

The Mac-V compound at Phan Thiet looked like a mini fortress with sandbags stacked around it and machine guns on the roof. Across the street from the Mac-V building was a walled off house with eight or ten guards armed with M-1 carbines and grease guns. It was most certainly some type of garrison. While I was standing there wondering about this fort, a civilian truck pulled up with an American civilian in it. The American was dressed in civilian clothes and had a machine pistol slung over his shoulder. The gates to the compound were opened and the civilian drove inside. I still question to this day just how Mac-V operated in Vietnam and don't have a clue as to why this compound in Phan Thiet existed.

I returned to the field that evening and the next day we went back on patrol in a populated area. My Eskimo was driving me nuts, although I liked having him on point in these populated villages because he looked a lot like a Vietnamese; he just didn't communicate with anybody. I guess the villagers thought he was an interpreter because they would approach him and immediately start speaking to him in Vietnamese, but all he did was plow through them pushing them aside. This approach to the locals just didn't help our ability to befriend the villagers we had been ordered to relocate.

We were ordered to evacuate these villages because this area was known to be a staging area for the NVA. As usual the villagers didn't want to leave their homes and most of them had little use for us. After all, we were the invaders. As a human being I had empathy for them, especially when you saw the women and children crying as they were forced out of their hooches. But we were under orders and I believe the NVA had given us little choice. They wanted to control this area and we had to make sure that didn't happen. This area was designated as a free-fire zone and had these villagers remained they would have become unintended targets for our gunships and artillery.

After we completed our job of evacuating the village, the rest of the company moved forward on patrol. They left our squad behind to guard the perimeter of LZ Virginia, and we were spread out guarding the airport. Once again, I was left to try and control the Eskimo. This was no easy task; he was a primitive type of guy and I had little control over anything he did. He had proven himself to be a crack shot, but truth be told, I was afraid of him because he was so unpredictable. It's next to impossible to control someone who not only doesn't communicate but exhibits no form of human compassion for anyone or anything.

I had been a fire team leader for a while, and I believed when it came time to make decisions I would lead by example and sprinkle in a little of the majority rules. I realize this is not the Army way and it probably would have pissed off some of the brass, but I was not an NCO and this method had worked for me up to this point. Clearly trying to set up the best and safest plan for my fire team was hindered by the quality of the soldiers I was expected to lead. When there were guys like the Eskimo and troopers like Mr. Untrustworthy who chose not to listen to anyone, it was impossible to lead. Taking my normal approach to leading a fire team was not an option and all I could hope to do was try and hang on until I had new fire team members who had some common sense.

12

Hurrah! I'm Out of the Field

DECEMBER 24, 1966. Well, you haven't gotten any letters from me for a while, but we have been on a four-day ambush and I just haven't been able to write. Guess what lover, good news! They have let me out of the field. I am working as S-4 (that's supply) back in Phan Thiet. I don't know how long it's going to be for but at least I'm out for now. Let me tell you about the second night of the ambush. We had set up on this trail just a little after dark, when my fire team and I heard some voices on the trail and they weren't speaking in English. So, we all dived into the prone shelter we had dug. Well, the gooks hit our trip flare and it didn't go off and we couldn't shoot because we weren't sure where they were, so on down the path they came right in front of our machine gun. The machine gun opened up and we opened up. My sixteen jammed (what a feeling) so we set off our claymore mine. Guess what, out of three on the trail our claymore got one. But listen to this, the one that we got was the most important VC ever captured in this part of Vietnam (he was an S-4 officer for a battalion). Applause! So, I guess you can say my fire team and I did a good job. Oh say, I just found out what I'm doing. I'm going back for a month and learn the job. Aren't you proud of your hubby? Yeah, well, so much for that noise. I'll let you know what's happening. Well lover, the beer and the ice just came in and I've got to get it out to the troops.

Wow! What a Christmas present I got on December 24, 1966. The first sergeant (Top) called me in from the field where I had been with the point fire team of the company battle formation and asked how I would like a job in the rear. My immediate answer was a resounding "Yes!" He laughed and said, "I thought that would be your answer," and then he asked, "Don't you want to know what the job is?" Please believe me I really didn't care. I had been feeling like I had used up all my luck in the field, so no matter what the job was I was relieved to know I would be getting out of the field. Then he told me my new job was S-4 (supply guy for Bravo Company). He asked me, "Do you want to know how you were selected?" and I answered yes. He said the captain and he had gone through the records of the Company and that I was the oldest remaining soldier still out in the field in Bravo Company. He said I had a clean record and had proven my combat skills in the field. I was pleased to hear this praise from him, and the fact that he picked me for this great job made me proud. The rest of my tour in Vietnam I spent in forward support areas and whether it was true or not, I felt safe and secure in these areas. In my last letter to my wife I went into some detail about the ambush we had gone on; I don't think I would have been as open with her about this ambush had it not been for the great news I was sharing about my getting out of the field.

It had been my experience while I was in Vietnam that very few ambushes resulted in any contact with the enemy. This ambush was different: suddenly things got real on this one when we could hear voices coming down the trail and they weren't speaking English. As they got closer, I waited for the trip flare to engage (our early warning signal to all the troops in the area). The flare did not engage and that was on me. I'd sent one of our new troopers out to set up our trip flare and he had failed to straighten the pin. Shame on me, I hadn't gone back, and double checked it myself. Because the pin had not been straightened, the flare failed to go off and nobody else in the area knew the enemy were coming down the trail. Then to top it off my rifle jammed as did the others on my fire team. The only working weapons we had were hand grenades, an M-79 and the .45 cal that the Eskimo carried.

Our machine gun was about 15 feet to our right. When the flare did not go off, I tried to warn the machine gun position by heaving chunks of dirt their way. The gunner didn't get my message until the VC were almost on top of them. This was a very dark night and not a bit of starlight could be seen. The gunner jumped up and got behind his machine gun just in time and opened fire. One of the three VC turned and ran back down the trail towards our location. Right then a new trooper yelled in my ear, "Should I set off the claymore?" I yelled back "set it off" and followed that by yelling as loud as I could "Claymore!" to warn all the others around us. This was SOP, so they knew to get their heads down before the blast.

When we had set up next to the trail, the ground was so hard it was like chipping granite, so we had dug as deep as we could to provide some sort of protection. We were just three feet off the trail, and I wasn't sure how I wanted to place the claymore. At first, I went out the length of the cord, about 25 feet, but placing it there was not an option because the trail was directly in front of us and we would have had little protection from the blast. So, I looked for an alternative location. Claymores have a killing radius of about 60 feet, so I decided the best and safest place was to put it flush up against a large tree two feet to the left front of our position. I selected this spot because I figured the tree would absorb the back blast generated by the claymore. I admit even though I thought this was the best placement for the claymore, it still made me very nervous. I'd never set off a claymore before, and though I'd been trained how to handle them I was never around one when it went off and didn't know what to expect. Turns out, it worked like a charm and none of our guys were hurt by the side and back blasts of the claymore. Most of the back blast was absorbed by the tree and the side blast had successfully nailed the one VC running back down the trail towards our position.

Once again, my rifle had jammed, so I began throwing the hand grenades I had laid out in front of me. Normally I didn't lay my grenades out like this, but I wanted to show our new troopers that there was another way to try and prepare for possible combat by having your grenades at the ready. I had thrown all but my last grenade and since we were so close to the trail and I didn't know if any VC were still alive in front of us, I decided to roll the grenade onto the trail just a few feet beyond the prone shelter we were occupying. When it went off, I swear I came about a foot off the ground, and my ears rang for a couple of hours. Thankfully none of our troopers were injured by the grenade. But we still didn't know if we could expect an onslaught of VC coming our way and here I sat with my useless *piece of crap jammed M-16*. Just like in the movies, my only option at that point was to affix my bayonet to my useless rifle and jump out onto the trail. I jumped over the dirt berm and immediately tripped over the VC that had been waylaid by the claymore. This guy appeared to be in pretty good shape, he had two holes in his chest from the Claymores ball bearings, but somehow the grenade I rolled out didn't kill or even wound him. He was one lucky son of a bitch.

While I was looking around to make sure there wasn't anyone still moving, I heard the Eskimo slamming a new magazine into his .45 pistol and jacking a round into the chamber. The Eskimo walked over to the VC who had been wounded and put his .45 down to the VC's head, so I grabbed his wrist and said, "Hey, we take prisoners." I'm certain he was about to blow this wounded enemy's brains out.

Just at that moment of mass confusion on this trail, with tracers going every which way, here comes the LT and the first sergeant. When they came upon this chaotic scene, they both were yelling at me, asking what the hell was going on. When I pointed out the wounded and now captured VC, they both scraped him up off the ground and called a medevac to pick him up.

When I observed the prisoner, I didn't think he had been seriously injured, but as it turns out the pellets from the claymore had penetrated his chest close to his heart. Years later I was told by the captain who had been our company commander during this incident that the VC we had captured had become a valuable asset for us. When the Army brass sent him to the Philippines for a heart operation, they found one of the ball bearings from the claymore had in fact penetrated his heart and without treatment he would have died. I'm told he was the most valuable prisoner captured in this area of Vietnam at the time. He turned out to provide a bonanza of information and gave the location of six safe houses and the names of 200 agents and undercover VC in the Phan Thiet area. When I found out how important this guy turned out to be, I was very happy I'd stopped the Eskimo from putting a bullet in his head.

Some time later after this successful ambush, the first sergeant told me he had put me in for the Silver Star, but as it turns out the machine gunner got it instead. I did however receive a Bronze Star for my part in this ambush and this was awarded to me at Fort Ord, California, after my return from the war in 1967.

Soon after starting my new job as S-4 my buddy Shelby stopped by for a visit and told me he was desperately seeking a job in the rear. He asked when I was due to leave, but after comparing our dates of arrival in country we discovered I had only arrived a few days prior to him. Turns out this was the last time I ever saw him; he was KIA on March 1, 1967. His loss stunned me because he had less than a month before he would have gone home to his family. I know for a very long time I tried my best not to think about Shelby, or any of the other troopers I knew who had paid the ultimate price in Vietnam. They're now frozen in time, young men who were here one minute and needlessly gone the next, and never able to go home to see their loved ones again. I'm certain this war and its indelible heartbreaking memories will stay with me until it's time for me to join my lost comrades.

The other soldier who had been S-4 before me was being fired. I took my new job seriously and really tried to do my best. Some of the guys in the rear (not all), drank too much and just didn't seem to give a damn about anything but themselves. When I'd been there a while, I learned to appropriate anything Bravo Company needed. Army red tape and regulations rarely stood in my way. Whenever something was requested for Bravo Company, I would find it and even if I had to lie, cheat or steal to get it, I did my very best to fill the order. Many of my supply contacts were just plain lazy: if I was looking for something and they refused to give it to me, all it took was to wait them out.

Any cold rainy night was a perfect time for procurement, because most of the guys in supply refused to go out in the rain. They would simply look over my supply order and sometimes cross things off, then sign off on it and direct me to go get it alone. I was like a kid in a candy store when they just sent me to get my own supplies. Occasionally I'd find things we had been told were not available and I made sure to pick up whatever I felt Bravo Company could use. Although I occasionally appropriated a few things that weren't on my current supply order, I never took an excess of anything. I just tried to make sure my guys in the field got their fair share of things that would make their job easier.

I now understood how the huge black market for our supplies and equipment had begun. It was clear that the supplies passed through many hands before they got to the field where they were needed most. Uniforms, weapons, American cigarettes and C-rations were big ticket items on the black market and dishonest soldiers found an easy way to supplement their income by selling whatever they could steal.

The job in S-4 was in fact a powerful one, and it had a lot of potential for abuse. I could see how easy it could have been to take a little here and take a little there and no one would have been the wiser. Since I had been a grunt for the past nine months and knew our guys were out in the field risking their lives daily, my only thought was to make sure they got whatever they needed as soon as possible.

DECEMBER 25, 1966. Merry Christmas on this Christmas night. Our hooch is right beside the landing pad of the 15th medical battalion, where the medevac choppers land. A chopper landed that wasn't a medevac, so I was watching, and I saw them help the pilot get out and I went over and got the story. The chopper had about six holes in it and the pilot was hit in the chin.

The pilot of this chopper had taken a bullet in the chin and was holding a rag on the wound to stop the bleeding when they landed. The Huey has a plexiglass window at the pilot's feet, and you could see the hole where the bullet had gone through the window. Luckily for the pilot the slug had gone through the plexiglass before hitting his chin, or he might have sustained life changing injury.

About this time General Westmoreland showed up in Phan Thiet and had the company gather around his jeep; then he climbed up on the jeep's hood and gave the troops a talk. I only heard part of his speech because the first sergeant had me doing things. The General was informing the troops of a possible medical issue: apparently a cook in the mess hall had come down with hepatitis. He told everyone that they would be required to get a shot. Hearing that, I immediately tried to escape the area, but the first sergeant knew how much I hated shots and caught me, then made me go first to make sure I got the shot. I was none too happy about having to go first and I swear the needle they used in my ass was a foot long.

One of my favorite pictures. Notice the sly smile on my face. This was a picture taken of me right after I got notice of transfer to S-4, December 1966.

JANUARY 1, 1967. [I used the stationery from the hotel and the letterhead began with the following: In country Rest and Recuperation for the troops welcome to the R&R center Hotel Vung Tau]. Well here I am at Vung Tau and so far it is a really nice place. The best part of all, everything is free as far as food and stuff goes but of course beer and drinks cost money. You should have seen the mess we had on New Year's Eve. I had planned on writing you around midnight but just before I was going up to write, the troopers started shooting weapons. It was unbelievable! The tracers just covered the sky and it lasted better than a half an hour. In our company area we had two hand grenades go off and one person was wounded. Isn't that just a senseless thing to do? I couldn't believe that someone would be stupid enough to throw a grenade in base camp, but I must have been wrong. I don't think I was ever so scared while I was in Vietnam. I was in a tent that caught some shrapnel, scary stuff. Say Vung Tau is out of sight. They have a regular dining hall and the hotel is really nice. I think when I go back through Saigon I'll try and see Sgt. Timmons at Long Binn. I hope it works out because I would sure love to see him. Tonight, we hit the bars as you can probably tell by my writing and tomorrow, we are going to the beach and go swimming in the ocean. It should be an interesting day and lots of fun. Oh, yea I borrowed 25 dollars to go on this R&R so your December pay should be a little on the short side, but then again you should be getting more because of the spec/4 pay.

I'm a little embarrassed to reveal I was scared to death when the hand grenades were thrown on New Year's Eve in base camp. I have described many stupid things that I'd seen in the past in base camp, but this night took the cake. The guy I mentioned who wounded himself was so drunk he nearly killed himself or injured others who were nearby. This soldier, for whatever reason, decided he wanted to see if he could outrun a live grenade. He released the spoon on the grenade but didn't get far before he tripped and fell flat on his face and that fall saved his life. Had he remained upright he more than likely would have been killed instantly. The grenade did leave him with some shrapnel in his back and his butt, but he was still

Me at In-Country R&R—Vung Tau R&R Center January 1967.

alive. Guess what? You can't outrun an exploding hand grenade. I certainly hope this bozo didn't get awarded a Purple Heart for this self-inflicted wound, but I'll never know.

The show the base camp perimeter guards put on that New Year's Eve was spectacular. This was a maximum display of our firepower and the mortar and artillery flares joined in after a while. The tracers covered the sky and the sound was indescribable. This impromptu show lasted for about a half an hour and I'm sure the brass was more than unhappy about this tremendous waste of ammo. Once things got going that night, it was soon out of control. This type of thing was inevitable once the troops were drunk and could get their hands on loaded weapons. Clearly there were no Cav helicopters flying anywhere near base camp that night. Looking back, I'd wished I had taken some pictures; the sky looked like a screen of tracers were circling base camp. I'm sure this wild display deterred any possible enemy attack. No NVA or VC in their right minds would have come near base camp that night.

> JANUARY 6, 1967. Well, here I am back at base camp. I haven't written for a couple of days because I have been traveling a lot. Guess who I stopped and saw while I was down near Saigon—Sgt. Timmons, and he looked good. We went down to his club and really put away some beer. He is in Long Binn near Binn Hoa, close to Saigon, see if you can find it on your map. When I got back to base camp, I got three letters from you, my do I ever love you. I wanted to get a letter from you so bad, but because I was down at Vung Tau there was no way. It sounds like you had a nice Christmas....

Sergeant Timmons was stationed at Long Binn and was the sergeant of the guard for the stockade used for American soldiers in Vietnam. He had been my sergeant at the stockade while I was stationed with the MPs at Fort Gordon. He showed me around and I had a chance to eat in the mess hall there. The hooch he lived in had wood floors and he shared it with three other soldiers. If you had to work in a war zone, this, in my opinion, was the way to live. They even had a hooch maid, who cleaned their beds, shined their shoes and kept everything in order. Incredibly their hooch had electric lights and a refrigerator. His living conditions made my own quarters seem primitive and in fact they were, but at least I had a home base now and didn't have to wonder just where I would be digging my next foxhole.

I said my goodbyes to Sgt. Timmons and headed back towards base camp. When I got back on the main road, I stuck my thumb out and it didn't take long before an Army deuce-and-a-half stopped and picked me up. This first night on my journey back to An Khe I stayed at Camp Alpha at Tan Son Nhut. I went to their mess hall and I was able to get some good food. The next morning, I went for breakfast before I left and soon discovered their milk in the mess hall at Camp Alpha hadn't improved a bit since I was there on my first day in Vietnam. I stupidly grabbed a glass of it and once again gagged and just about ruined my breakfast.

When it came time to leave, I went in search of a ride back to An Khe. Normally I would just look for one of our cavalry aircraft and catch a ride. But the cavalry rarely utilized Tan Son Nhut, so after a brief search I put my name on a list for a plane that was heading my way. They told me it would be a while, so I looked around and found some shade and just waited. While I was waiting, I needed to take a leak and noticed there was a single-story solitary building with a huge sign that said Restrooms a short distance across the tarmac. At a distance it looked nice, but when I got inside, I almost upchucked my breakfast. Every toilet was filled with shit and there was crap everywhere. It was so bad I couldn't even stay long enough to take a leak. I headed back to the shade I had been in and stepped around the corner and took my leak.

A short time passed, and two air force types showed up and opened the doors of the hanger I had been using for shade. One of these guys came out with a case of beer and asked if I wanted one, and as I said sure. I thought these guys didn't have any better than we did and their beer would be warm just like ours. How wrong I was! One of the airman rolled over a big CO_2 fire extinguisher, the kind normally used to put out aircraft engine fires, then he put the case of beer on the floor and sprayed the entire case with the CO_2 and voilà we instantly had iced cold beer. I was impressed with their ingenuity; I'd never seen this done before and right about that time this iced cold beer sure did hit the spot.

JANUARY 13, 1967. Well I didn't get a letter from you today, but I got a couple yesterday, so I guess it's all right. Days are passing kind of fast and I just hope they keep it up so we can be together very soon. It's hard to believe that we have been apart for so long. It will be nice to be back to your willing and warm arms. Just remember that our day will come soon. Tonight, a helicopter crashed while I was serving chow and I just happened to have my camera. I got some good shots and there went three-hundred thousand dollars of our taxpayer's money (wait a minute, I'm a taxpayer). Nobody was hurt. It looks like we're going back to An Khe very shortly....

JANUARY 16, 1967. Well, that's what the date on my watch looks like. I just got back from the movies. All I could do was think about you. I'm sitting right now listening to one of the guy's tape recorder. Wow do some of those songs bring back memories. Here's a picture of my jeep taken today with the driver's swinger. Now if you look close under the right headlight you might see what I was trying to do with this picture. If you can remember a few months ago you sent me a picture of you sitting on the Chevelle, well, here is my answer to that picture. I knew you'd just love to have this one. By now you've taken a second look at the picture so let me tell what you're seeing, that's our jeep I'm sitting on.... Well sweets, give my usual to J.R. for his papa.

JANUARY 17, 1967. I got your letter today with the picture of you in it. My but you are skinny. Wow.... Here's a paper and the L.Z. Bird story, well, we had just come from that place just before that happened. As I said before, someone is watching over me lover and I hope he's watching over you and J.R.

I was doing a lot of traveling for the company during this time. One morning the first sergeant gave me a pile of papers and said to take them to

Me sitting on my S-4 Jeep—Trying to imitate a picture my wife had sent with her sitting on our new Chevelle—January 1967.

base camp and distribute them to the different addressees. I took a Caribou from LZ Virginia to Nha Trang.

At Nha Trang I looked around for a 1st Cav aircraft and finally found one who said I could hitch a ride back to An Khe. The aircraft was a Caribou and I noticed the cowling was off the left engine compartment and the pilot and co-pilot were tinkering with something. They told me to come back in about a half hour. When I returned to the aircraft, they had just started up the left engine and blue smoke rolled across the pavement. Wow! Could I pick them! Here I was carrying a huge packet of documents marked "Confidential" and boarding a plane with obvious mechanical issues. When we took off there were four of us onboard. The crew chief had me help him tie off some loaded pallets that were stowed onboard, and at the same time showed me how he wanted them unhooked when they needed to be dropped. Silly me, I thought he meant we would be dropping them from the air. After an hour I sat down next to the crew chief and asked why we weren't at An Khe; he said we had to drop the pallets first. Then I looked out the port hole and it appeared we were circling. Finally, we were down to tree-top level and seemed to be coming into a small airstrip. As the back ramp let down, I could see lots of smoke from the artillery explosions and it was obvious whoever was fighting on the ground was involved in a serious firefight.

It turns out this was a landing strip at a Special Forces camp somewhere in the central highlands, who knows where. They were under attack and the crew chief and I slid the pallets out of the plane as fast as we could, then the pilot lost no time getting out of that place. That whole thing was scary. Here I was finally doing what I considered to be a safe job and the dangers of war continued to follow me wherever I went.

> JANUARY 19, 1967. Well, the company is back in, so I have really been going. I got back those pictures and here are some I thought you might like. I'll send the rest little by little. That big one is of me and my girlfriend over here. Her name is Susie and she is something else. She loves to be held by her hind legs while she's getting some peanuts....

In my last letter I mentioned my girlfriend Susie. She lived in a hole in the ground she shared with a generator at LZ English and her roof was a piece of plywood propped up against the side of the hole. She was leashed on a 25-foot piece of rope and anytime I got within her range she would dash out, hit my leg at full speed and climb up to the pocket she knew would be holding peanuts or gum. After she had taken what she came for,

Caribou taking off from Central Highlands.

she would scamper down my leg and kick up her hind legs up in the air for me to grab and swing her in a circle. Every time I did this, she would scream bloody murder, but once you started it was next to impossible to put her down. Each time it was an ordeal to end our little game; she had to be completely worn out before she would allow me to leave. She knew exactly how far she could go on the rope and believe me if you got within her radius, she'd come flying out of that hole to rummage through your pockets. If I was in a hurry, I had to make sure to avoid her bunker.

> JANUARY 21, 1967. I had a nice letter from you today and the best part of it was that you added another day for us to be together on our vacation. But I'm sorry that you missed out on a three-day weekend. Well sweetheart, here are some more of those pictures. How did you like those of me? … My goodness only 62 days at the most and I can hardly wait.

About this time, I began keeping a short-timer's calendar and I still have it. Most everyone I knew did this at about the two-month mark. I found as I crossed off each day a combination of excitement and apprehension crept into my mind. On one hand I just couldn't wait to get home and as I marked off each day, I was reassured my life might soon return to normal. Towards the end of my tour in Vietnam I had an ever-present sense

My girlfriend "Susie" the monkey sitting on my shoulder looking for treats.

of unease; thoughts that I might be killed or injured just before I was to go home kept me on edge. Sadly, I'd seen too many soldiers who never got to cross off that last day on their calendars and return home to those they loved.

> JANUARY 30, 1967. Well I'm back at Phan Thiet. I just got about all the equipment that I went after, but we still need some stuff. Say lover guess what? They have me up for a medal, the Bronze Star. How about that! It's for outstanding duty and you wouldn't believe all the things they say about me. Well maybe I'll get it and then you'll have a real war hero. It's stopped raining in An Khe at last and it was sunny, bright and warm. The weather at Phan Thiet is just wonderful. It is warm all the time but not too hot. We still have no word on how long we are going to be down here. It's almost February lover and that means just a little over a month away from your loving arms. I can hardly wait, and I know you feel the same way.

Back in base camp I had just walked by the battalion medical tent when I saw Doc Bell, my medic from the 2nd Platoon. We had served together in the 2nd Platoon for a long time; in fact, he was the one who had patched up my leg when I got the punji stake wound at the end of May. As

Playing with "Susie." She loved to be held by her legs and swung in a circle.

with most grunts I pretty much worshipped our medics; they were a special breed of soldier. They proved their bravery over and over and most of the time put our welfare above their own.

When Doc Bell noticed me, he called me over and told me he thought I had already rotated home and I told him I was going home soon. He asked me if my shot record was up to date. I looked at him and all I could do was cringe, since I had purposely ducked most of the shots they'd tried to give me while I was in Vietnam. He said, "Well, I better pull your record and have a look." He then let me know that some of the shots I needed had to be given a certain number of days or months before leaving Vietnam. Then he told me, "If you haven't had them, they won't let you go home," and that got my attention. Of course, when he checked my shot record, he only found two shots, one for hepatitis and one that they required before I went on R&R. I pleaded with Doc Bell and asked if he could just sign off on them, but I noticed as I was talking he had begun pulling bottles from the refrigerator and needles out of the cabinet and lining them up on the tray in front of me. He ended up with a total of seven needles.

When I saw the needles, I said, "No way!" and Doc Bell said, "No way you're not!" He held all the cards in this poker match, so I rolled up my left sleeve and told him I wanted all the shots in my left arm because I needed to write with my right hand. Well, I made it to shot number four before I made him switch to my right arm. This was torture for me, but at this point getting out of Vietnam was all I could think about and I wasn't going to let a little pain stand in my way. When Doc Bell finished, he was kind and backdated some of the shots so my departure from Vietnam was not delayed. I admit I was less than appreciative at the time, but of course when I looked back, I could see he was only helping me to get home. I tried looking him up after the war to thank him for what he did, but I could never locate him to properly thank him.

> FEBRUARY 5, 1967. Well, I didn't get any mail today but maybe some will be along tomorrow. Guess what, I am now the S-4. The guy I was working for got sent back out to the field and I took over his job. We had a sergeant come out from An Khe and we will work together. Well lover, I'm getting shorter and shorter and it won't be very long now. Assignments came out for the people leaving in March, but mine isn't down yet.

About this time our first sergeant offered me a promotion to Sergeant E-5, but in the same breath he said, "But you can't stay back here, you'll have to go back in the field." I quickly weighed my options and although this promotion would have made me an NCO, I knew my wife would kill me if I willingly returned to the field. I told him no thanks and he said he understood. He told me he had five sergeant slots open, which was no surprise to me; combat sergeants came and went like flies. It was hard to keep low level NCOs in the field. They either transferred out, were demoted, or worst of all were injured or killed and I was certain I didn't want to be included in the last three of those categories.

I wrote two letters, February 6 and 7. Both had little to do with what I was doing; they mostly relayed how excited I was that I would be leaving Vietnam soon.

FEBRUARY 15, 1967. Well, haven't written in a while we have been fixing up our C.P. and supply tent here at LZ English. I have been filling lots and lots of sandbags. The Vietnamese would fill sandbags for me for one and a half or two cents, but you know the Scots blood in me, and I wouldn't hear of it. We finally found a little girl who helped by holding the bags and we paid her 20 cents. We are about a mile and a half to two miles from the place where we had that big battle last May. I hope they don't get into it again the way we did back then. I'll write soon as I can again.

We left LZ Virginia around this time and moved with B Company north to LZ English near Bong Son. As soon as I arrived there, I started building a bunker. It was mostly underground and was two sandbags thick. At first, I had passing soldiers help fill the sandbags, and then a little girl (see the above letter) who held the bags while I filled them. I built in an escape hatch in the top that was level with the road that ran behind the bunker. The windows were constructed of old ammo boxes and I procured some runway steel planking (PSP) to use as support for my sandbag covered roof. The steel planking was hard to come by, but I figured no one would miss a few panels, so in the cover of night I slipped over and took a couple at a time from the nearby runway. I guess I wasn't the only one finding another use for the PSP, because an order came down from the LZ English base commander that anyone caught taking PSP from the runway would be subject to court-martial. Luckily, I had enough to finish my bunker by then.

My letters were becoming sparse. My new job in S-4 took up a lot of my time and I wasn't doing anything interesting to write about.

As I said before some of the guys in the supply units were just plain lazy and that was good for making sure B Company remained well supplied. The prime example were the guys at the ammo dump: they'd let

Me resting outside my hooch while working S-4. Notice the stack of sundry rations behind me.

me go out alone and load it myself. Each trip I took a little extra and that proved to be a wise move, because before I'd come to S-4, B Company was made to stand down because they were short of ammo and I didn't want to see that happen on my watch.

One time, while getting mortar ammo, I dug down to the bottom of the stack of boxes and there were three boxes of mortar flares. These were impossible to get, and our First Sergeant was constantly requesting them. It was a great find and I was sure I'd make some brownie points when I returned with the mortar flares. When I found them, I restacked everything on my mule and then piled all the ammo I could on top of the mortar flare boxes. I didn't have to take much effort to hide the mortar flare boxes from the ammo guys because it was raining that night and I knew they never, ever came outside into the rain to check. Sure enough, I parked out in the rain and no one even offered to come out and see what I was taking. When I got back, I called the first sergeant and told him I'd "found" some mortar flares and he was pleased. He told me to send a couple of mortar flares out with the next supply run.

Though I thought I was now in a safe job, it still had its own dangers. I heard a supply guy from one of the other companies had some guys helping unload a truck full of mortar rounds and they were tossing them around like sacks of potatoes. They dropped one of the boxes and boom. I was told three were killed. Once I heard this story, I had a lot more respect for mortar rounds and handled them more carefully myself.

My job in S-4 kept me busy and all I could think about was getting on that airplane and heading back to the world. Then on March 1, 1967, my world fell apart. I got some heartbreaking news that day and thinking about it now still can bring tears to my eyes.

I got word that my old squad had been sent out to set up an ambush and while they were in the process of setting up, a group of villagers passed them. I guess visibility was next to zero at the time so the guys on the ambush paid little attention to the villagers and continued to set up in a rice paddy where two dike paths crossed. Having been on many ambushes I knew if you had contact with anyone you didn't know, you needed to abort and move your ambush location. This time, whoever was making the decisions made a fatal error in judgment and the squad didn't move. The villagers must have been lookouts for the VC and the squad paid the price for not moving. The VC crawled up alongside the dike and tossed a U.S. Army grenade in on them. Two were killed and four were injured by the grenade. But it was the news of who had been killed that tore me up. Two of my closest buddies in 2nd Platoon, Jay Shelby and James Wheeler, were just gone in an instant. This was how it was—young men with their whole lives ahead of them were never going to see another sunrise or be able to leave this hell hole of Vietnam alive.

I went up to grave registration at LZ English to see Shelby and Wheeler, but I just couldn't go in. I stood and then sat outside for a couple of hours, but I couldn't get up enough courage to go inside. Tears were streaming down my cheeks and I couldn't stop them. The anguish I felt from their deaths was indescribable and to this very day the sorrow of their loss haunts me.

Shelby and I had been best friends and at the time he was killed he was a short timer just like me. At one of the reunions after the war, one of the guys from the 2nd Platoon told me that the others in the platoon had tried to get the platoon sergeant to let Shelby stay behind because he was due to leave the field the next day. The platoon sergeant said no way and Shelby's fate hung on that sergeant's decision. As I've said many times in this book, life was cheap in Vietnam and you never knew just when yours might come to an end.

This paramount event in my life took what little optimism I had left away from me for a time. I stopped writing letters home and became hyper aware of where I went and what I did. More than anything I just wanted to make it home in one piece and the fear that something terrible might happen to me seemed to overshadow my every thought.

I was beginning to wonder just how I could ever leave this terrible war behind me and try to return to a law-abiding society. Having been a grunt in Vietnam and seeing the things I'd seen, I doubted my transition back to my life in the states was going to be easy.

I'm no angel, but I was certain I hadn't done things I couldn't live with later. I didn't allow myself to boom-boom, so I wasn't in any danger of carrying home a disease to my wife. When I shot at or killed someone, it was only because they were trying to shoot me first. Looking back on that terrible year, I still believe I'd done my best to retain my values. Purposely subjecting anyone or anything to unnecessary injury or death just wasn't part of my make-up. My main objective was to try and keep my buddies and myself alive so that we all could return home.

This war brought out the best in some guys and the very worst in others. Some guys just lost it over there, and I saw them do unthinkable things. I don't know how they were able to return home without feeling some remorse for their actions and can't imagine how they could live with themselves for some of the awful things they did. I purposely did not describe the many thoughtless and vicious acts I had seen during this terrible year and after all these years they rarely show up in my nightmares.

I hadn't written my wife since the last week in February 1967. Shelby and Wheeler's deaths left me reeling and I just couldn't come to terms with their loss. I did write her on March 8, 1967. I tried to keep things light and that letter focused on my upcoming departure from Vietnam, never hinting I was grieving for the recent loss of my friends.

MARCH 12, 1967. Well, after you receive this letter don't bother writing anymore because you can say it to me in person. I got my port call. It's for the 22nd of March so that's when I'll be home. I imagine you'll get this on about the 20th so it should give you a couple of days to prepare. Expect a call from me sometime on the 22nd. Oh joy, I can hardly believe this has come true. We can put into operation all those plans that we have made and most import- ant of all we'll be together. I hope you're not working that day. I'm glad you're starting your leave on the 23rd that works out perfect. Huh. Would you believe only 10 days to go! Wow it's going to be so nice.

I had forgotten we had to cross back over the International Date Line, so I was confused about what day I really would be arriving home. My last ten days I just roamed around base camp. There was no one to bother me and I felt like a lost puppy. I wandered around and took a trip down mem- ory lane, taking pictures of the green line and its guard tower. I went to An Khe and took some pictures of downtown An Khe and its Marketplace. Looking at these pictures now everything there looks so primitive, but at the time this was the nearest thing to civilization we could visit while in base camp.

Last picture I took of downtown An Khe in March 1967.

Marketplace at An Khe, March 1967.

You would think I would be happy just having some time to myself, but after a year of almost constant activity and very few days off I didn't know what to do. Boredom finally got the best of me and I started to look around for something worthwhile to do. I noticed a group of soldiers preparing to go out on patrol of the green line and asked if I could tag along. I was carrying my new 35mm camera that I had just purchased to take home, so I guess they may have thought I was a reporter of some type. It wasn't long before I realized none of these troopers were grunts and I was extremely happy when we headed back and hadn't accidentally stumbled over any VC. When I got back, I realized it wasn't too bright volunteering to go along on a patrol with guys I didn't know. Try as I might I still don't know what I was thinking when I decided to go along on that patrol. When I returned, I came to my senses and stuck close to my bunk until my orders came. I hung around the Bravo company orderly room and just waited for the magic words that would send me back to the world.

Finally, I got the word and was sent out to Pleiku to catch the "Freedom Bird" home. Pleiku was still a nasty area and though I was happier than happy to be returning home, I still was worried that something bad might happen before we left.

We had been ordered to wear our stateside khaki uniforms, so I dug mine out of my pack. They were wrinkled and didn't look too sharp, but it didn't matter to me. All I could think about was getting on that plane and getting the hell out of Vietnam.

I got in line and prepared to enter the plane. I watched the soldiers who were filing off the plane we were about to board and as I did thoughts of my arrival at Tan Son Nhut airbase one year ago swirled in my head. These new arrivals looked so young and innocent and I wondered just how many of them would return home in one piece. Sadly, I'm sure some would never return to the U.S. alive and that thought broke my heart.

This air strip at Pleiku was not the safest place to be. During my year in Vietnam this area had been a hot bed of activity and I still worried we might be mortared before we could leave for home. The pilots of the plane may have had a similar opinion of this air strip's safety, because we loaded up quickly and they wasted no time getting it back in the air.

At long last we were headed home and the relief I felt brought tears to my eyes. Once on board it seemed as though everyone was waiting for some sort of sign before they could completely relax; that came when the pilot announced we had reached 3,000 feet and a gigantic cheer went up from everyone on board.

Once I'd settled down, here came the tears again. I believe you would have had to walk in my shoes to understand my emotional state. This was my final trip out of Vietnam, and the

"Happy Soldier" picture of me in doorway of B 1/7 orderly room. I had less than a week to go before returning "Back to the World"!

realization that I could never leave this war behind me was clouding the joy I should have had at that moment. I had seen too much and suffered too much to ever be the same again.

Our last stop on this very long trip was the Army fort at Oakland and by then I was biting at the bit to get home. But the Army in all its wisdom decided that we all had to wait and be issued new Class A uniforms, with all of the necessary insignia's, etc. So, four hours later they finally released me, and I headed for the San Francisco Airport and bought my ticket home to Los Angeles.

When I landed in L.A. I quickly found my wife and we hurried out of the airport. She told me she wanted to make sure she was on time and had been there a couple of hours. I'd seen pictures of the Chevelle she bought while I was in Vietnam and as we neared the car, I could see the headlights were on. My wife suddenly panicked and said, "Oh no, I left the lights on" and that she had locked the keys inside. Then a look of relief crossed her face and she said, "Oh, I have a gift for you" and she handed me a little box with a set of car keys she had made for me, so all was well.

Once we settled into the car, she asked if I'd like to drive, but I said no. At that moment everything seemed new to me; I had been away too long and couldn't relax. As we entered the freeway, I panicked and asked her to stay in the slow lane and not go over 45 m.p.h. I'd lived through Vietnam and knew one thing for sure—I didn't want to die in a car accident on my first day home. I just couldn't shake the feeling of uncertainty and unease I was experiencing at that time. I remember the trip home on the freeway was frightening. I couldn't settle down and every brake light made me jump. It was a couple of weeks before I got behind the wheel of a car and could enjoy driving again. I was fortunate to have a 30 day leave and had a wonderful month with my family. Slowly I began to unwind and appreciate life again.

I was one of the lucky ones though. I still had a year to go in the Army when I got back to the states and the Army and its discipline helped me maintain my sanity. I soon became a sergeant and the perks that came with that promotion improved my outlook on everything. I got a great job for my last year and went home to see my family most weekends. This transition gave me time to get to know my wife and son again and allowed me to wind down from the constant uncertainty of the war in Vietnam.

Many grunts didn't have the opportunity to slowly assimilate back into society. They came home and were just let loose out into a country that was becoming unhappy with the Vietnam War and its participants. It's a sad fact, but I believe the government let many of my comrades down. They were thrown away and little effort was made to help them recover from the damage the war did to their minds. The movie version of the "crazy" Vietnam veteran wandering the streets seemingly ready to kill irritates me. The fact is some guys just never truly made it home from that terrible war and continued to be tormented by their horrific memories. Some tried to heal themselves with alcohol and others could no longer maintain their personal relationships. Simply said, many of them lost all hope and just never saw the light at the end of the tunnel again.

When I left the Army in March of 1968 my discharge papers had a block filled in showing I was an "Expert in Light Weapons." The block next to it was the civilian equivalent and in capital letters it said–*NONE!*

Through these many, many years since the war I have been able to go forward and try to forget Vietnam. I have lived a good life; I have a wonderful son and daughter-in-law, three grandsons, two great-grandsons, and my wife and I just celebrated our 55th wedding anniversary. I managed to graduate from two colleges and enjoyed jobs in both the public and private sectors. Vietnam may have taken away much of my confidence about my future, but I have been able to overcome the uncertainty of war and enjoy the life I have been given.

The Vietnam War changed my life forever and I will never forget the friends I needlessly lost in Vietnam. I still look back at times and the old anxiety returns. *Vietnam may be in my rearview mirror ... but it's never far behind me.*

Operations I Was On

My tour of 1st of the 7th Cavalry operations by date:

25 March–8 April 66 Lincoln

11–17 April 66 Mosby

26–28 April 66 Bee Bee

29 April 66 Browning

4–16 May 66 Davy Crockett

19 June–1 July 66 Nathan Hale

2–30 July 66 Henry Clay

18–31 July 66 Hayes

1–25 August 66 Paul Revere II

2–24 October 66 Irving

25 October until end of 66 Operation Thayer II

Glossary

AFO: Artillery forward observer

Air Assault: Four to sixteen Huey slicks bringing in troops to an unsecured LZ.

Airborne: Troopers who had gone through airborne training.

AIT: Advanced individual training.

AK-47: The 7.62mm .30 caliber Russian assault rifle, the automat Kalashnikov model 1947. Ugly and crude but effective, this weapon brought the fire-power of an NVA/PAVN unit to the equivalent fire-power of a similar size American unit.

Allies: In Vietnam the allies in country were the ROKs, Philippines and Australians.

Ambush: As small as 4 or 5 soldiers or large as a company waiting on well traveled routes to waylay enemy troops. Usually a foxhole was not dug and if contact was made you immediately returned to the mother unit.

An Khe: Town borders on base camp.

An Khe Plaza: Sin city.

AO: Area of operation.

APO: Army post office with a zip code in San Francisco.

ARA: Aerial rocket artillery. The Huey chopper had two 48 rocket pods which fired 2.75 inch rockets.

Artillery: Large cannons of 105mm, 155mm, and 175mm.

ARVN: Army of the Republic of Vietnam soldier.

B-52: U.S. Air Force bomber.

Ba Muoi Ba: Literally beer 33, a local Vietnamese beer.

Back in the World: Anywhere but Vietnam.

Base Camp: Camp Radcliff was the division base camp for the 1st Cavalry Division.

Battalion: A military unit of three Infantry Companies and one Weapons Company. This would be approximately 800 to 1,000 soldiers.

Battery: Artillery unit, usually six 105mm or 155mm howitzers, or two 8-inch or 175mm self-propelled howitzers.

Beaucoup: Many.

Beaucoup Dinky Dau: Real crazy.

BIC: Vietnamese for understand: no bic, I don't understand.

Biere Leroux: Local Vietnamese beer, quart bottles only.

Bird Dog: Forward air controller. Flying above the action the O1 aircraft would coordinate artillery and air support.

Body Bag: Plastic bag to transport killed in action bodies out of the field.

Body Count: Tally of the enemy you have killed.

Boom-Boom: To have sex.

Boom-Boom Girl: A prostitute.

Boonie Hat: A camouflage or O.D. hat often worn in the field in place of the steel pot.

Boonies: Out in the field (jungle).

Brigade: A military unit of three battalions in the 1st Cavalry Division.

Bronze Star: Military decoration for heroic or meritorious service in combat.

Bush: Out in the field (jungle).

Butterfly Sweeps: Patrols looping out in the shape of a butterfly's wing.

C & C: Also Charlie Charlie, the command and control helicopter carrying the commander in charge overseeing his troops on the ground.

C-4: Plastique explosive.

C-123: A cargo plane with wing-mounted engines.

C-130: Large four engine transport aircraft.

C-141: Large military transport aircraft.

C-Rations: Combat field meals, sometimes called C's.

Call Sign: Your signature on the radio.

Camp Alpha: Where soldiers arriving from the United States were processed upon first arriving in Vietnam.

Camp Radcliff: Name of base camp at An Khe.

Caribou: Twin engine transport aircraft that held one platoon and could land on small dirt airstrips.

Cav: Nickname for cavalry.

Cavalair: 1st Cavalry Division's newspaper.

Cavalryman: Nickname for 1st Cavalry soldier.

Charlie: Nickname for communist soldiers from the Army phonetic alphabet for "Victor Charlie."

Chieu Hoi: Open arms amnesty program for VC and NVA to rally to the side of the RVN government. Offer could be found on pamphlets usually.

Chinook: Nickname for the CH-47 transport helicopter, a large twin-rotor transport helicopter.

Chop Chop: Food.

CIDG: Civilian Irregular Defense Group. Mercenaries hired by the CIA and led by the army special forces.

Claymore: Antipersonnel mine, very effective. These propel in a 60 degree arc 700 double-ott size steel projectiles. This weapon was deadly up to 50 meters. Used on ambushes and defensive positions.

Close (With): Arriving at a destination.

CO: Commanding officer.

Cockadau: Vietnamese slang meaning to kill.

Code of Conduct: Rules of how a U.S. G.I. should conduct himself.

Coke Girl: Usually young girls who sold everything except boom boom to G.I.s.

Conex: Container used for storing stuff.

Contact: When a U.S. unit would strike an enemy unit and a combat engagement ensued.

CP: Command post.

CQ: Charge of quarters.

Crew Chief: The enlisted person in charge of the care of the helicopter and in charge of other crew the door gunner.

CS: Riot control tear gas.

Daisy Cutter: Huge bomb blu-82 dropped from C-130 to clear a small LZ.

Danger Close: An air strike or artillery which was close enough to cause friendly casualties.

Davy Crockett: Operation in Bong Son early 1966.

Deros: Date eligible for return from overseas.

Detcord: A cotton cord rope used to set off small explosions with C-4.

Deuce-and-a-Half: 2½ ton truck.

Didi: Sometimes dd or Dee Dee, leaving to go, get out.

Didi Mow: Go quickly.

Dink: Slang for Vietnamese person.

Dinky-Dao (dien cai dau): Vietnamese for crazy.

Doc: Nickname for a medic in the field.

Dong: Vietnamese money, like American cents.

Donut Dolly: American ladies from the American Red Cross.

Door Gunner: Soldiers who operated the M-60 machine guns at the door-ways of the Hueys.

Dustoff: Nickname and call sign for medevac.

E (Rating): E-3 would be a rating of a private first class.

Elephant Grass: A tall course grass which cut a soldier as you passed through.

Entrenching Tool: Name for army folding shovel.

Envelop: Surrounding or encircle.

ETS: Estimated termination of service or day you get out.

F-4D Phantom: U.S. air force jet used in ground support.

F-5 Freedom Fighter: U.S. air force jet used in ground support.

FAC: Forward air controller.

Fast Movers: FAC radio code for jet aircraft.

Fatigues: Army O.D. work uniform.

Field: Anywhere out in enemy territory.

Fire-Team: A military unit with a leader, two riflemen and one M-79 man.

Firebase: Forward support area usually with artillery.

Firefight: An exchange of small arms fire with enemy.

Flare: An illumination device fired from mortars or dropped from Puff. Trip flares were put out by hand, attached to a trip wire, as an anti-intrusion device. Hand flares were for signaling.

FNG: Fucking new guy.

FO: Forward observer, who coordinated artillery or mortar fire.

.45: U.S. issued pistol, .45 caliber.

Four-Point-Duce: A very large mortar.

Foxhole: Dug as nighttime defense. This defensive measure was usually about four feet deep with two by four feet dimension at the top.

Frag: Nickname for fragmentation grenade, author's weapon of choice.

Fragging: An armed grenade rolled into a friendly position or tent etc. on purpose, usually happened in base camp.

Fratricide: Friendly troops killing friendly troops.

Friendlies: Troops or others considered friendly. When they are to the front of your position restricted firing in effect.

Friendly Fire: Called misadventure by the DOD when friendly fire does you damage.

G.I.: Government Issue.

Giap, General: Command officer of the North Vietnam army.

Golf Course: Open area in base camp where the 400 or so helicopters parked, later in 1966 runways were installed.

Gooks: Slang for Vietnamese.

Grease Gun: ..45 caliber World War II era machine pistol.

Green Beret: Special Forces soldiers who did recon for the Cav from time to time.

Green Line: Barrier line around base camp at An Khe. This detail was considered very good and safe duty when infantry could guard it.

Grids: USA map broken into 1,000 meter squares.

Grunt: Slang for an infantry soldier in the field.

Guns: Slang for gunship.

Gunship: Huey that had a 9 rocket pod and two M-60s on each side plus the door gunners and later a 40mm grenade launcher on the front.

H&I: Harassing and interdiction fire by the artillery usually fired during the night.

Happy Valley: Area just north/northwest of base camp.

HE: High explosive.

HHC: Headquarters and Headquarters Company.

HHQ: Headquarters Company.

High Jumper Two Six Mike India: Authors call sign as RTO with the platoon sergeant.

Hmong: Montagnards of Laos and Vietnam who often fought in CIDG companies for the United States.

Ho Chi Minh: Leader of North Vietnam in 1966.

Ho Chi Minh Slippers: Sandals cut out of truck tires usually with tread still showing on bottoms.

Hon Kong: Mountain overlooking base camp at An Khe.

Hong Kong: R & R center for soldiers.

Hong Kong Tea: Bar girls order tea instead of whiskey, caught on to quickly by the soldiers.

Hooches: A house, shack or open sided shed. Also our temporary shelters we put up nightly using ponchos.

Horn: The radio, "prick 25".

HQ: Headquarters.

Huey: Bell UH-D1 troop carrying helicopter. This was the workhorse of the Cav in Vietnam. This chopper made a very distinctive "whop" sound so you knew when one was coming your way.

Humping: The infantry term anytime you're on the move in the bush.

Hunter/Killer: Tactic where many small units hunt for the enemy and when the bastards were found the rest of the unit piled on.

Ia Drang: Where LZ X-Ray, Albany & Juliet were located next to the Cambodian border.

Illumination: Flares.

In Country: To be in Vietnam.

Incoming: Mortars or rockets coming in on top of you.

Indirect Fire: Usually supporting artillery or mortar fire, not line of sight support.

Irving: Operation near Phu Cat, October 1966.

Jakis: Class a uniform for the tropics. This was also the color of the NAV and PAVN uniforms. Sometimes they wore the Vietnamese peasants black pajamas as a disguise.

Jolly Rings Two Six India: Authors first call sign as RTO for LT.

JP-4: Aviation jet fuel.

Jungle Boots: Boot with canvas sides and very light weight, lugs on the bottoms for grip, two holes in the side for ventilation and water draining after stream crossing.

Jungle Pants and Shirts: Tropical fatigues, light weight and fast drying.

KIA: Killed in action.

Kinnard, General Harry: 1st Cavalry Division commander, 1965, 1966.

Klick: One thousand meters, a kilometer.

La Die: Come out (Vietnamese).

Lagger: To remain in an area usually out of sight waiting until a unit would be called into action.

Law: 66mm light antitank weapon.

LBJ: Long Binh jail. Also the president's initials in 1966.

Leg: Nickname in the Cav for a standard infantry soldier as opposed to being airborne.

LP: Listening post, same as outpost except at night. This was the most dangerous duty a grunt could pull.

LRRP: Long range reconnaissance patrol. These patrols consisted of only six or seven to reconnoiter what the enemy was up to and their strength and report back to HQ.

LRRP Rations: Rations which were different from C's, used on LRRP missions. Freeze dried and reconstituted with hot water.

LT: Nickname for the platoon leader usually a second lieutenant. Like the medics, the LTs and Captains only had to spend six months in the field.

LZ: Landing zone, for helicopters.

LZ Betty: Forward LZ near Virginia in Phan Thiet.

LZ English: Large rear base area in the Bong Son area close to huge battle in May 1966.

LZ Hammond: Forward supply base south of LZ English.

LZ Juliet: Forward LZ, artillery base in the Ia Drang valley close to large battle in August 1966.

LZ Virginia: Rear base area in Phan Thiet at the airport.

M-1: .30 caliber WW II era semi-automatic rifle.

M-1 Carbine: Lightweight .30 caliber World War II era carbine with selector for full automatic.

M-14: 7.62mm .30 caliber infantry semi-automatic rifle.

M-16: 5.56mm 2.23 caliber colt manufactured full automatic, standard rifle for the 1st Cavalry Division and the First division to adapt to this new rifle.

M-60: 7.62mm .30 caliber belt fed machine gun.

M-79: 40mm grenade launcher.

Mad Minute: Originated by Col. Moore, battalion commander 1/7 Cav in the Ia Drang at LZ X-Ray. The entire perimeter would open fire at a predetermined time from fixed positions for about one minute. This was to spring any pending ambushes and/or test weapons. Usually this was done just before first light.

Magazine: A clip which usually held 20 rounds of ammo and was inserted into the rifle.

Main Force: A large enemy force usually NVA.

Malaria: Serious parasitic disease spread by the female anopheles mosquito.

Mama San: Any older Vietnamese woman.

Marbling: Anytime a unit was moving in the field.

MASH: Mobile army surgical hospital.

Medevac: A helicopter designed for medical evacuation, usually a Bell UH-D1 Huey with red crosses on the sides.

Medic: Medical aid soldier in the field.

MIA: Missing in action.

Military Payment Certificate: MPC or script used everywhere.

Mini Gun: Gatling gun capable of firing up to six thousand rounds per minute.

MM: Millimeter, physical size of shell.

Mo-Gas: Nickname for gasoline for motor vehicles.

Montagnard: Pronounced mountain-yard, the mountain people who didn't much care for Vietnamese, north or south.

Moore, General Harold: Commander of the 1st of the 7th Cav at LZ X-Ray and brigade commander during author's tour.

Mortar: Tube artillery used for indirect fire with one platoon dedicated to carry and fire the mortar.

MOS: Military occupation specialty, job title.

MP: Military police.

MPC: Military payment certificate, the funny money used instead of U.S. greenbacks which were contraband in the RVN.

Mule: Four wheel drive flat bed vehicle.

Nathan Hale: Operation around Dong Tri, June 1966.

NCO: Noncommissioned officer.

Number One: The best.

Number Ten: The worst.

Nuoc Mam: Really repulsive fish smelling sauce Vietnamese put on everything.

NVA: North Vietnamese Army or also could be a North Vietnamese soldier.

OCS: Officer Candidate School.

OD: Olive drab.

OP: Outpost, out in front of the main body as an early warning to the rest of the unit during day time.

Operations: My tour of 1st of the 7th CAV operations by date.
    13–28 March 66 Jim Bowie
    25 March–8 April 66 Lincoln
    11–17 April 66 Mosby I
    26–28 April 66 Bee Bee
    29 April 66 Browning
    4–16 May 66 Davy Crockett
    19 June–1 July 66 Nathan Hale
    2–30 July 66 Henry clay
    18–31 July 66 Hayes
    1–25 August 66 Paul Revere II
    Phan Thiet OP Byrd: B Co. attached with 2nd of the 7th Cav.

Out Going: Mortar or artillery fire going out.

Overran: A unit which had been completely over-powered by an enemy unit.

P-38: G.I. can opener about the size of your car key.

Palace Guard: Infantry guarding a forward base area usually occupied by brigade or division HQ.

Papa San: Any older Vietnamese man.

Patrol: Sweeps by a unit looking for the enemy.

Paul Revere II: Operation in the Ia Drang, August 1966.

PAVN: People's army of (North) Vietnam, a North Vietnamese soldier.

Perimeter: Foxhole line around an area guarded by infantry with the HQ and usually weapons platoon (mortars) inside.

Pershing: Operation in Bong Son, February 1966.

PF: Popular forces. Nicknamed ruff puffs. Local villager soldiers recruited out of hamlets for a home guard.

Piaster: Vietnamese money traded at 124 piasters to the dollar (1966 rate). Sometimes these were called p's. There are one hundred dong to the piaster.

Platoon: A military unit of four squads consisting of about 42 soldiers at full strength. 1 Lieutenant and RTO, 1 platoon Sergeant and RTO, 1 medic, 2 machine gun crews, 4 squad leaders, 6 grenade launchers, 6 team leaders (riflemen) and 12 riflemen. Others could be attached.

Point: Lead soldier of a unit maneuvering in the field.

Pop Smoke: Pull pin and ignite a smoke grenade for identification and wind direction for chopper landings.

POW: Prisoner of war.

PRC-25: Radio used in the field nicknamed "prick 25". Range was 5-10 kilometers.

Prep: Nickname for preparatory fire on an LZ usually by ARA or artillery or sometimes both.

Prone Shelter: Shallow shelter dug instead of a foxhole. Usually dug during the heat of an engagement, these were not recommended for defensive positions.

PSP: Pierced steel planking. These were used to strengthen runways.

Puff the Magic Dragon: Converted C-47 aircraft gunships with 7.62mm miniguns.

Punji Stake: Two foot long piece of bamboo sharpened at both ends. Used as simple booby-trap.

Purple Heart: Military decoration award for a wound received in combat.

PX: Nickname for Post Exchange.

PZ (Papa Zulu): Pick-up zone for helicopters.

R & R: Rest and relaxation. Each soldier in the Cav was allowed one six day R & R out of country and one in-country for three days.

RA: Regular army.

Ration Card: Card given to the G.I.s rationing certain goods.

Recon: Nickname for reconnaissance.

Recon by Fire: Firing a weapon in concert with others even though you're not under fire. This was done to try and draw enemy fire in order to locate the enemy in the surrounding jungle.

Reconnaissance by Force: Larger unit doing recon.

Regiment: NVA units used this designation rather than brigade. They were usually three to six battalions.

REMF: Rear echelon mother fuckers, a soldier in the rear.

Rock N Roll: Open fire on full automatic.

ROK: Republic of Korea. These soldiers serving in Vietnam were from Korea.

Round: A bullet or shell one at a time.

Round Eye: Caucasian female.

RPG: 82mm rocket-propelled grenade. Usually an antitank weapon, the NVA/PAVN used it as an antipersonnel and bunker busting weapon.

RTO: Radio Telephone Operator, a radioman in a field unit.

Rucksack: Slang for the packs taken from PAVN and used by grunts.

RVN: Republic of Vietnam.

S & D: Search and destroy. This was the type of operations we usually went on.

S-1: Personnel.

S-2: Intelligence.

S-3: Operations.

S-4: Supply.

Saddle-Up: Get your gear on and get ready to move.

Safe Conduct Pass: Leaflets that were dropped in enemy held territory that all allied forces were to honor.

Saigon Tea: Tea served in bars instead of whiskey. Bar girls at first asked G.I.s to buy them a shot of whiskey but the soldiers grew wise and so the girls would just asked for Saigon tea.

Sameo Sameo: In like manner.

Sappers: Infiltrators usually carrying satchel charges for sabotage.

Script: MPC.

Search and Destroy: Operations to locate and destroy the enemy and any of their supplies and sanctuaries.

Sham: Avoiding the field or going on operations.

Short: Close to completing one's tour of duty.

Short Round: Artillery falling short of its mark.

Sin City: Bars and whorehouse outside base camp at An Khe servicing the 1st Cavalry Division.

Sinh Loi: Vietnamese for sorry about that.

Six: On the radio, unit commander.

SKS: 7.62mm .30 caliber semi-automatic carbine the Samozaryadnyi Karabin Simonova used by the NVA/PAVN.

Slick: Nickname for a Huey troop carrying transport helicopter, a Bell UH-D1.

Sloop: Slang for Vietnamese.

Smoke Grenade: Grenade that released colored smoke for ground identification by aircraft of friendly troops.

SNAFU: Situation normal, all fucked up.

Snoopy Scout: H-13 observation helicopter used for scouting.

SOP: Standard operating procedure.

SP Pak: Sundry pack containing stuff you couldn't usually get in the field.

Spider Hole: Small NVA fox hole we couldn't fit into.

Squad: A military unit made up of two fire-teams.

Stand-Down: Rest time for field soldiers in rear support areas known to be secure.

Stand-To: All gear in place and soldiers in the field at the ready down in their foxholes and prepared for an attack.

Starlight Scope: A night vision enhancement scope which intensifies available light to help a soldier see better in the dark. Looking through the scope, everything is green.

Steel Pot: Helmet worn for protection with camouflage cover.

Strongpoint: A strongly defended position usually at a bridge or other target the NVA would like to attack.

TAOR: Tactical area of responsibility.

TDY: Temporary duty assignment.

Tee Tee: A little bit.

1049: Ten forty-nine. This form was paperwork for an inter-army transfer.

Tet: Vietnamese holiday or festival for the New Year and the year 1966 was the year of the horse.

Thayer II: Operation in Bong Son, October 1966.

33: Local beer, Ba Muoi Ba.

Thompson: .45 caliber World War II era submachine gun.

Titi: Very small, little bit.

Top: Nickname for the Company First Sargeant.

Tour: One year in Vietnam.

Toy coy zip: Sorry about that.

Tracer: Round of ammunition chemically treated to glow red for the U.S and green for the NVA/PAVN. These glow so a soldier can follow the bullet's flight.

Trip Flare: Ground flare set off by a trip wire. This was an anti-intrusion device.

UCMJ: Uniform code of military justice.

Uncle Ho: Ho Chi Minh.

USARV: United States Army Republic of Vietnam.

USO: United Service Organizations.

VC: Viet Cong, the irregulars or South Vietnamese guerrillas fighting the RVN government and us. These troops were usually armed with lots of old U.S. equipment taken from the ARVN.

VC Main Force: Full time VC.

VCS: Viet Cong suspect.

Victor Charlie: Phonetic name for VC.

The Wall: Monument in Washington D.C. with the names of the 58,158 U.S. soldiers killed in Vietnam.

Webbing: The gear and suspenders and harness we used to support all the equipment carried by us grunts.

White Wing: Operation after masher in Binh Dinh province in 1966 (Bong Son).

WIA: Wounded in action.

The World: Any place except Vietnam.

WP: White phosphorus or Willie Peter, artillery or mortar rounds that exploded in huge white clouds of smoke.

Xin Loi: Vietnamese for sorry about that.

XO: Company executive officer. Number two in command.

Yards: Affectionate name for the Montagnards.

Index